Interface Explorations 31

Editors
Artemis Alexiadou
T. Alan Hall

De Gruyter Mouton

The Morpheme

A Theoretical Introduction

by
David Embick

De Gruyter Mouton

ISBN 978-1-5015-1621-4
ISBN (PDF) 978-1-5015-0256-9
ISBN (EPUB) 978-1-5015-0258-3
ISSN 1861-4167

Library of Congress Cataloging-in-Publication Data

A CIP catalog record for this book has been applied for at the Library of Congress.

Bibliographic information published by the Deutsche Nationalbibliothek

The Deutsche Nationalbibliothek lists this publication in the Deutsche Nationalbibliografie; detailed bibliographic data are available on the Internet at http://dnb.dnb.de.

© 2015 Walter de Gruyter Inc., Boston/Berlin
This volume is text- and page-identical with the hardback published in 2015.

Printing and binding: CPI books GmbH, Leck
♾ Printed on acid-free paper

Printed in Germany

www.degruyter.com

Contents

Chapter Dependencies — ix

Preface — xi

1 Morphemes in the Grammar — 1
1.1 Introduction — 1
1.2 The Architecture of the Grammar — 3
1.3 Syntactic Terminals — 5
1.3.1 Morphemes and Features — 6
1.3.2 Roots — 7
1.3.3 Functional Morphemes — 9
1.3.4 Pieces and *Non-Affixal* Morphology — 11
1.4 Lists and Decomposition — 11
1.4.1 Lists and Lexical Information — 13
1.4.2 Decomposition — 17
1.4.3 Lists and Their Motivation — 19
1.5 Summary and Core Properties — 20
1.6 (P)review: Main Themes — 22
1.6.1 Interface Transparency — 22
1.6.2 Realizational Sound/Meaning Connections — 24
1.6.3 The Morpheme-Locus Effect — 28

2 Morphemes and Features — 31
2.1 Introduction — 31
2.2 Functional Morphemes — 32
2.2.1 Features and Functional Morphemes — 32
2.2.2 *Bundling* and Possible Morphemes — 34
2.2.3 Differences in Active Features — 36
2.2.4 Summary: Features of Functional Morphemes — 40
2.3 Roots — 41
2.3.1 Roots and Phonological Features — 41
2.3.2 The Categorization of Roots — 43
2.3.3 Roots and Lexical Semantic Meanings — 47
2.3.4 Roots and Synsem Features — 49

2.3.5	Roots and "Morphological" Features	51
2.3.6	A Root is a Type of Morpheme	55
2.4	Conclusions	56

3 Structures and Linear Order — 59
3.1	Introduction	59
3.2	Structures	60
3.2.1	An Illustration	62
3.2.2	Movement and Complex Heads: Summary	66
3.3	Some Definitions: *M-Words* and *Subwords*	67
3.4	Linear Order	71
3.4.1	The Concatenation of M-Words and Subwords	71
3.4.2	Syntactic Structure and Morpheme Order	73
3.4.3	Structure and Order	76
3.4.4	Bracketing and Order Mismatches	79
3.5	A Note on Structure and Phonological Wordhood	82
3.6	Conclusions	84

4 Vocabulary Insertion: An Introduction — 85
4.1	Fundamental Notions	85
4.2	The Vocabulary Insertion Process in Detail	88
4.2.1	Adding Phonological Content	88
4.2.2	Vocabulary Insertion and Synsem Features	91
4.3	Ordering of Vocabulary Items	92
4.4	Vocabulary Insertion and Blocking: A First Look	96
4.5	The Order of Insertion in Complex Structures	99
4.6	Illustration: A Fragment from the Latin Conjugation	100
4.6.1	Preliminary Observations	100
4.6.2	Vocabulary Items	103
4.6.3	Non-Deletion of Features	107
4.7	Summary	109

5 Syncretism and (Under)specification — 111
5.1	Introduction	111
5.2	Syncretism and Underspecification	113
5.2.1	An Example: Hupa Agreement	114
5.2.2	Implementing an Analysis of Syncretism	117
5.2.3	Comparison	119

5.2.4	Some Additional Points	120
5.3	Specification	121
5.4	Syncretism versus Homophony	125
5.5	Illustrations	127
5.5.1	Seychelles Creole Pronominals	127
5.5.2	Mongolic Possessors	129
5.5.3	Barbareño Chumash Pronominals	131
5.5.4	Anêm Possessive Suffixes	134
5.6	Conclusions	136
6	**Further Topics in the Analysis of Syncretism**	**139**
6.1	Introduction	139
6.2	Impoverishment	140
6.2.1	Spurious *se* in Spanish	141
6.2.2	Norwegian Adjectives	143
6.2.3	Default Vocabulary Items	146
6.3	Impoverishment and Patterns of Syncretism	149
6.3.1	Illustration in the Abstract	150
6.3.2	Latin Dative and Ablative Plurals	151
6.3.3	Second/Third Plurals in Latin American Spanish	153
6.3.4	Syncretisms in Macedonian Verbs	155
6.3.5	Person and Number in Amele	157
6.4	Underspecification and Impoverishment	161
6.5	General Conclusions: Syncretism and Vocabulary Insertion	166
7	**Contextual Allomorphy, and Blocking**	**169**
7.1	Introduction and Review	169
7.2	Types of Allomorphic Conditioning	170
7.2.1	Inwards versus Outwards	172
7.2.2	Grammatical versus Phonological Conditioning	173
7.2.3	Contextual Allomorphy and (Morpho)phonology	176
7.3	Conditions on Contextual Allomorphy	178
7.3.1	Cyclic Domains	179
7.3.2	Concatenation	183
7.3.3	Inside-Out Insertion	191
7.3.4	Summary	193
7.4	Blocking, Morphemes, and Vocabulary Insertion	194
7.4.1	Blocking and Words: The Intuition	196

7.4.2	*Glory*, **gloriosity*, and the Morpheme	197
7.5	Non-Affixal Morphology and Blocking	201
7.5.1	An Analysis of Non-Affixal Changes	202
7.5.2	Pieces, Processes, Blocking	203
7.5.3	Non-affixal Morphology: Concluding Remarks	206
7.6	Conclusions	208

8 Concluding Remarks   211

Appendix: Fusion and Fission   213
A.1	Introduction	213
A.2	Fusion	213
A.3	Fission	216

Notes   221

Bibliography   233

Index   244

Chapter Dependencies

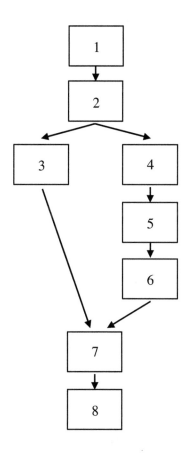

Preface

"I'm not as dumb as you think...I've seen how it worked out. I guess I can put two and two together."
   "Sometimes the answer's four," I said, *"and sometimes it's twenty-two."*

—Dashiel Hammett, *The Thin Man*

*

As far as its contents and title are concerned, this book could have been called *The Morphemes*, since the distinction between Roots and functional morphemes is central to the theory that is developed here. But because my main focus is on the central importance of the discrete piece—that is, the morpheme—I have opted for the singular version.

There is also something to be said about the book's subtitle (*A Theoretical Introduction*). This classification reflects my primary goals for this work. There are three of these.

The first goal is that it will function as a component in a course (or course sequence) on morphology, at the introductory graduate (or advanced undergraduate) level; this is the kind of course that I have been teaching at the University of Pennsylvania over the past several years, and a fair amount of the material that has found its way into the work, especially in chapters 4-6, is drawn from those classes.

The second goal is that it will serve as a clear statement of some of the central themes in Distributed Morphology, and thus prove useful to advanced researchers from other subareas (or adjacent areas of language research) who are interested in the general theoretical issues that are addressed here, and in the particular view of the morpheme that has been developed in this framework.

The third goal is that it will connect a number of ideas that have been investigated within Distributed Morphology and related frameworks—notably, the relations between the theory of the morpheme and the Vocabulary Insertion operation on the one hand, with the phenomena of syncretism, blocking, and allomorphy on the other—in a way that will be of interest to researchers working in a variety of areas. My impression from the literature is that, while substantial progress has been made in understanding the phenomena just mentioned, there is a need for a systematic overview of how the different parts of the theory might fit together.

Along with the three goals just mentioned, it is worth mentioning what this book is not. For one, it is not intended to be a textbook per se, even if it is a book that could be used in a class. While it offers an introduction to the morpheme, its concerns are often directed at theoretical points that are complex and open to many directions of resolution. It does not start with a slow introduction to the phenomena that are considered to be part of "morphology"; instead, it starts with a core notion—the morpheme—and proceeds from there to two of the central theoretical questions for the morpheme, syncretism and allomorphy. Moreover, there are no exercises of the type that are central to texts. This might mean that it is somewhat closer to being a handbook. In a limited sense, this is probably true. However, a handbook is typically regarded as a comprehensive overview of the literature up to a point, and I have made no attempt to give a detailed overview of the literature here. Instead, I have tried to connect the essential components of *one* view of the morpheme into a coherent system. My hope is that the overarching system will allow specific points of theoretical interest to be understood and developed further; i.e., that those who use the book will be in a position to understand the primary literature, and to make contributions to it.

* *

Regarding what is covered in the book, and the scope of the background literature that is cited—

As far as the time-period of the work covered here goes, I think it is fair to say that there is no good time to finish a work like this one. Looking back into the work I see several things that could have been done differently, connected in a completely different way, and so on. Looking at the present, it is, of course, impossible to keep updating a book in a way that reflects a field that is developing continuously. In practical terms, this means that the book omits some of the most recent research in this area; a large component of this book took its current form in the summer and fall of 2010, and in making revisions and additions over the past few years I have not included works published after that time.

As far as the scope of the work is concerned, I have tried to concentrate on the theory of the morpheme (and on the attendant theory of Vocabulary Insertion) as much as possible. The focus on Vocabulary Insertion (and on syncretism, allomorphy, and blocking) reflects this primary concern. A number of other issues that are part of the "theory of morphology" (understood in an informal sense) are not addressed in this work. In my view, an overview of the morpheme would ultimately have to be supplemented by (1) an overview of the theory of *affixation* (connecting with syntax); and (2) an overview of the theory of *morphophonology* (connecting primarily with phonology). But those books have not been written yet.

The book assumes that readers are familiar with many themes in current theoretical work in linguistics. For reasons that will become obvious in the pages to come, it is not practical (or desirable) to cut off the theory of the morpheme from syntax, phonology, and semantics. Thus, much of the discussion in this book assumes that readers have ample background in current approaches to generative syntax, and, to a lesser extent, phonology.

It is possible to use this book in a few different ways; I have tried to summarize these in the graph of chapter dependencies that appears a few pages back.

* * *

The material in this book was developed over the course of several years. At one point in around 1999, Morris Halle and I worked out an analysis of the verbal system of Latin. One idea was that the introduction to that piece of work would be a general introduction to Distributed Morphology. This project did not materialize in the form that was originally conceived (although a few small parts of the analysis of Latin verbs have surfaced in various places, including here). I hope that some of the insight and clarity that is found in all of Morris's work has made its way into these pages.

Chapters containing a general introduction to the theory slowly took form after 2000, and I used early versions of these in classes I taught in Brazil and Argentina in 2004. I also used these chapters as introductory material in a few of the seminars I taught at University of Pennsylvania in the following years. After several thorough rewritings, this initial material was turned into something like the current form in 2010, when the contents of most of the later chapters was added as well. After that the draft was edited substantially, with an emphasis on overall coherence, and on the introduction of illustrative examples. A draft was nearly completed during the summer of 2013, but I was not ready to let it go at that time; then work on other projects dominated my attention. Finally, the conclusion and the final preparations for publication were completed during the 2014-2015 academic year.

* * * *

I am particularly thankful to Morris Halle and Alec Marantz for providing me with a number of helpful comments during many stages of this project. Andrés Saab also has my special thanks for careful reading and extensive comments on some earlier drafts which (I can definitely say) were not necessarily a pleasure to read. I'm also especially grateful to the many, many individuals who were exposed to this material in classes and lectures over the last 10+ years, whose comments, corrections, understandings, and misunderstandings have contributed immensely to the work. Finally, thanks to Beatrice Santorini and Tricia Irwin for invaluable help with the final preparation of the manuscript, and to Lara Wysong and Mouton de Gruyter (and the Interface Explorations series in particular) for working with me on publishing this material.

* * * * *

My work in the summers of 2012-2015 was supported by the Eunice Kennedy Shriver National Institute of Child Health & Human Development of the National Institutes of Health, under Award Number R01HD073258.

D.E., Philadelphia, Summer 2015

Chapter 1
Morphemes in the Grammar

1.1 Introduction

At the most basic level of description, a grammar consists of a set of primitive elements and a set of rules for deriving complex objects out of these primitives. According to the view that is developed in this book, the primitive elements are *morphemes*, and the system responsible for combining morphemes into complex structures is the *syntax*. The syntax generates expressions that relate sound and meaning. In the particular model of grammar that is assumed here, sound- and meaning-specific representations are created by distinct sets of computations that apply to the objects derived by the syntax. The sets of computations related to sound and meaning are referred to as Phonological Form (PF) and Logical Form (LF); these are the *interfaces* of the syntax.

My focus in this book is on the theory of the morpheme. This is one subpart of an area of investigation that is typically or traditionally called *morphological theory*. As mentioned above, the particular morphological theory that I will advance in this book starts with the assumption that morphemes are syntactic objects—i.e., the terminal nodes of syntactic derivations—and proceeds from there to develop an account of how morphemes are represented in memory, and of how they connect sound with a particular type of meaning (specifically, semantically interpreted features). Given the fundamentally syntactic orientation of this theory, it must be stressed from the outset that terms like *morphology* and *morphological theory* are used in this work in an informal sense: there are often no principled answers to questions about where "morphology" stops, and where e.g. "syntax" or "phonology" begin or end. A consequence of this view, which is emphasized throughout this book, is that it is not possible to understand the morpheme in isolation from the syntactic and phonological components of the grammar.

In terms of the model of grammar that is assumed here, there are two large questions that define research in morphological theory. The first of these is the question of the morpheme: this is the focus of the present work, and its general properties and orientation take the form sketched in the preceding paragraph. The second question concerns the rule system or systems responsible for the derivation of complex forms. This is a primary concern of morphological theory because the objects of study often consist of more than one morpheme, and it must be asked how morphemes are composed into these larger objects. In terms that are inherited from traditional grammar, the rules governing the construction of phrases are in the domain of *syntax*, while the rules that are responsible for the derivation of complex words are the purview of *morphology* or *word formation*. Whether or not these are truly distinct domains—i.e., whether or not the grammar of human language employs one set of computations for the derivation of words and phrases, or two—is an empirical question. On the assumption that there is some kind of derivational system at play in the generation of both words and phrases, every model of the grammar must specify whether words and phrases are derived by the same rule system, or by different systems.

The questions outlined immediately above can be stated as Q1 and Q2:

Question 1 (Q1): What is the nature of the primitive units of derivations; i.e., what is the nature of the *morpheme*? How do morphemes relate to syntactic, semantic, and phonological information?

Question 2 (Q2): What is the nature of the rule system that assembles morphemes into words? How does this system relate to the syntax?

The theory of the morpheme that is developed in this work assumes and articulates some specific architectural assumptions that are drawn from the framework of Distributed Morphology, which was initially presented in Halle and Marantz (1993) (building on Halle 1990); see Embick and Noyer (2007) for a short overview. With respect to Q2, Distributed Morphology takes the position that the syntax is the generative system responsible for the derivation of all complex objects; this assumption was introduced in the first paragraph of this chapter. At a number of points in this chapter and in later chapters, some additional assumptions will be made about the types of structures that are relevant for morphological concerns. However, it is not my intention in this book to consider the arguments for a syntactic approach to morphology; nor will I look in detail at the syntactic processes and structures that are implicated in the affixation of morphemes to each other. Rather, assumptions about structure are introduced only as a means of advancing the primary focus of the work, which is directed at Q1, the question of the morpheme.

To look at the morpheme in detail, it is necessary to begin with some assumptions about the organization of the grammar. Because Q1 and Q2 each implicate the relationship(s) between morphology and other components of grammatical competence—in particular, computations and representations relevant for syntax, semantics, and phonology—the study of morphology must, as pointed out above, be pursued in conjunction with a theory of how the grammar as a whole is organized. This chapter outlines the essential components of grammatical architecture in a way provides the context for an initial perspective on the morpheme.

Before considering these very general questions about the organization of the grammar, some remarks are in order concerning the "word", an object which is often (in fact, almost always) taken to be at the center of morphological theory. The theory that is presented here posits no architectural differences between words and phrases. This means that to the extent that there is any role played by the word in the theory, both words and phrases are derived syntactically. For this reason, uses of the term "word" in the pages to come are to be understood non-technically, as a way of picking out objects which, because of their structure (and because of how the phonology interprets such structures) have the properties that linguists typically associate with (phonological) words. More precisely, the use of the term *word* is informal because the actual work in the theory is done by theoretical objects with technical definitions—in particular, representations that are defined in terms of **morphemes**, and the ways in which they are composed—that are introduced as the discussion proceeds (see in particular chapter 3). In short, even though I will follow standard practice in referring to the "word" in its familiar sense, this is a matter of convenience, nothing more.

1.2 The Architecture of the Grammar

The model of grammar that is assumed here is shown in (1). The syntactic part of the grammar generates syntactic structures, which are "spelled out" and subjected to further operations relevant to sound and meaning: these are the PF and LF interfaces respectively. For concreteness, I will speak of the derivations in (1) in terms adapted from the approach of Chomsky (2000, 2001) and related work; in principle, though, the theory of the morpheme that is advanced here is compatible with a number of different assumptions about syntactic theory.

(1) The Grammar

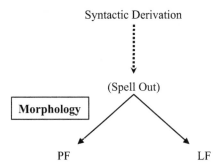

Above, I introduced the idea that the primitive elements of syntactic derivations are morphemes. In terms of (1), this means that morphemes are the terminal nodes in the syntactic derivations that appear at the top of the diagram. The status of morphemes as basic objects—that is, in what form(s) they are represented as primitives in memory—is a matter of central importance in the theory of morphology. The basic representation of morphemes does not, however, exhaust what there is to be said about morphology and its connections with other components of the grammar, as can be seen from the presence of the **Morphology** box in (1). This box stands proxy for a set of computations that apply to the output of syntactic derivations, in the PF component of the grammar. With reference to (1), then, the primary goals of this book are to present (i) a theory of the basic representation of morphemes, along with (ii) a theory of the computations and representations in the Morphology box that are most relevant to the theory of the morpheme.

Some further comments are required with respect to the second of these goals. PF serves as an interface between syntax and sound-related cognitive systems.[1] Among the computations that apply to serve this purpose, there are some that are primarily morphological in nature, while there are others that serve a more general purpose. For example, one operation that applies in the PF branch of the grammar adds phonological content to syntactic nodes. It is called *Vocabulary Insertion*, and it is examined in detail in chapter 4. This operation is specifically "morphological" in the sense that I intend here: its sole function is to supply a sound form to (certain) morphemes. On the other hand, other PF operations have a much more general character. For example, the

PF component is responsible for the computation and representation of linear information. These linear representations play a role both in the serial realization of syntactic objects, and in phonological interactions of various types. Linear computations and representations are not "morphology-specific" in any obvious way, since they are not directed exclusively at the morpheme, in the way that Vocabulary Insertion is. Or, put slightly differently, there is much to be said about the representation of linear order in language that has nothing to do with the typical concerns of morphology. Overall, then, while there are some aspects of PF that are tailored directly to what might be considered morphological concerns, one of the primary claims of Distributed Morphology is that morphological phenomena implicate several parts of (1) beyond the Morphology box. Connecting with a theme introduced earlier in this chapter, a consequence of this view is that a great deal of what there is to be said about morphology involves connections with articulated theories of syntax, semantics, and phonology.

Distributing the analytical mechanisms that are central to the theory of morphology has significant architectural consequences. In a grammar with the properties of (1), there is one system for building complex structures. Thus, the theory of constituent structure and the theory of syntactic derivations (including, for example, the idea that syntactic derivation is cyclic) are directly relevant to a number of morphological phenomena. This point is important. Although the emphasis in this work is on the morpheme, and on some of the operations that are specifically morphological in the sense identified above, the syntax is at the center of the framework. According to one way of thinking about this, this means that the *principles of syntax* comprise a non-trivial component of the *principles of morphology*. While this point is especially clear in the analysis of affixation—and, more generally, when the derivation of complex objects is analyzed, along the lines framed in (Q2)— its importance is also seen in various places in the discussion of (Q1) that occupies most of the pages to come.

1.3 Syntactic Terminals

In the grammar shown in (1), syntactic derivations produce hierarchical structures of the type that are standardly represented with trees. The terminal nodes of these trees are morphemes. With this idea in mind, I will sometimes use the terms *morpheme* and *(terminal) node* interchangeably in this book.

The morphemes that serve as the terminal nodes of syntactic expressions are objects stored in memory. As such, they have a *basic* (i.e., *underlying*) representation; the theory of the morpheme starts with this.

1.3.1 Morphemes and Features

Morphemes must ultimately relate *sound* and *meaning*; more precisely, they connect a particular type of phonological representation with a particular type of semantic representation. Exactly how they do this is a matter of central theoretical importance. A standard (or, at the very least, familiar) view of this relation is that morphemes are specified from the beginning (i.e., in memory) with features of each of these types. The theory presented in this book rejects this view. As will be seen below, it is not the case that all morphemes are represented underlyingly with both a meaning component and a sound component. Instead, some morphemes possess only a representation of meaning- (and syntax-) related features, and acquire phonological properties only after they have been combined into complex structures.

An important component of the theory of the morpheme is the idea that the grammar contains representations of the sound and meaning facets of language: that is, representations of sound and meaning in terms of *features*. There are two kinds of features to be considered initially: *phonological* features and *syntacticosemantic* (henceforth, *synsem*) features. The former are featural representations of the type familiar from phonological theory. The latter are features like the [past] feature that is responsible for past tense interpretation, or the [def] feature that is found in definite determiner phrases, and so on.

(2) Feature Types: Sound and Meaning

   a. **Phonological Features:** Features from the universal inventory of phonological features; e.g. [±voice], [±labial], etc.

   b. **Synsem Features:** Features from the universal inventory of syntacticosemantic features; e.g. [past] ('past'), [def] ('definite'), [pl] ('plural'), etc.

Depending on further hypotheses, it could very well be the case that (certain) synsem features are binary, like the phonological features referred to in (2a), so that (2b) would have [±past] and [±def]. Some questions along these lines are addressed in subsequent chapters. I will employ binary synsem features by default in the pages to come, with further complications to this picture introduced only when necessary.

The two types of features in (2) are a preliminary to understanding the basic representation of morphemes. As a next step, a distinction must be made between two types of morphemes in the grammar: the *Roots*, and the *functional morphemes*. While both the Roots and the functional morphemes function as the terminal objects in syntactic derivations, they differ with respect to how they relate the features in (2):

(3) Two Types of Syntactic Terminals

   a. **Functional Morphemes:** These are, by definition, composed of synsem features such as [±past], or [±pl], or [±def]. A further hypothesis is that they do not possess phonological features as part of their basic representation (see below).

   b. **Roots:** These make up the open class or "lexical" vocabulary. They include items such as $\sqrt{\text{CAT}}$, $\sqrt{\text{OX}}$, or $\sqrt{\text{SIT}}$. Roots do not contain or possess synsem features; a working hypothesis is that in the default case, they have an underlying phonological representation.

An important aspect of (3) is that not all morphemes are specified for each of the feature types in (2). In particular, the *functional morphemes* contain no phonological features as part of their basic representations; instead, they receive phonological content after the syntactic structure is spelled out, in the PF component of the grammar. On the other hand, *Roots* do not possess (or consist of) synsem features; and they (unlike functional morphemes) have an underlying phonological representation, at least in the default case.

1.3.2 Roots

The Roots—items like $\sqrt{\text{CAT}}$ or $\sqrt{\text{SIT}}$—are typically spoken of as members of the traditional *lexical categories*; while this description is commonly adopted, it is perhaps more accurate to say that they are members of the *open class* vocabulary.[2] They are language-specific combinations of sound and meaning—crucially, though, they relate to lexical or conceptual meaning, *not* the type of (grammatical) meaning encoded in synsem features. For example, the fact that the Root $\sqrt{\text{CAT}}$ in English has the phonological representation /kæt/, and that it has something to do with *felis catus* (and not something else), is particular to English. This aspect of the Root—the arbitrary connection between sound and meaning—must simply be memorized. Crucially, this type of sound/meaning connection does not involve synsem features; another way of putting this is that $\sqrt{\text{CAT}}$ cannot be *decomposed* (that is, constitutively broken down) into synsem features.

While the way in which a Root connects a particular phonological representation with a particular meaning is arbitrary, it is nevertheless quite likely that there are significant universal constraints on what could be a possible Root in human language; particularly with respect to what kinds of meanings could be associated with a Root. This is a substantial topic in its own right, one which must take into account both the nature of conceptual representations and their relationships with objects in the grammar, and the "differential" contributions to meaning of the type associated with Saussure's theory of the sign. As the details of Root semantics and representation are beyond the scope of the present work, I will focus primarily on matters of morphosyntactic and morphophonological representation in the discussion to come.

In this book, it is assumed as a working hypothesis that Roots possess a phonological representation as part of their primitive make-up. In this sense, then, the Root $\sqrt{\text{CAT}}$ in English is specified with the phonological matrix /kæt/ from the beginning. While in many cases a phonological representation might suffice to uniquely identify a Root in a language, this is not always true. In particular, it is sometimes necessary for a Root to possess an index that uniquely identifies it. The need for this type of index is clearest when there is homophony between Roots. For instance, the Roots underlying *bank* 'financial institution' and *bank* 'shore of a river, etc.' have phonologically identical underlying forms, but are nevertheless distinct Roots. Using numbers for the indices, these Roots could be specified as e.g. $\sqrt{\text{BANK}}_{254}$ and $\sqrt{\text{BANK}}_{879}$, in addition to possessing a phonological form. In representations of this type, each Root has a unique *non-phonological* identifier in addition to its phonological features. Beyond the indices just mentioned, it is also conceivable that Roots in some languages are specified with "morphological" features of the type associated with systems of conjugation or declension (or grammatical gender); some questions along these lines are addressed in chapter 2.

The assumption that Roots can have a phonological representation underlyingly has important consequences in a number of domains. It means, for example, that in the default case Roots are not subject to "late insertion" of phonological material in the PF component of the grammar in the way that functional morphemes are (see 1.3.3 immediately below). If Roots are specified for phonological representation underlyingly, then the ways in which the same Root may be realized in different forms are predicted to be restricted compared to what is found with functional morphemes. It is not clear at this point whether these predictions are borne out empirically. If it turns out to be the case that certain Roots do in fact show suppletion, in a way that requires them to be represented without phonology underlyingly, the general theory of Vocabulary Insertion that is outlined in this book could be extended to them straightforwardly (see section 3 of chapter 2).[3]

1.3.3 Functional Morphemes

As stated in (3a) above, functional morphemes lack phonological content as part of their basic representation. One of the basic functions of "morphology proper" in the framework presented here—i.e., one of the aspects of morphology that is not syntactic in nature, or part of what PF does more generally—is to supply phonological features to functional morphemes. The mechanism responsible for this operation, which is outlined in this chapter and studied in detail in chapter 4, is called *Vocabulary Insertion*. Vocabulary Insertion is an operation that takes place in the PF component of the grammar; it is one of the computations in the Morphology box of (1). It makes crucial reference to a list of objects called *Vocabulary Items*, in which *phonological exponents* (or, sometimes, just *exponents*) are paired with conditions on insertion, stated in terms of features of functional morphemes.

Schematically, a Vocabulary Item takes the form in (4), where synsem features $\alpha, \beta, \gamma...$ are paired with a phonological exponent /X/; the bidirectional arrow relating these two components specifies the nodes to which that item may apply, in a way that is made precise in chapter 4.

(4) Vocabulary Item

$$[\,\alpha\beta\gamma\,] \quad \leftrightarrow \quad /X/$$

synsem features 　　　*(phonological) exponent*

Collectively, the set of Vocabulary Items like the one schematized in (4) comprise the *Vocabulary* of a language.

As an illustration, it can be seen that in terms of representations like (4), the (regular) plural in English nouns like *cat-s* is derived with a Vocabulary Item that pairs the synsem feature [+pl] for 'plural' with the phonological exponent /-z/ (by convention, this exponent is sometimes shown with a hyphen to its left to indicate that it is a suffix):

(5)   [+pl] ↔ /-z/

The Vocabulary Item in (5) is an object in the memory of speakers. It applies to terminal nodes in a syntactic structure (specifically, those that are [+pl]) when the syntactic structure containing that node is operated on at PF.

Concretely, it can be assumed that the syntax combines [+pl] with a noun that contains the Root √CAT, as shown in (6). The *n* head in this structure is a morpheme that creates a noun (a *categorizer*; see chapter 2); the label # indicates that [+pl] is a type of number morpheme:

(6)   Structure for *cats*, before Insertion

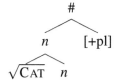

When the item in (5) applies to the node [+pl], the effect is that the phonological exponent /-z/ is added to that node. Informally, it is said that [+pl] is *spelled out* or *realized* as /-z/; correspondingly, the Vocabulary Insertion operation is sometimes referred to informally as *spell out*.[4] Terminologically, theories that allow for morphemes to receive phonological form after they are combined in this way are said to have *late insertion*; sometimes the term *realizational* is applied to theories of this type.

The results of Vocabulary Insertion applying to (6) are shown in (7), which also shows the *n* head with a null exponent (i.e. -Ø):

(7)   Structure for *cats*, after Insertion

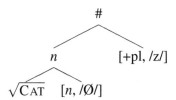

All Vocabulary Items have the form shown in (4). The only modification to this picture is found in cases in which morphemes in the context of the morpheme undergoing Vocabulary Insertion are referred to in a Vocabulary Item. This results in a phenomenon called *contextual allomorphy*. For example, while the [+pl] node is given its form by the Vocabulary Item in (5) when it is attached to *cat*, this is not the case when [+pl] is attached to *ox*. In this latter case, the [+pl] morpheme is realized as (orthographic) *-en*. In this situation, it can be said that the [+pl] morpheme has two distinct (contextual) allomorphs, *-s* and *-en*.

Vocabulary Insertion is central to the view of the morpheme that is advanced in this book. Chapter 4 provides a much closer look at this operation, and the motivations for it are examined in chapters 5 and 6. Contextual allomorphy is treated in detail in chapter 7.

1.3.4 Pieces and *Non-Affixal* Morphology

A basic tenet of the theory developed here is that morphemes (whether Roots or functional heads) are *pieces*, and that morphological phenomena can only be understood in a theory that is piece-based. In light of this claim, it might look as if the approach fails to consider some other issues that are traditionally regarded as part of morphology. This is particularly true of various types of *non-affixal* morphological changes; for example, the change seen in English *sing/sang*, where it is the vowel seen in the Root (and not a segmented affix) that—informally speaking—distinguishes the past tense from the present tense form. This kind of effect is put to the side for the moment, because several more issues have to be addressed before it can be seen how non-affixal processes can be understood in terms of functional morphemes and Roots. Ultimately, it will be seen that the Distributed Morphology framework treats piece-based morphology and non-affixal morphology with distinct mechanisms. The motivation for distinguishing affixal and non-affixal morphology in this way is discussed in chapter 7.

1.4 Lists and Decomposition

Both computations and lists play an important role in the theory of grammar. In this section I will briefly comment on the computational part of the theory, before looking in more detail at some specific assumptions about lists that are part of the theory of Distributed Morphology.

Distributed Morphology holds that **all** complex linguistic objects are derived by the syntax. A consequence of this view is that there is no architectural difference between the manner in which words and phrases are derived. Or, put another way, this means that the grammar does not contain two distinct generative systems, one responsible for the creation of complex words, the other for the creation of phrases. Rather, the theory answers (Q2) above by holding that there is a single generative component in the grammar.

With this architectural position in focus, it is important to emphasize that it is the **basic** derivation of complex objects that is syntactic in this theory. This leaves open the possibility that structures created by the syntax may be further operated on by computations of the PF branch of the grammar, in ways that are relevant to morphology and phonology. For example, in some contemporary views of the mechanics of affixation, the creation of the complex heads that are at the center of the theory of morphology (see chapter 3) may occur either in the syntax, or in terms of PF relations that are derived from syntactic representations. The second disjunct here refers to postsyntactic affixation operations, which create complex heads in the PF component of the grammar. These PF affixation operations apply to the output of a syntactic derivation; from this, it follows that the syntax plays a defining role even when complex heads are created at PF. Because the syntactic structure is the input to PF, and because linear relations are derived from syntactic constituent structures, it is the syntax that determines which nodes are in local PF relationships. Thus, the theory is syntactic at its core, even if PF operations are required for the analysis of certain phenomena.

Beyond having a syntax that derives complex structures, it is also necessary for grammars to *list* certain types of objects (or information about objects) that play a role in the architecture in (1). For example, the morphemes themselves, which are the basic building blocks of the theory, are not derived by any operation—they exist in memory, on a list that is accessed in the course of a syntactic derivation.

Questions about how lists and the property of listedness fit into the theory of grammar are extremely important: first, because the theory must specify precisely how listed information interacts with different aspects of the architecture in (1); and second, because of commonly held understandings (and misunderstandings) about the nature of lists and what is often associated with the notion of *lexical* information in the grammar. In the remainder of this section, I briefly review some key assumptions about the lists that play a role in Distributed Morphology, beginning with some background discussion concerning some of the senses of the term *lexical* that are employed grammatical theory.

1.4.1 Lists and Lexical Information

Because it builds all complex objects in the syntax, the theory of morphology that is presented in this book is sometimes referred to as a *non-lexicalist* theory. What this means is something that must be approached in a few steps, since there are many different theories and ideas to which the term *lexicalist* has been applied. I will focus on two key senses of the term: one that concerns architectural assumptions about the derivation of complex forms, and another that is relevant for listed information and how (and where) it is represented.

In the way that I use the term, a non-lexicalist theory stands in contrast to theories that posit a non-syntactic generative system that is responsible for the derivation of words. Many approaches that derive words in a component of the grammar that is not the syntax originated in the 1970s, and this idea is still an active part of many frameworks. In theories that attribute a special architectural status to words, the term *lexicon* is used for the non-syntactic generative component of the grammar; accordingly, having a lexicon in this specific technical sense results in what is called a *lexicalist* view of grammar (see e.g. Carstairs-McCarthy 1992 for an overview and background discussion).

As mentioned above, the term *lexical* is used in many ways in addition to the technical sense "having a generative Lexicon" introduced immediately above (Aronoff 1994 examines this point in its historical context). Of these further uses of the term, perhaps the most important one uses *lexical* to describe information that must be listed. As it turns out, this list-related sense of what it means to be lexical actually subsumes two distinct notions. The first is that the lexicon is a list of the basic building blocks of the grammar: that is, the primitives that are employed in the construction of complex forms. Primitive building blocks have to be listed in some way, since they are, by definition, not derived. The second type of listing associated with the term *lexical* is related to certain kinds of unpredictability that are associated with prima facie *non*-primitives. In this second sense, the lexicon is seen as a repository for information about complex forms whose behavior is unpredictable in some way, and which therefore must be recorded. For instance, the fact that a certain noun (e.g. *ox*) takes an irregular plural form (*ox-en*), or the fact that a certain phrase (e.g. *buy the farm*) has a "special" meaning (something like 'die'), is not predictable from anything else in the system; therefore such special properties must be listed.

The two types of information just described—(i) the representation of the primitive building blocks, and (ii) the irregularities of larger objects—are logically distinct from one another. This means that, in principle, these two types of information could be encoded in distinct lists; this is the approach that is advocated in the present work. However, a frequently encountered proposal, one which plays a role in many theories of grammar, is that there is a **single** list that performs both of the functions identified in the last paragraph. This view stems from the influential discussion of Bloomfield (1933), whose definition of the lexicon is taken at face value in much later work. A central passage expressing his view is the following:

> A complete description of a language will list every form whose function is not determined either by structure or by a marker; it will include, accordingly, a *lexicon*, or list of morphemes, which indicates the form-class of each morpheme, as well as lists of all complex forms whose function is in any way irregular. (1933:269)

It is clear from the second half of this quote that Bloomfield's lexicon performs the two distinct functions that are discussed earlier: it is both a list of morphemes, and, in addition, a list of (the unpredictable properties of) irregular complex forms.

Putting things together, there are now three different ways in which the lexicon and lexical information have been implicated in the discussion to this point. These correspond to the different notions or senses of *lexical* that are outlined in (8); and it bears repeating that (8a-c) are logically distinct from each other.

(8) Notions of *Lexical*

    a. The idea that the lexicon is a generative system in which words (as opposed to syntactic objects) are derived.

    b. The idea that basic elements (morphemes) must be listed, because they are underived.

    c. The idea that the unpredictable behavior of complex objects must be listed.

With (8) at hand, we are now in a position to understand one of the important architectural claims of many lexicalist theories: the idea that the grammar contains a lexicon that—in addition to combining (8b,c), as Bloomfield's lexicon does—also derives words (8a). In terms of the overall organization of the grammar, a further assumption that characterizes theories of this type is that the lexicon is "prior" to the syntax, in the sense that it provides the syntax with its terminal elements (which, in theories of this type, are words).[5] With some non-trivial differences, theories that incorporate a single lexicon covering all of (8) are explored in Lieber (1980), Selkirk (1982), Kiparsky (1982), and much related work.

This is not the place to review the details of how the functions in (8) are accounted for in lexicalist theories, or the distinct ways in which the lexicon has been defined, or the manner in which different lexicalist theories have defined crucial notions like *listedness*, *wordhood*, etc.[6] The point that is crucial for present purposes is this: the non-lexicalist theory developed in this book does not have a lexicon of the type identified in the last paragraph, i.e., a single component of the grammar that performs all of the functions in (8). Nor does it have a lexicon that performs the two functions associated with Bloomfield's lexicon, i.e., it does not have a single list covering (8b) and (8c). But—and this point is crucial—this does not mean that the approach dispenses with the need to list certain types of information. A non-lexicalist theory must still make use of lists, and must in some form account for all of the list-related phenomena discussed in this section (that is, (8b) and (8c)). As will now be shown, Distributed Morphology employs three distinct lists, and situates access to these lists in different places in the architecture in (1).

Two of the three lists have already been introduced above: first, the list of *Syntactic Terminals*, which consists of the functional morphemes and Roots; and second, the *Vocabulary*, the list of Vocabulary Items that insert phonological content into functional morphemes. These lists are accessed at different points in the model in (1). The list of Syntactic Terminals is accessed by the syntax, when complex objects are built. The Vocabulary is consulted after syntactic structures are sent to the PF component of the grammar. The list of morphemes (= Syntactic Terminals) and the Vocabulary Items are both central to morphological concerns. Using separate lists for them in the way just described and putting these lists in different parts of the grammar are thus ways in which morphology is *distributed* in the present approach.

Moving beyond the Syntactic Terminals and the Vocabulary, something remains to be said about (8c): unpredictable information associated with complex objects. This information comes in different types. A certain amount of unpredictable information is associated with the Vocabulary. For example, the fact that the Vocabulary Item used in the formation of regular plurals in English has the exponent /-z/ is unpredictable. This information is encoded as part of the relevant Vocabulary Item. Other unpredictable information—in particular, the kind associated with allomorphic irregularity—is listed in the Vocabulary as well. So, for example, the fact that $\sqrt{\text{O}\text{X}}$ takes an *-en* plural is encoded in a Vocabulary Item as well (the specific way in which this is done is treated in later chapters; see also section 1.6.2 below).

Something beyond the Vocabulary is required in order to represent unpredictable information about meanings. It has been proposed that at least some information of this type is found on a list that is called the *Encyclopedia* (Marantz 1997). At first glance, there appear to be different types of information that could in principle be present in this list. One kind of unpredictable information on the interpretive side is found with the meaning of Roots. So, for example, the fact that the noun *cat* (which is derived from the Root $\sqrt{\text{CAT}}$) means what it does is not predictable. This information about its meaning must be listed, and one possibility is that this is done in the Encyclopedia. Although this part of the theory of meaning is centered on Roots, it involves functional morphemes as well. An important aspect of the theory of Roots is that grammatical contexts (i.e., local morphemes) play a role in determining the interpretation of a Root—this phenomenon is what is called *polysemy*. Thus, beyond whatever "basic" meaning is represented with a Root, some additional information about how Roots are interpreted in the contexts they appear in has to be listed as well; see chapter 2.

Beyond Root interpretation, other types of idiosyncratic semantic information must be listed as well; for example, as mentioned earlier, the fact that the phrase *buy the farm* in English has a meaning like 'die' in addition to its literal meaning. There are different conceivable approaches to storing this kind of special (= unpredictable) meaning. As long as the phrase *buy the farm* is built in a syntactic derivation, a number of alternatives are compatible with the overall view of grammar that is assumed here.

The last two paragraphs introduce two types of unpredictable meanings that have to be listed in some form. A question of some interest is whether Root interpretations are represented in the same list that contains idiomatic meanings of the *buy the farm* type. It is possible that both of these types of special meanings are encoded in a single Encyclopedia, as Marantz 1997 might suggest. But it may very well turn out to be the case that these aspects of language are distinct, and require distinct representations (see e.g. Marantz 2010). Numerous questions of this type could be examined in a more sustained study of this part of the theory of meaning; but since my concerns here are more morphosyntactic and morphophonological, I will put these to the side.

In summary, the theory developed here does not have a *Lexicon* in the way that many *lexicalist* theories of grammar do. Rather, it employs three lists: the list of *Syntactic Terminals*, the *Vocabulary*, and the *Encyclopedia*.

1.4.2 Decomposition

The previous subsection looks at the kinds of information that must be listed in the grammar, and outlines an approach that employs three distinct lists. Specifying what must be listed, though, is only part of the picture. Distributed Morphology also takes a stance on what kinds of objects *cannot* be listed. In particular, the theory holds that all **complex** objects—i.e., all objects that consist of more than one morpheme—are derived syntactically, every time they are employed. In other words, every word and every phrase is built every time it is used. This position manifests a strongly *decompositionalist* view of language, in which there is no possibility of storing non-primitives. It is stated as *Full Decomposition* in (9).

(9) **Full Decomposition:** No complex objects are stored in memory; i.e., every complex object must be derived by the grammar.

The particular sense of *complex* that is at issue in (9) is important. In principle, *complex* could mean either "consisting of more than one primitive", or it could mean something like "a single primitive with some internal structure". It is the former sense that is crucial here: primitives—which in this theory are morphemes in memory—may be internally complex, in that they may be composed of multiple features. What is ruled out by (9) is storage in memory of a representation that consists of more than one morpheme.

Decomposition is a central component of the theory because it takes the strongest possible generative stance on *lexical relatedness*: the way in which different words are related to one another in the grammar. A theory of morphology must specify what connections exist between related words, such as *play*, *played*, and *plays*; or *vapor*, *vaporous*, and *vaporousness*; and so on. By Full Decomposition, complex objects are related when they share a common part—that is, when they can be decomposed into a shared element. In the case of *plays* and *played*, for example, the relatedness of these forms is found in the fact that both contain the Root √PLAY. Full Decomposition holds that there is no possibility in the theory of storing *plays* and *played* as separate objects in memory, and stating relationships of "relatedness" between them. Rather, they are related because they are built from a shared piece, the Root √PLAY; that is, relatedness is defined decompositionally, in terms of morphemes.

While Full Decomposition might appear obvious (at least in some quarters) when applied to "regular" forms like *plays* and *played*, its strength is much more apparent in the case of "irregular" past tense forms like *sang*. In particular, Full Decomposition rules out an analysis in which *sang* is stored as a combination of the Root √SING plus the past tense morpheme T[+past]. By way of contrast, this kind of "whole word storage" is a property of many other theories of morphology, where it is assumed that any form that is irregular must be "stored", not "derived by rule".[7]

With respect to *sing/sang*, implementing an analysis that complies with Full Decomposition begins with the observation that both the Root √SING and past tense morpheme T[+past] exist as independent morphemes. This is clear from the fact that √SING appears in a number of other contexts (e.g. *sing-Ø*, *sing-s*, *sing-ing*, etc.), while T[+past] appears with a number of other verbs (*play-ed*, *pass-ed*, *plaster-ed*, etc.). Thus, by Full Decomposition, the only way that √SING and T[+past] can be combined is in a syntactic derivation: one that produces the complex head shown in (10). (Also included here is a categorizing *v* head that creates verbs (see chapter 2); the T[+past] morpheme is shown adjoined to *v*, for reasons having to do with how English tense-affixation works):

(10) Past Tense of √SING

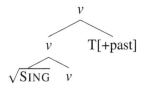

After Vocabulary Insertion and the application of a morphophonological rule that changes the stem vowel, the structure in (10) surfaces as *sang*. (For discussion of this "stem change" (= *stem allomorphy*), see chapter 7). In the terms that were introduced above, *sing* and *sang* are related in the sense that they can be decomposed into a shared part: each of these forms is the result of a derivation that contains the Root $\sqrt{\text{SING}}$.[8]

The predictions that derive from Full Decomposition are the topic of ongoing research both in the theoretical domain, and in psycho- and neurolinguistic studies (for the latter see e.g. Embick and Marantz 2005 and Stockall and Marantz 2006 for perspectives that connect with the present work). The importance of Full Decomposition is seen in many of the case studies that are examined later in this book: particularly in the analysis of contextual allomorphy (where irregular forms are at issue) and of blocking effects (where lexical relatedness is crucial); see chapter 7.

1.4.3   Lists and Their Motivation

The framework of Distributed Morphology uses three lists: the list of Syntactic Terminals; the Vocabulary; and the Encyclopedia. It is worth mentioning that with respect to "conceptual" questions about the nature of the grammar, these lists might not all be on equal footing. Two of them are more or less impeccable as far as considerations of parsimony ("Minimalist" or otherwise) are concerned: the Syntactic Terminals and the Encyclopedia. This is because every theory needs to have a list of building blocks and to list certain types of unpredictable interpretations.

The motivation for the Vocabulary, on the other hand, is not as self-evident as the motivation for the other two lists is. Even though it deals with information that has to be listed—since the phonological forms that realize morphemes are not predictable—there are ways of encoding this information that do not require a third list; by representing phonological information with morphemes in the list of Syntactic Terminals, for example. That is, admitting the Vocabulary into the ontology of the theory is a consequence of denying that functional heads are "traditional" morphemes (= morphemes that possess both sound and meaning from the beginning) in favor of a realizational approach to sound/meaning connections.

It is not clear whether or not there is any sort of conceptual motivation for the Vocabulary. However, the motivation for Vocabulary Insertion is not meant to be conceptual; it is empirical, and is based on the need to state certain cases of morphological identity—instances of the phenomenon of *syncretism*—systematically. Section 1.6.2 of this chapter provides an introduction to syncretism, which is then examined in detail in chapters 4-6.

1.5 Summary and Core Properties

The theory developed in this book is centered on the idea that morphemes are the primitive elements of derivations in the grammar in (1). The theory employs the three lists in (11):

(11) Lists

   a. **The Syntactic Terminals:** The list containing the *Roots* and the *Functional Morphemes*.
   b. **The Vocabulary:** The list of *Vocabulary Items*, objects that provide phonological content to functional morphemes.
   c. **The Encyclopedia:** The list of special semantic information.

These lists are accessed at distinct stages, as shown in the diagram in (12):

(12) The Grammar, with Lists

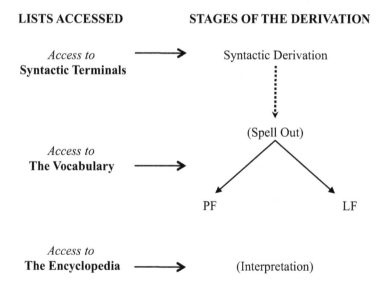

Morphemes are drawn from the list of *Syntactic Terminals*, and serve as the terminal elements of syntactic derivations. The *Vocabulary* is consulted at PF, where phonological exponents are added to functional morphemes. Finally, the Encyclopedia is accessed in the interface with interpretation. For convenience, I have shown this after the LF interface (which I take to encode the more "structural" aspects of compositional interpretation). There are some oversimplifications involved in this treatment of Encyclopedic knowledge, but these do not impact the central claims of this work.

The rest of this book articulates the central claims of Distributed Morphology, with respect to the morpheme and the Vocabulary Insertion operation in particular. Although Distributed Morphology is a framework in which different theories can be explored, there are some core positions that define its boundaries. As I see it, these are as follows:

Syntactic: The theory is non-lexicalist; there is no pre-syntactic lexicon in which words are derived or stored. The only generative component in the grammar is the syntax. Thus, words have no privileged architectural status.

Morphemes: The approach is piece-based. The fundamental units of morphology are discrete pieces arranged in hierarchical structures: morphemes.

(Some) Late Insertion: For certain morphemes—in the approach assumed here, at least the functional morphemes—phonological material is supplied only on the PF branch, via the operation of Vocabulary Insertion.

Full Decomposition: No complex objects are stored in memory; rather, every complex object must be derived by the grammar, every time it is employed.

Different varieties of Distributed Morphology have been proposed within the boundaries defined by these four distinct positions, and their differences continue to be investigated empirically. Abandoning any one of these central positions, however, results in an approach with quite different properties from those of the theory discussed here.

1.6 (P)review: Main Themes

Note: This section outlines a number of themes that recur throughout the book, in a way that might require a more advanced background than the preceding sections. Much of this background is presented in later chapters of the book. Thus, readers who are directly interested in the development of the nuts-and-bolts of the theory might wish to continue on to chapter 2, and return to this section at a later point (e.g. when specific themes are referred to later, or in conjunction with the concluding remarks in chapter 8).

Although it is primarily directed at the morpheme, this book also touches on a number of further theoretical questions. This is perhaps not surprising, since the discussion starts with the representation of morphemes in memory, touches on the composition of morphemes into complex objects, and looks in detail at the phonological realization of morphemes at PF. That is to say, despite the book's focus on the morpheme, the chapters to come examine a number of distinct parts of the grammar, in a way that gives substance to the general idea that the analysis of most "morphological" phenomena cannot be pursued without reference to syntax, semantics, and phonology.

All the same, there are a number of main themes that are present in the entire book. By *themes* here I do not mean theoretical principles or assumptions per se. Rather, these are recurring areas of interest—both consequences of the approach, and ways of framing its basic properties—that are manifested both throughout the pages to come, and in the literature as well. Three of the most important of these are outlined in the remainder of this chapter.

1.6.1 Interface Transparency

An important topic in linguistic theory is how objects of morphological interest like morphemes (and words, in the informal sense) interact with the syntactic structures in which these objects appear. This is part of the question (Q2) that is posed in the first section of this chapter. Treating morphemes as syntactic objects, as in the present approach, produces a theory in which there are **direct** connections between syntax and morphology. This is a significant point, because not all morphological theories treat the relationship between words and syntactic structures in this way. Indeed, many theories of morphology explicitly deny that morphemes are syntactic objects (e.g., theories with a lexicon of the type defined in 1.4.1), or deny that the form of words is based on a decomposition into morphemes in the first place (e.g., Anderson (1992) who develops an *affixless* or *amorphous* theory, for inflectional morphology anyway). Theories of the syntax/morphology interface thus range from the more opaque (where the structure of words and the structure of clauses in which those words appear have nothing to do with one another) to the more transparent (where morphological structures are syntactic structures). The latter type of view, which I refer to as *interface transparency*, constitutes one of the main tenets of Distributed Morphology. In essence, it amounts to the claim that mismatches between syntax and morphology are minimal. More precisely, the idea is that transparent syntax/morphology connections are the norm, and that deviations from the norm are the result of operations that apply in the PF component of the grammar.

Within transparent theories of the syntax/morphology interface, a standard view is that *complex heads* are the most important syntactic objects of morphological interest. A complex head consists of two or more morphemes that have been combined by an affixation operation. For example, a Root that appears in a syntactic structure with heads X and Y (13) can be combined into a complex head (14) with these heads. The affixation shown in (14) could, for example, be produced by the process of head movement, taking the $\sqrt{\text{ROOT}}$ to X, and then [$\sqrt{\text{ROOT}}$ X] to Y:

(13) Structure   (14) Complex Head

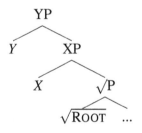
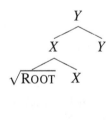

In this schematization, the object of "morphological interest" (14) is created in the structure in (13); i.e., the word has a direct relation to the phrase that it appears in, since the word is created in that phrase. There is no further question about how the structure of words like (14) might relate to phrasal structures like (13), beyond the theory of affixation itself, which specifies under what conditions affixation may take place (so that, for example, the presence of other material in a structure like (13)—e.g. a head Z between X and Y—could prevent head movement from taking place).

In theories that do not derive words syntactically, the question of what to do with word/syntax relations is a pressing one: something must regulate how it is that words like $\sqrt{\text{ROOT}}$-X-Y are created in one system (e.g. a Lexicon), and used in syntactic environments in which the features X and Y are expressed. Moreover, such a theory does not have a clear answer to why the position (linear order) of the -X and -Y morphemes appears to be systematically related to the clause structure in which XP and YP appear, an effect that relates to the so-called *Mirror Principle* (see chapter 3).

On the other hand, a syntactic approach offers straightforward answers to questions of this type: words that express the features X and Y express these features because they are derived in syntactic structures where X and Y are syntactic terminals. Moreover, the morphemes appear where they do for reasons that are directly related to the syntactic structure (see chapter 3 below), by virtue of (i) the locality conditions on affixation, in conjunction with (ii) conditions that regulate how syntactic structures are linearized.

In summary, the relationship between syntactic structures and morphology is maximally transparent in this framework because in the default case, there is no difference between the two. When "mismatches" between syntax and morphology (or phonology) do arise (as in the case of e.g. "bracketing paradoxes", or with post-syntactic movement; see chapter 3), it is because of the application of specific PF operations. Following a long line of such research (one that is initiated in the discussion of prosodic mismatches in Chomsky and Halle (1968), and developed in the 1980s in works like Marantz (1984, 1988) and Sproat (1985)), the goal of Distributed Morphology has been to develop a restrained view of the PF operations that render syntax/morphology connections less transparent. For an overview of these operations, see Embick and Noyer (2007); for discussion of mismatches that specifically implicate morphemes and their features, see the Appendix.

1.6.2 Realizational Sound/Meaning Connections

The idea that Vocabulary Insertion provides phonological forms to certain morphemes—or the idea that at least some morphemes do not possess an underlying phonological representation—constitutes a significant theoretical move. It is motivated empirically, by the finding that sound/meaning connections at the level of the morpheme are quite complex.

The easiest way to approach this complexity is through the observation that sound/meaning connections for morphemes are not always *one-to-one*. Under ideal circumstances, each functional morpheme in a language would be paired with a unique phonological exponent. This type of situation (which does not, evidently, occur in any natural language) would, at the level of the morpheme, be maximally transparent. One of the main topics in the theory of the morpheme concerns the possible departures from the one-to-one ideal, and the implementation of analyses that take these departures into account. As in the case of section 1.6.1 above, the theoretical imperative in this domain is to account for the attested departures from the ideal, while maintaining the most transparent (= strongest) theory of sound/meaning connections possible.

The lack of full transparency in sound/meaning connections is manifested in different ways. Informally, the two ways that are of immediate interest involve sound/meaning connections that are *many-to-one* and those that are *one-to-many*. The first type (= many sound forms, one meaning) is found in the phenomenon of *allomorphy*, where a single morpheme like T[+past] shows multiple, distinct phonological realizations, as it does in *play-ed*, *ben-t*, and *hit-Ø*. This is a complication to the simple one-to-one ideal, since a single synsem object (T[+past]) has more than one distinct phonological underlying representation associated with it (/d/, /t/, Ø). Allomorphy figures prominently in the introduction to Vocabulary Insertion that is developed in chapter 4; and a more detailed treatment of allomorphy occupies much of chapter 7.

Another significant complication for the one-to-one ideal is found in the phenomenon of *syncretism*, where morphemes composed of distinct sets of synsem features are realized with the same phonological exponent. Compare, for example, the present tense verb forms from Latin and (Latin-American) Spanish in (15) (Latin *laudāre* 'praise'; Spanish *hablar* 'speak'):

(15) Illustration of Syncretism

p/n	Latin	Latin American Spanish
1s	laud-ō	habl-o
2s	laudā-s	habla-s
3s	lauda-t	habla-Ø
1p	laudā-mus	habla-mos
2p	laudā-tis	habla-**n**
3p	lauda-nt	habla-**n**

While Latin shows distinct agreement morphemes for the six combinations of person and number features shown in (15), Latin American Spanish shows only five distinct phonological exponents, with an *-n* appearing in both the second person plural and third person plural contexts. The fact that *-n* appears in these two morphosyntactically distinct environments is not an accident; that is to say, it is not a case of homophony of the type found with *bank* 'side of river' and *bank* 'financial institution', or with plural /-z/ versus third person singular present agreement /-z/ in English. Rather, in the analysis of Latin American Spanish there needs to be a way of saying that **the same** *-n* appears with two distinct sets of synsem features; this effect is what is referred to as a *(systematic) syncretism* in this work.

Syncretisms are pervasive in natural language, and the theory of the morpheme must be able to analyze them as non-accidents. The Vocabulary Insertion operation, introduced in section 1.3 of this chapter, is designed to provide a systematic (that is to say, non-accidental) analysis of syncretism. It does this by providing a mechanism by which a single phonological exponent can occur in multiple synsem contexts; i.e., as the phonological realization of distinct morphemes.

The key idea is that Vocabulary Items may be *underspecified* with respect to the functional morphemes that they apply to. In order to see this point in a specific example, consider the functional morphemes involved in Spanish agreement (AGR) in (16); the synsem features are [± 1] and [± 2] for person, and [$\pm$pl] for number:

(16) Spanish Agr Morphemes

    a. [+1,-2,-pl] = '1st person singular'
    b. [-1,+2,-pl] = '2nd person singular'
    c. [-1,-2,-pl] = '3rd person singular'
    d. [+1,-2,+pl] = '1st person plural'
    e. [-1,+2,+pl] = '2nd person plural'
    f. [-1,-2,+pl] = '3rd person plural'

In a particular derivation involving a finite Spanish present tense verb, one of the functional morphemes in (16) is present prior to Vocabulary Insertion. These functional morphemes are spelled out at PF by the Vocabulary Items in (17):

(17) Vocabulary Items for Spanish Agr in (15)

$[+1,-2,+pl] \leftrightarrow$ -mos
$[+1,-2,-pl] \leftrightarrow$ -o
$[-1,+2,-pl] \leftrightarrow$ -s
$[-1,-2,-pl] \leftrightarrow$ -Ø
$[-1,+pl] \leftrightarrow$ -n

The Vocabulary Items in (17) compete for application to a given morpheme. In order to apply, a Vocabulary Item must have a (not necessarily proper) subset of the features on the morpheme that it is to apply to. When more than one Vocabulary Item could in principle apply to a morpheme, the Vocabulary Item with the most specific content (i.e., the one with the largest subset of features on the target morpheme) wins the competition. In the case of the 2nd and 3rd person plural forms, the most specific Vocabulary Item that can apply is the last one in the list in (17); this is because there is no Vocabulary Item in (17) that refers to $[-1,+2,+pl]$ or to $[-1,-2,+pl]$. As a result, the exponent -*n* is inserted into two nodes that are distinct in terms of their synsem features; thus, it is found with both the second person plural and third person plural agreement morphemes (16e,f).

As mentioned earlier in the text above (16), this analysis of syncretism relies on the idea that Vocabulary Items may be underspecified with respect to the morphemes that they apply to. In a way that will be made precise in chapter 4, this means that Vocabulary Items need not make reference to all of the features that appear on the morpheme that they apply to. In the particular case of (17), the Vocabulary Item that inserts -*n* is underspecified with respect to the two morphemes it applies to—(16e) and (16f), in that it does not make reference to the feature $[\pm 2]$ that is present on each of these morphemes.

It is important to observe that the analysis of syncretism in (17) accounts for the syncretism in (15) by using a **single** Vocabulary Item, and not by using two distinct Vocabulary Items that each happen to have the exponent -*n*. By definition, the syncretism is analyzed as systematic. Even though second and third person agreement morphemes are distinct objects at one level of analysis, since they have distinct synsem feature content, they receive their phonology from the same Vocabulary Item.[9]

Underspecifiying sound with respect to meaning—or, in the terms of this work, exponents with respect to synsem features—requires Vocabulary Insertion (or something like it). It crucially requires the idea that sound forms are added to morphemes that do not possess phonological representations underlyingly. If there were no Vocabulary Insertion operation, and functional morphemes were represented with their phonological form inherently, the Spanish pattern could not be analyzed as a systematic effect. Rather, the grammar of Spanish would contain two distinct functional morphemes [-1,+2,+pl,/n/] and [-1,-2,+pl,/n/] whose phonological form just happens to be the same. This latter analysis, which treats the identity in form as accidental homophony, is not capable of stating the important generalization that (featurally) similar meanings are realized with the same morphology in language after language.

In summary, the Vocabulary Insertion operation is required as a way of systematically accounting for syncretism, one of the most important ways in which languages deviate from a one-to-one relation between sound and meaning. As noted earlier in this chapter, theories that add phonological exponents to morphemes in this way are called *realizational* theories of morphology.[10] One of the central goals of Distributed Morphology is to develop a realizational theory of morphology that maintains the strongest possible theory of sound-meaning connections, while at the same time being flexible enough to account for syncretism and some related phenomena. This theme is developed in detail in chapters 4-6 below; and the question of how to maintain a strong realizational theory occurs throughout the entire book.

1.6.3   The Morpheme-Locus Effect

A final thread that extends through the following pages is extremely general; in some sense, it is one of the main arguments of Distributed Morphology. This is the idea that the morpheme is essential for explaining a number of phenomena in the grammar. This may sound unsurprising, especially given the assumptions that are articulated above; at a minimum, the morpheme must have an important status in a theory like the one outlined here, because it is a syntactic theory, and morphemes have the privileged status of being the terminal elements in syntactic derivations. But if the central claim of this book is correct, then the morpheme is special in ways that go beyond this. In particular, it appears that the morpheme as defined in this work is the object that is referred to by a number of formal operations and representations which, taken together, cover a large part of the theory of morphology. To highlight this facet of the theory, I refer to the convergence of distinct subtheories on morphemes (and not objects of other sizes) as the *Morpheme-Locus Effect*.

This effect manifests itself in a number of distinct domains. One of the most fundamental is with respect to sound/meaning relations, and follows on the discussion of the last subsection. Functional morphemes receive their phonological form via the Vocabulary Insertion operation; and, part of the theory of Vocabulary Insertion to be developed below is that morphemes are the *only* targets for phonological realization. This means that there is no possibility of treating entire "words" as subject to phonological realization in a single step, nor is it possible to realize other syntactic objects (i.e. non-terminal nodes) with Vocabulary Insertion. Thus, the primary locus of sound/meaning relations in the grammar is the morpheme, because it is only in that type of object that "basic" sound/meaning relations are established.

Empirically, this morpheme-only view of insertion turns out to have important consequences in a number of domains. One is in the theory of *blocking effects* in the grammar. In a view that derives from the influential work of Aronoff (1976), competitions for grammaticality can be waged between entire words, so that, in a famous example, it is possible to say that *glory* blocks **gloriosity*. In the theory that is developed here, word/word competition cannot take place. The only locus for competition is the morpheme, because that is the only object to which Vocabulary Insertion applies (the assumption of Full Decomposition is also relevant here). It appears that restricting phonological realization in this way produces correct predictions about the full range of blocking effects seen in natural language, as is discussed in chapter 7. The key idea in this analysis is that the morpheme is the special object: an instance of the Morpheme-Locus Effect.

Another phenomenon that plays a central role in most morphological theories is contextual allomorphy, where a morpheme takes different forms that are determined by items in its context. In chapter 7, I will articulate a theory in which the locality conditions on allomorphic interactions are stated in terms of morphemes: roughly, one morpheme may see another for allomorphic purposes only when the two morphemes are adjacent. Again, this is a manifestation of the Morpheme-Locus Effect. It could have turned out to be the case that allomorphy in natural language required reference to larger objects (whole words), to properties of non-terminal nodes, and so on, but this does not appear to be the case. Rather, the theory of contextual allomorphy requires insertion of phonological material at morphemes, and relies on locality conditions defined in terms of morphemes.

There are other places where the Morpheme-Locus Effect can be seen in the pages below, both in very specific case studies, and in connection with very general architectural points. For instance, much of what is called Interface Transparency above is centered on the morpheme, and would be impossible without it.

In sum, the Morpheme-Locus Effect is a shorthand way of referring to the central claim of this book: *the theory of morphology requires morphemes, because it is only in this way that a number of grammatical phenomena can be explained in a principled way.*

Chapter 2
Morphemes and Features

2.1 Introduction

The first chapter of this book outlines the essential properties of a piece-based view of morphology in which morphemes are the terminal nodes in syntactic structures. A central idea in the theory is that morphemes are of two distinct types: the *functional heads* and the *Roots*. The present chapter looks in greater detail at each of these types of morpheme, with particular emphasis on how they relate to different types of features.

As stressed in chapter 1, morphemes are the **primitive** elements of syntactic derivation; that is to say, they are *atomic*, as far as the syntax is concerned. This means that the morpheme is the smallest object manipulated by syntactic operations. But the idea that morphemes are atomic does not mean that they have no subparts. Indeed, according to the view that I will adopt here, some morphemes (functional morphemes in particular) are bundles of features. In the words of Chomsky (2007:6), such morphemes are "a structured array of properties (*features*) to which Merge and other operations apply to form expressions".

The precise sense in which morphemes are *structured* objects is of some interest. As an initial hypothesis, a morpheme consisting of different features F_i can be represented as a set like (1):

(1) $\{F_1, \ldots, F_n\}$

Beyond the minimum of (1), how much internal structure morphemes possess is an empirical question. The simplest position is (presumably) that morphemes are sets of features and nothing more, so that positing any additional structure (e.g. "geometries", or other hierarchical representations of features) requires significant empirical motivation.[1]

While (1) is the basic way in which morphemes are represented, some notational conventions are often employed in representing morphemes, particularly with respect to how *category* is treated. Following standard practice, morphemes in this book are sometimes represented with a category label separate from further specification of feature content. So, for instance, when this convention is employed, a past tense morpheme is represented as in (2):

(2) T[+past]

This type of representation is shorthand for a representation like (1), where all features—including those that make the morpheme a tense morpheme—are represented in a single set, so that the "category label" is just another feature.[2]

2.2 Functional Morphemes

The idea that morphemes are sets of features is most clearly relevant to functional morphemes, where the approach developed here extends a view that is standard in syntactic theory: functional morphemes are the familiar *functional categories*, by definition, bundles of grammatical features. As will be seen below, however, Distributed Morphology expands the use of functional categories, by making use of functional heads to provide the "lexical categories" like *noun*, *verb*, etc. to Roots; see section 2.3.4 below.

This section looks at the non-phonological aspect of functional morphemes: their synsem features. Questions about the phonological representation of functional morphemes are put off until chapter 4, where the Vocabulary Insertion process is introduced.

2.2.1 Features and Functional Morphemes

I assume that the grammar contains a universal set of synsem features. To a first approximation, the features in this set are those that are required for semantic interpretation; that is to say, they are *interpretable* features, in the sense of Chomsky (1995) and related work.

The universal synsem feature set includes features related to Tense, Aspect, Number, Person, etc.: all of the different feature types that are relevant for semantics, or, more precisely, that are responsible for those aspects of meaning that are encoded in the grammar. Some preliminary versions of features of this type are referred to in chapter 1: for instance, [±def] for definiteness, [±pl] for plural, [±past] for past tense, and so on. Following a convention introduced in the last chapter, it will be assumed that such features are binary in the default case.

Taken together, the set of synsem features is called the *Universal Feature Inventory*, or, for convenience, the UFI. A particular language employs a subset of features from the UFI. Terminologically, a feature that is selected by a language is said to be *active* in that language. The active features in a language are employed (either individually or bundled with other features) as the contents of the functional morphemes of that language.

The contents of the UFI are the topic of one of the basic research questions about the substantive universals of human language (cf. Chomsky (1965)). With respect to the particular concerns of this section, there are two properties of the UFI that relate to the theory of functional morphemes. The first is the idea that languages draw from the same inventory of features. The second property is that there are evidently universal constraints on what could be a possible morpheme in a language, so that not any subset of features from the UFI could be bundled together into a functional morpheme.

These two positions place some quite general boundaries on the morpheme inventories of natural languages, with the result that languages are expected to overlap considerably in their morpheme inventories. Nevertheless, there is also a language-particular aspect of the theory of functional morphemes—the exact set of functional morphemes in any given language is something which shows cross-linguistic variation. This is because individual languages may differ in two ways. First, a feature from the UFI may be active in one language, but not another. Second, languages may differ in terms of how they package their features into functional morphemes.

The UFI has parallels in the feature theory of phonology, where it is standardly assumed that different languages employ different subsets of features from the same universal inventory, and package them into segments in different ways.

In phonology, a substantial literature (e.g. Jakobson and Halle (1956), Chomsky and Halle (1968), Clements (1985), Halle (2002), and much related work) has produced large-scale agreement about most of the feature inventory. For the UFI, there is less consensus, relatively speaking, about the nature of functional morphemes and their features, making this an extremely active area of ongoing research. Bearing this in mind, we can nevertheless look at some illustrations of how languages differ in their morpheme inventories.

2.2.2 *Bundling* and Possible Morphemes

As mentioned in section 2.1 above, it is assumed in this work that a single morpheme can consist of more than one synsem feature. Terminologically, it can be said that functional morphemes that consist of multiple sysem features contain *bundled* features. As an example of this bundling, a first person plural pronominal is represented with two features [±1] and [±pl], as shown in (3), which puts to the side the feature(s) that define the category of a pronoun:

(3)   First Person Plural = [+1,+pl]

In this morpheme, the two features together produce the relevant interpretation: the [+1] feature is responsible for the first person part, and [+pl] provides the plurality.

Many languages possess the functional morpheme in (3). But it is by no means *necessary* for the two features in (3) to be bundled together into one morpheme. As far as the claims of this chapter go, it could very well be the case that some languages have [±1] and [±pl] in separate morphemes. This latter scenario is perhaps what is found in languages like Mandarin Chinese, where personal pronouns show separate morphemes for person and number:

(4)   Mandarin Chinese Pronominals (Corbett 2000)

p/n	form
1s	wǒ
2s	nǐ
3s	tā
1p	wǒ-men
2p	nǐ-men
3p	tā-men

So, whereas English has a single morpheme (3) that receives the pronunciation *we*, Mandarin Chinese has two separate morphemes, [+1] and [+pl], which are used to derive the meaning of first person plural. The general idea that languages differ in terms of how they bundle features—and that these differences have interesting empirical consequences—has been explored in a number of domains.[3]

While it will be assumed throughout this work that languages may differ with respect to how they bundle features along the lines just illustrated, some general comments are in order concerning how alternative hypotheses about functional morphemes might be brought to bear on the analysis of phenomena like the one seen in English and Mandarin. In particular, certain general assumptions about morphemes and features could force analyses in which either (i) Mandarin would look like English (with person and number bundled, and subsequently split), or (ii) English would look more like Mandarin (with person and number as separate morphemes, and subsequently combined). Informally speaking, the former scenario would be motivated in a theory in which the bundling of features is preferred to their independent representation as morphemes; and the latter would arise in a theory that assumes the reverse (i.e., as little bundling as possible). Although neither of these hypotheses will be examined in detail in this work, operations that have the effect of splitting and fusing morphemes, which would be required on the alternatives (i) and (ii) above, are discussed in Appendix A.

Moving past questions about how languages may differ, there is a universal question concerning which features can be bundled together into a functional morpheme. For example, while person and number features are often bundled together in pronouns in many languages, in the way that is illustrated in (3), the same does not appear to be true for many other conceivable combinations of features. It does not seem to be the case, for instance, that languages employ morphemes that consist of bundled Tense and number features, or preposition and adjective features, and so on.

While it is possible to point to many examples of prima facie impossible morphemes like the ones just mentioned, there is, as far as I am aware, no comprehensive theory of possible morphemes. At least, there is no **explicit** theory of impossible morphemes. By this I mean that many (often tacit) aspects of syntactic theory, concerning the nature of grammatical categories and their interactions with each other, constitute a working theory of possible morphemes. They do this because they employ morphemes with certain combinations of features (and certain selectional properties, etc.), and not others. Thus, the absence of many conceivable but apparently impossible morphemes "makes sense" given what is known about the syntax of natural languages (e.g., that Tense and number do not have similar distributions). However, this kind of observation falls short of a general theory of *possible morpheme*, which would be an important component of a comprehensive theory of the UFI. In practice, most approaches—including the present one—assume that there is some notion of syntactic and semantic coherence that determines what kinds of features may be bundled together. But how exactly this kind of coherence is defined, and what motivation(s) there might be for it, are important questions that are at present open for further investigation.

2.2.3 Differences in Active Features

It is well known that languages differ in terms of the morphological distinctions they make. This is true even when we put to the side relatively superficial morphological properties like systems of (arbitrary) conjugation and declension classes, which are notorious for their language-particular character (see 3.3 below).

There are two main ways in which cross-linguistic differences in morphological distinctions are manifested. One way is in terms of the selections that languages make from the UFI: in some cases, a feature that is active in some languages is not active in others. A second possibility is that different languages possess the same features in some domain, but differ in terms of how these features are bundled. We saw a preliminary example of this type in the discussion of English versus Mandarin pronouns in the preceding section.

As will become clear below, the two potential types of difference may or may not be difficult to distinguish from each other. This point can be illustrated with systems of number of the type associated with pronouns, number marking in nominals, and attendant verbal agreement, which exhibit some fairly well-studied differences in morpheme inventories. For instance, some languages distinguish only between singular and plural numbers, whereas others mark in addition to these a *dual*, for two referents. Classical Greek is a language of the latter type; it has singular, plural, and dual numbers, so that nouns are in principle marked in three distinct ways, as shown for the noun *níkē* 'victory' in (5). For simplicity, I have not attempted to segment the number morphemes in these forms:

(5) *níkē* 'victory', Nominative Case

singular	níkē
dual	níkā
plural	níkai

The same number distinctions are found in verbal agreement as well. The present tense verb forms in (6) show different endings that reflect the three-way division of number:

(6) Present Tense lú-ō 'loose'

p/n	form
1s	lúō
2s	lúeis
3s	lúei
1d	lúomen
2d	lúeton
3d	lúeton
1p	lúomen
2p	lúete
3p	lúousi

The number system of Classical Greek can be compared with that found in a language like English, where there are only two numbers: singular and plural. In a language of the latter type, a single binary feature suffices to make the needed synsem (and hence morphological) distinctions; for convenience, we can take this feature to be [±pl]. Then, [-pl] and [+pl] encode "singular" and "plural" respectively (the terms in quotes can be understood as a shorthand way of referring to the more basic feature distinction).

Clearly, a single binary feature [±pl] is insufficient to make the semantically relevant distinctions in a language that has a dual in addition to singular and plural. On the assumption that features are maximally binary, another feature is needed. Here, it will be assumed that dual number arises in systems with two binary features, [±sg] and [±pl]; the dual is found when the value for each such feature is negative, as shown in (7):[4]

(7) Number Features

	+sg	-sg
+pl	– –	"plural"
-pl	"singular"	"dual"

With reference to (7)—and the assumptions about English outlined above—it can be seen that Classical Greek employs functional morphemes that are not found in English. In English, number morphemes contain either [+pl] or [-pl]:

(8) English Morphemes, with Number

    a. singular: [-pl]

    b. plural: [+pl]

Classical Greek, on the other hand, employs functional morphemes with the number features shown in (9):

(9) Classical Greek Morphemes, with Number

    a. singular: [+sg,-pl]

    b. dual: [-sg,-pl]

    c. plural: [-sg,+pl]

In this analysis, English and Greek differ in terms of features selected from the UFI: English uses [±pl], but makes no use of [±sg]. In terms that are employed at the beginning of this section, this means that a feature that is active in one language (Greek) is not active in another (English). (Secondarily, Greek also differs from English on this analysis in having [±sg] and [±pl] features bundled in the same node).

    It should be evident from even this introductory discussion that the precise nature of the difference between these languages depends on assumptions about the representation of features. Suppose, for example, that (perhaps because of some other assumptions about uniformity of features) English were treated with [±sg] and [±pl] features. Then, English singular and plural would be defined as in Classical Greek: that is, they would be [+sg,-pl] and [-sg,+pl] respectively, while [-sg,-pl] would not exist as a morpheme in the language. Under this second scenario, English and Classical Greek would both have the same features from the UFI, in the sense that both would employ [±sg] and [±pl]. The difference between them would then be that Classical Greek would have functional morphemes with [-sg,-pl], whereas English would not. Thus, the languages would differ in how features are bundled into morphemes, but not in terms of which features are active in the languages in the first place.

    On the basis of just the information considered above, it is difficult to distinguish between the first (inventory-based) and second (bundling-based) treatments. There might be additional empirical and theoretical considerations favoring one or the other when systems of number are analyzed in detail. However, because the comparison of Greek and English suffices to illustrate the basics of how individual languages make use of the UFI, I will not examine this point further here.

Speaking informally, it is often clear when one language makes a distinction that is not found in another, as in the case of the dual above. Sometimes, though, many difficult questions arise when even simple-looking differences are examined in detail. Consider, for example, the domain of "tense", broadly construed for present purposes so as to refer to tense and aspect together. Verbs in even relatively similar languages often differ in terms of the tense distinctions they express. For example, English has present and past tense forms of the verb, whereas Spanish verbs manifest a further distinction between imperfective and preterite (= perfective) past tenses:

(10)   Tense Forms

    a. English

        i. Present: play, play-s

        ii. Past: play-ed

    b. Spanish *hablar* 'speak'; 1s, 2s, 3s, ...

        i. Present: habl-o, habl-a-s, habl-a, etc.

        ii. Imperfect: habl-a-ba, habl-a-ba-s, habl-a-ba, etc.

        iii. Preterite: habl-é, habl-a-ste, habl-ó, etc.

Clearly, English and Spanish differ in terms of the number of distinct finite verb forms they possess. What this means at the level of synsem features active in the language is, however, less obvious. For instance, one of the meanings of the Spanish past imperfective form is past progressive. In English, past progressive meaning is expressed with what is called the *progressive* form, which consists of a form of *be* along with an *-ing* form of the main verb:[5]

(11)   John was playing.

Determining how the Tense (and Aspect) morphemes of English and Spanish might differ thus ultimately depends on an analysis of how the meaning of the English (past) progressive relates to the meaning of the Spanish imperfective. It is possible that the languages use very similar features that are "packaged" differently: that is, so that the same features are realized as a single "verb" (= complex head) in Spanish, but as an auxiliary plus a participle in English.

There are, of course, alternatives to this analysis, according to which, for example, English and Spanish employ different (though semantically similar) features and morphemes in this part of the tense system. Answering questions of this type requires an integrated theory of semantics and syntax along with morphology; it is a good example of why many topics of morphological interest cannot be investigated in isolation.

The question of how morphemes are packaged into complex heads is an important topic and will be taken up again in chapter 3. For immediate purposes, the comparison based on (10) shows that superficial differences in morphosyntax are not necessarily always reducible to differences in synsem feature inventories or morphemes in a simple way. Rather, such differences might involve either differences in features and their bundling into morphemes, or the arrangement (through affixation operations) of morphemes into complex heads, or both.

2.2.4 Summary: Features of Functional Morphemes

Functional morphemes are bundles of synsem features: binary features, at least in the default case. The working hypothesis adopted in this book is that the features have no additional internal structure; however, the general framework is compatible with many different types of theories of feature content and organization.

A final question to consider with respect to synsem features is whether or not they are specific to particular categories. Morphemes like D[+def] and T[+past] make it look as if synsem features are specifically geared towards particular grammatical categories (so that, e.g., Determiners may be [±def], and Tense nodes [±past], but not vice versa). It is certainly possible that features are very specific to different categories in this way. But it is conceivable that the semantic operations that are applied when synsem features are interpreted are much more general than this. One attractive possibility is that the grammar does not contain features that are specific to notions like "person" or "number" or "tense" or "deixis"; rather, it possesses a small number of features corresponding to general-purpose semantic operations whose precise interpretation depends on what grammatical category the features apply to. For illustration and semantic execution of proposals along these lines, see in particular Schlenker (1999, 2006) and Harbour (2008).

2.3 Roots

In addition to functional morphemes, the grammar contains morphemes that are called *Roots*. By definition, Roots are the members of the open-class vocabulary of a language. This part of the vocabulary is typically thought of as connecting with *concepts*: a system of mental representations of classes, which exists outside of the grammar (see Murphy (2002) for an overview). The representation and use of Roots is a complex issue, because of their dual nature as grammatical objects that have important connections with (presumably) extragrammtical cognitive systems.

The discussion below concentrates primarily on the more grammatical aspects of Root representation—i.e., on how Roots are represented in memory, and how they relate to different types of features. Some assumptions about the meaning and conceptual side of Roots are outlined as well, but these are kept to a manageable minimum.

2.3.1 Roots and Phonological Features

A hypothesis that has been adopted in much work is that Roots are represented with phonological features underlyingly. In terms of the standard notation that is used for this type of morpheme, the Root underlying the noun *cat* is shown in (12):

(12) $\sqrt{\text{CAT}}$

On the further assumption that the Root $\sqrt{\text{CAT}}$ has a phonological matrix underlyingly, (12) can be thought of a shorthand for a more explicit representation that is minimally the one in (13) (using the set representation of morphemes employed earlier in this chapter for functional morphemes):

(13) $\{\text{/kæt/}\}$

As with functional morphemes, the discussion below will alternate between the less explicit ((12)-type) and more explicit ((13)-type) representations, depending on immediate concerns.

In the case of the Root $\sqrt{\text{CAT}}$ in (12) and (13), it is taken for granted that the phonological underlying representation suffices to uniquely identify the Root. However, phonological representations alone are not able to do this for all Roots in a language. As noted in chapter 1, a modification to (12) is required in order to distinguish homophonous Roots from one another. This can be accomplished with indices. In terms of the more explicit set representations, this means that such indices are included in the set as well. Thus, the Root underlying *bank* in the sense of "financial institution" can be represented as in (14a), with the Root that is part of *bank* "side of a river" in (14b):

(14)   Two Homophonous Roots

    a. {/bæŋk/, 254}

    b. {/bæŋk/, 879}

The indices are chosen arbitrarily; all that is needed is a minimal way of distinguishing these two Roots from each other, since the phonology is not able to perform this function. Various other means might be appealed to in order to distinguish homophonous Roots from each other. For example, there are languages in which homophonous Roots behave differently in terms of conjugation, declension, gender, or other such "morphological" features (see below); when this occurs the morphological features can be used to identify each of the homophonous Roots uniquely, such that arbitrary numerical indices are in principle unnecessary. For example, different Roots with the same underlying phonology are found in Latin *aud-ī-re* 'to hear', and *aud-ē-re*, 'to dare'. However, these two Roots belong to different conjugation classes, as is reflected in the different theme vowels that appear with them (*-ī* and *-ē* respectively). In a theory that encodes conjugation classes with diacritic features (see section 2.3.5), the diacritics could be used to uniquely identify the two Roots.

If (at least some) Roots are subject to Late Insertion, numerical indices are essential for all Roots, since only these distinguish one Root from another. More specifically, Late Insertion of Roots can be formalized as the insertion of a phonological form that makes reference to a numerical index, so that a Vocabulary Item realizing the Root in *cat* would be represented as follows:

(15) $\sqrt{766} \leftrightarrow$ /kæt/

In an approach that employs Vocabulary Items like (15), the object $\sqrt{766}$ functions as a unique identifier of the relevant Root, which then receives its phonological form via Vocabulary Insertion. Using Vocabulary Insertion for Roots might be useful for the analysis of (stem) suppletion, the phenomenon seen in light verbs (= bundles of grammatical features; see section 2.3.6) like *go/went*, if this truly exists for Roots. However, the primary motivation for Vocabulary Insertion is syncretism; and, because syncretism is most evident in the realization of functional morphemes, I will put the question of Vocabulary Insertion for Roots to the side in the pages to come, with the understanding that Vocabulary Insertion can be extended to them if necessary.

2.3.2 The Categorization of Roots

An important property of Roots is that they have no grammatical category inherently. This assumption derives from earlier work on derivational morphology; see in particular Chomsky (1970), Marantz (1997, 2001), Borer (2005), and the implementation in Embick and Marantz (2008), which is adopted here.

According to the category-free theory of Roots, traditional lexical categories like 'noun' or 'verb' or 'adjective' are convenient shorthand labels that refer to syntactic structures in which a Root combines with a *category-defining* functional head such as *n* or *v* or *a*. A Root that is categorized in this way is shown in (16) for the noun *cat*:

(16) The Root $\sqrt{\text{CAT}}$ as 'Noun'

$$
\begin{array}{c}
n \\
\overbrace{\sqrt{\text{CAT}} \quad n}
\end{array}
$$

Category-defining morphemes come with different features, so that a single language possesses several types of *n*, *v*, and so on. The different types of features on these morphemes are responsible in part for the semantic side of derivational morphology.[6]

Representations like (16) show complex heads, created by adjoining the Root to the category-defining head (by head-movement, for example). Depending on what is assumed about constituent structure, it is possible that some complex heads are formed in structures involving a Root that is in the complement of a category-defining head *x*, as in (17a); affixation of the Root to the head produces the complex head (17b):

(17)   a. Syntactic Structure

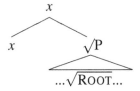

   b. Complex Head created in (17a)

Another possibility is that Roots are merged directly with functional heads, so that something like (17b) is created in the absence of a phrasal projection of a Root (the two possibilities are not mutually exclusive). The exact range of structures like (17a) in which complex heads like (17b) are formed is a topic of ongoing research. For the most part, the analyses presented in this book will concentrate on complex head structures like those in (17b), without dwelling on details of the pre-affixation structure (see chapter 3 for further comments).

The assumption that Roots must always be categorized by a functional head is called the *Categorization Assumption*:

(18)   CATEGORIZATION ASSUMPTION: Roots cannot appear without being *categorized*; Roots are categorized by combining with category-defining functional heads. (Embick and Marantz 2008)

By the Categorization Assumption, Roots never appear "bare". Rather, they surface only in syntactic derivations in which they have been merged with category-defining heads. A consequence of this view is that many words that are by standard description "simple" members of a particular lexical category—e.g., the "verb" *play*, the "noun" *cat*, the "adjective" *red*, and so on—are structurally complex. Minimally, they consist of a Root and a categorizing functional head:

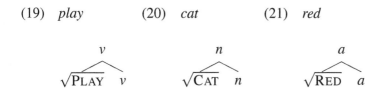

According to this theory, then, Roots are not words, where *word* is understood in its informal sense to refer to *cat* etc. Rather, (some) words contain Roots, but Roots by themselves can never surface on their own.

While this claim might seem prima facie counterintuitive for languages like English, where, for various reasons, the underlying form of Roots is often quite close to what we think of as a word in certain cases (e.g., the Root √CAT underlies the noun *cat*), in other languages it is more immediately evident that Roots do not surface by themselves. For example, in languages with theme vowels or "word markers", such as Spanish, a Root like √ALT 'high' cannot appear as **alt* on the surface. Rather, this Root always appears with further morphemes, associated noun class (which is related to gender): *alt-o* 'high-MASC', *alt-a* 'high-FEM', and so on. The overt *-a* and *-o* suffixes express features of noun class, an "arbitrary" morphological property of nouns in many languages (cp. section 2.3.5 below). The fact that Roots like √ALT cannot appear without them illustrates the point that what we identify as the Root must appear with other morphemes in forms that actually surface. When these additional morphemes have overt phonology, the point that Roots always surface in combination with other morphemes is easier to see than it is in English.

In other languages, the differences between Roots and words are even more striking. In Semitic languages like Arabic, for example, Roots are represented phonologically as sequences of consonants like √KTB for 'write'. These consonant sequences are syllabified and put into a prosodic shape (descriptively, a *template*) of consonants and vowels, in a way that is determined by morphemes in the local context of the Root. For example, *kataba* 'to write' is derived from √KTB, as is *kitaab* 'book' (see section 2.3.3 for more examples). A Root of like √KTB cannot be pronounced on its own (unlike what we might think about the phonological representation of √CAT); rather, it is capable of being pronounced only when it has combined with other morphemes.

As stated in (18), it is not just any functional morpheme that can categorize a Root. There is a special set of morphemes in the grammar that perform this function; they are sometimes called *categorizers*. In terms of their phonological realization, categorizers sometimes have overt exponents and sometimes do not. In the case of the words shown in (19-21)—*play*, *cat*, and *red*—the category-defining heads are not realized phonologically. In other words, like *dark-en*, *marri-age*, and *glob-al*, these heads do have overt phonology, as shown in (22-24).

(22) *darken*   (23) *marriage*   (24) *global*

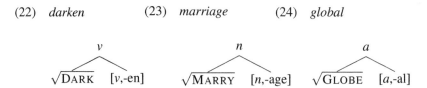

In words like *vaporization*, there are two overt categorizing heads, as shown in (25):

(25) *vaporization*

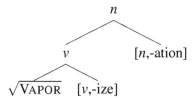

Category-defining heads are subject to Vocabulary Insertion, just like other functional morphemes. This is how the *-en*, *-age*, and *-al* exponents come to be inserted into *v*, *n*, and *a* in (22-24) respectively. With respect to forms like *play* etc., in which there is no overt realization of a categorizer, some different analyses are possible. For present purposes, it can be assumed for these examples that the category-defining head has a null (-Ø) exponent; so, for example, the verbal form of √PLAY can be represented as *play-Ø* when this level of detail is required.[7]

In addition to showing category-defining heads with overt exponents, the structure in (25) for *vapor-iz-ation* illustrates an additional point: category-defining heads can appear outside of other category-defining heads, to produce words with multiple morphemes of this type (compare *break-abil-ity*, *fool-ish-ness*, etc.). When multiple category-defining heads of different types appear in a single word, true "category-changing" occurs, because an object from one category (i.e., the verb *vapor-ize* in (25)) is converted into a member of another category (in the case of (25), the noun *vapor-iz-ation*). The idea that multiple category defining heads can appear together in a derivation is particularly important when phase-cyclic derivation is implemented; see chapter 7 for discussion.

A final point concerning Roots and their categorizers is that the structures containing these objects are built syntactically; they are not stored. Because it treats the derivation of all complex forms syntactically, the theory has no modular split between derivational morphology and inflectional morphology. Rather, derivational morphemes like *n*, *v*, etc. are syntactic objects, just like morphemes like Determiner (D), Tense (T), and so on.

2.3.3   Roots and Lexical Semantic Meanings

In addition to being grammatical objects that are categorized in the way described in the preceding section, Roots are related to both lexical semantic and conceptual representations (note that I am making no claims about where the lines might be drawn between these two types of information). Because questions about Root meaning intersect both with general questions about the nature of concepts, and with more specific questions about how the grammar treats lexical semantic information in the first place—both extremely complex questions—meaning will be treated in only a cursory fashion here.

Part of the theory of Root meanings is directed at the Root itself, and part of it is directed at immediate grammatical contexts in which a Root appears. By the former, I mean that Roots possess an inherent meaning (at least in the typical case); by the latter, I mean that categorizers (and perhaps other morphemes local to a Root) play a role in determining which meaning(s) of a Root are active in a given grammatical context.

With these two components of Root meaning in mind, a working hypothesis about Root meaning that will be adopted here is that Roots possess lexical semantic representations that are legible to a semantic system that interprets syntactic objects. (Recall from chapter 1 that the Encyclopedia is sometimes referred to as encoding meanings of this type; other assumptions are possible as well.) The system in question determines how to interpret a Root when it appears in different grammatical contexts: e.g., when it appears as a noun (with *n*), or as a verb (with *v*), or as a member of some other category.

In these different grammatical environments there is a shared component of interpretation that is centered on the Root's "basic" meaning, but perhaps some context-specific differences as well. For example, when the Root

√FEATHER in English is employed as the noun *feather*, it refers to an object that has a number of properties. Part of what English speakers know about this Root, though, is that in another context, as the adjective *feather-y*, it can also have a more restricted meaning, where the weight aspect of √FEATHER is prominent: (*feather-y* in this sense means "light or airy", with no actual objects (feathers) involved (example from Taft (2004)). Collectively, the different facets of lexical semantic meaning that are found with Roots in different contexts constitute the phenomenon of Root *polysemy*, a phenomenon that is widespread in human language.[8]

The way in which Root meanings are manipulated in different grammatical contexts is particularly striking and easy to illustrate in Semitic languages like Arabic, where, famously, a single Root can typically appear in a number of different "templates" (sequences of consonants and vowels), with interpretations related to the Root's core meaning. These templates are a morphophonological manifestation of the different grammatical contexts (defined by different functional morphemes) in which the Root is found.

Some illustrations for the Root √KTB, which is roughly 'write', are shown in (26) (see Wehr (1976), Kaye (2007)); note that some of these examples involve overt affixes in addition to changes in templatic pattern, but for the sake of simplicity the examples are given without segmentation:[9]

(26)   Some Forms of the Root √KTB

>   kataba 'to write'
>   kitaab 'writing, book'
>   kutubii 'bookseller'
>   kuttaab 'Koran school'
>   kutayyib 'booklet'
>   kitaaba 'act or practice of writing'
>   kitaabii 'written, literary'
>   maktab 'office'
>   maktaba 'library'
>   miktaab 'typewriter'
>   kaatib 'writer, scribe'
>   maktuub 'written down'

Each of these forms is based on the consonants /k/-/t/-/b/, which, together (and in that sequence), constitute this Root's underlying phonological representation. These consonants appear in different prosodic patterns in ways that are determined by morphemes in their context to produce a number of derivatives, which have related forms and meanings.

While Arabic (and Semitic languages more generally) offer a particularly striking example of Root-based derivation, the same general phenomenon is hypothesized to exist in all languages, even if not all languages have the same kind of intricate system of morphophonological possibilities for Roots that is manifested in Semitic.

Regarding the notion of *core meaning* invoked above, it can be assumed that each Root possesses a lexical semantic representation of meaning, which I abbreviate as $\mathscr{R}$. In a particular derivation in the grammar, a Root appears in a syntactic context, i.e., with functional heads local to it. When the syntactic object containing the Root is spelled out, the semantic system that interprets syntactic structures operates on $\mathscr{R}$ (and the meanings of the morphemes in the context of the Root) to produce a semantic representation that specifies the meaning(s) of the Root that are activated in that grammatical environment.

2.3.4 Roots and Synsem Features

To this point we have discussed two types of representations related to meaning in the broad sense: first, the synsem features; and second, the $\mathscr{R}$-meanings associated with Roots. This section addresses the relation between these meaning types, which, in effect, is part of the larger question of how Roots and synsem features are connected.

The view that I will take here is that Roots are represented in a way that does not involve synsem features, period. In particular, Roots are not specified for any such features, nor can they be decomposed into them. These two positions are stated in (27):

(27) Roots and Synsem Features

    a. **No Synsem Specification on Roots:** Roots do not possess synsem features.

    b. **No Root Decomposition:** Roots cannot be decomposed into synsem features.

The first position (27a) places a restriction on the types of features that Roots may be specified for. It allows Roots to possess only phonological or morphological features inherently (on the latter see 2.3.5).

The second position (27b) is closely related to the first. It says that whatever the semantic or conceptual content of Roots might be (in terms of $\mathscr{R}$-meanings), Root meanings are not reducible to the synsem feature inventory of human language (i.e., to features in the UFI). While it is possible that $\mathscr{R}$-meanings can be defined in terms of a feature system that classifies Roots along different semantic dimensions (e.g. certain Roots are semantically stative, others relate to entities, and so on), this system of Root classification is not the synsem feature system. Another way of putting this is that the $\mathscr{R}$-meaning system and the synsem meaning systems are disjoint, even though these systems might have to interact in a way that accounts for the fact that Roots have different distributions (i.e., appear in different syntactic contexts; see below).

The claim in (27b) prohibits a particular kind of *lexical decomposition* in which Roots are collections of grammatical features. Some care must be taken terminologically here, because the term "lexical decomposition" is (unfortunately) used in distinct and incompatible ways in the literature (this confusion of uses relates to the many senses of *lexical* that are mentioned in chapter 1). The sense of "lexical decomposition" that is prohibited by (27b) amounts to the claim that Roots (Root meanings) cannot be broken down (i.e., constitutively decomposed) into synsem features. It is worth emphasizing the terminological point because "lexical decomposition" is also used in another way to refer to the idea that "words" as typically understood can be decomposed into a number of morphemes that are discrete syntactic objects. This latter type of lexical decomposition is, of course, not only admitted by the theory; it is at the heart of it.

Both of the statements in (27) are negative. This does not mean that Roots have no properties whatsoever (although the idea that Roots are effectively without syntactically visible properties or absent from syntactic derivations has been explored in this framework; see Marantz (1995), Embick (1997, 1998, 2000) for some relevant views). At a minimum, there must be a theory of Root meanings, i.e., of $\mathscr{R}$ representations, to account for the simple fact that Roots possess inherent meanings.

A further question is how $\mathscr{R}$-meanings relate to syntactic distributions. Empirically, it is clear that some Roots are deviant in certain syntactic environments. For example, $\sqrt{\text{RUG}}$ is impeccable as a noun, i.e. *The rug is red*, but deviant as an intransitive verb in the author's English, i.e. *#John rugs*. If Roots are not specified for synsem features, then it cannot be the case that this distributional fact is encoded by specifying the Root as $[-v]$ (or $[+n]$, or whatever would achieve the desired result). Rather, the deviance must be attributed to how the $\mathscr{R}$-meaning of the Root connects with the syntactic context in which it appears.

In the discussion of *rug* above, the symbol # is used for 'deviance' because it is an open question whether this sentence is *ungrammatical*, or grammatical but unacceptable (presumably due to being semantically deviant, i.e. *infelicitous*). Different positions on this point appear in the literature. Borer (2003), for example, allows all Root/context combinations to be grammatical in the technical sense. Another possibility is that restrictions on Root distributions arise from the fact that they have inherent semantic properties (in the form of $\mathscr{R}$-meanings) that determine their distribution (see the comments in Embick and Marantz 2008). According to the latter view, deviance arises when the $\mathscr{R}$-meaning of a Root cannot be reconciled with the meaning contribution of the syntactic environment in which the Root appears, in a way that is part of the grammar, and not some other (e.g. conceptual or pragmatic) system. There are many ways in which the differences between these views could be explored, and the distinctions between competing approaches are often quite subtle. On a unifying note, it is important to observe that on either one of these views, some aspect of Root meaning (i.e., $\mathscr{R}$ meanings) must interact with the grammatical meanings derived from morphemes in the context of the Root; this reiterates the point (introduced in 2.3.1 above) that $\mathscr{R}$-meanings and synsem feature meanings must be visible to each other in some way, even if they are distinct.

2.3.5 Roots and "Morphological" Features

There are two components to the analysis of Roots that has been outlined to this point. The first is that Roots are specified with phonological representations, and perhaps "numerical" indices. The second is that while Roots have ($\mathscr{R}$-) representations of lexical semantic meaning, Roots are not represented with synsem features, nor are they decomposable into them.

These components of the theory revolve around the two types of features introduced earlier in this work, phonological features and synsem features. It seems, however, that Roots are sometimes related to (and perhaps specified for) another type of feature that has not been introduced yet: a type that is primarily morphological in nature. The need for such features is seen when the Roots (and some functional morphemes) in a language belong to specific morphological classes, classes whose members cannot be predicted on the basis of anything else in the language.

A common manifestation of this effect is seen in the nominal and verbal systems of many languages, where nouns and verbs are divided into distinct *declension* (for nouns, and sometimes adjectives) or *conjugation* (for verbs) classes. For instance, the verbs of Classical Latin fall into five conjugations, each of which is exemplified in the present tense indicative form in (28). The different conjugations show distinct *theme vowels*, the vowel immediately after the Root; I: /-ā/; II: /-ē/; etc. (secondarily, there are also some conjugation-related differences in how agreement endings are realized as well—compare e.g. 3pl *-nt* and *-unt*):

(28) Present indicative forms of some Latin verbs

	I	II	III	III(i)	IV
	'praise'	'warn'	'lead'	'seize'	'hear'
1s	laud-ō	mon-e-ō	dūc-ō	cap-i-ō	aud-i-ō
2s	laud-ā-s	mon-ē-s	dūc-i-s	cap-i-s	aud-ī-s
3s	laud-a-t	mon-e-t	dūc-i-t	cap-i-t	aud-i-t
1p	laud-ā-mus	mon-ē-mus	dūc-i-mus	cap-i-mus	aud-ī-mus
2p	laud-ā-tis	mon-ē-tis	dūc-i-tis	cap-i-tis	aud-ī-tis
3p	laud-a-nt	mon-e-nt	dūc-unt	cap-i-unt	aud-i-unt

Following a more or less standard classification from the descriptive literature, the different conjugation classes are identified with labels (I, II, etc.). All verbs in Latin belong to one of the five classes in (28), with the exception of a few verbs that are *athematic* (that is, they show no theme vowel). Membership in one of the classes cannot be predicted on the basis of the meaning of a Root, nor is it determined by a Root's phonological properties. Instead, the class that a particular Root belongs to simply has to be memorized. It is thus arbitrary, from the point of view of the synchronic grammar. Because this arbitrary classification has effects on morphological realization (and not on syntax, or semantics), the features involved are referred to as *morphological*.

One way of encoding unpredictable morphological information is with *diacritic* features, whose sole purpose is to derive relevant morphological differences between the classes. In the case at hand, the Latin Root $\sqrt{\text{AUD}}$, which belongs to Conjugation IV, can be represented as in (29):

(29) $\sqrt{\text{AUD}}_{[\text{IV}]}$

In (29), the Root √AUD possesses a feature [IV], which has an effect in the morphology of the language (it causes the theme vowel to be realized as /-ī/).

In terms of the (syntactically oriented) classification of features that is introduced in chapter 1, diacritic features are not interpretable—i.e., they are not synsem features, and so by definition they have no effect on semantic interpretation. Rather, their effects are seen in the PF component of the grammar.

The representation of the Latin Root in (29) includes a single diacritic [IV]. There is nothing in principle that prevents a single Root from possessing multiple diacritics of this type, with the different features being visible in different contexts. Multiple specification for diacritic features is sometimes needed because there are languages in which e.g. both the nominal and verbal systems show class-based behavior, and in which a single Root can surface either as a noun or as a verb. For example, the Latin Root √DUC appears both as the conjugation III verb *dūcere* 'lead' (cf. (28) above), and as the declension III noun *dux*. The fact that the numeral III is employed as the name of both the nominal and verbal forms of this Root is, of course, an accident of the descriptive tradition. The important point is that this Root belongs to one arbitrary class as a noun, and another arbitrary class as a verb, and this information must be encoded in the grammar somewhere. The behavior of this type of Root suggests that it is specified for two separate diacritics: one that plays a role in the nominal environment [*n*-III], and one that plays a role in the verbal environment [*v*-III], where the *n* and *v* annotations here play the role of identifying these features as relevant in a particular environment.

Systems of verbal conjugation and nominal declension are standard examples of phenomena for which diacritic specification seems to be necessary. Terminologically, an analysis that makes a diacritic part of a Root's basic representation as in (29) employs what is called the *inherent specification* of features, since the features in question are possessed by Roots underlyingly.[10]

Inherent specification (or something like it) is required with other types of phenomena beyond conjugation and declension classes. For example, the cross-linguistically common division of nouns into arbitrary *genders* may be thought of in the same terms. The fact that 'bridge' in Spanish is masculine *el puente*, or that 'table' is feminine *la mesa*, is something that must be memorized. In the same way that conjugation class features like [IV] serve as diacritics on Roots like Latin √AUD, Spanish gender features can be specified on Roots as well, so that e.g. the Root √MES underlying *mesa* possesses a feature [+fem]. The particular example of gender (both in Spanish, and in many other languages) raises a number of important questions that have been discussed in the literature, because gender features interact with semantically interpretable features that encode the sex of a referent. In the case of Spanish, gender also interacts with the realization of noun class features that determine the realization of the final segment of most nouns (typically *-o* or *-a*). See Harris (1991) for extensive discussion of these points.

Beyond the specific examples just considered, a general question in the theory of features concerns the limits of inherent specification. The idea that Roots may not be specified for synsem features, which is advanced in section 2.3.4, is a substantive proposal in this vein. For general discussion along these lines that takes into account further feature types, see Embick (1997, 2000).

Another very general question that can be asked is why languages employ diacritic features in the first place, given that such features are (by definition) semantically irrelevant. This question connects with issues in diachrony and acquisition, and may very well implicate the properties of cognitive systems (e.g., memory) that are external to the grammar.

Concerning details of implementation, it is also important to ask whether the phenomena associated with inherent specification all require analyses in which diacritic and other (e.g. gender) features are specified on Roots. As far as this goes, it is probably safer to say that some sort of memorized information about class is associated with Roots, but need not be represented with the Root per se. For example, Kramer (2009) argues on the basis of data from Amharic that gender features are not exclusively specified on Roots, but can also be found on the *n* heads that categorize Roots.

Along these lines mentioned in the last paragraph, it should be noted that there are some other mechanisms that could be used to account for some arbitrary class phenomena. Representations like $\sqrt{\text{AUD}}_{[\text{IV}]}$ make arbitrary class membership a featural property of the Root. An alternative to encoding arbitrary class information in this way would be to employ contextual allomorphy (see chapters 4 and 7). My view of this matter is that it is difficult to completely eliminate diacritics by appealing to this or related alternatives. However, I will not dwell on this matter further here, since distinguishing alternative proposals in this domain is a subtle matter, and implicates many questions that go beyond the scope of this work. In the pages to come, diacritic specification of Roots along the lines outlined here will be employed whenever morphological features are required.

2.3.6 A Root is a Type of Morpheme

A Root is a particular type of morpheme. This means that being a Root is an inherent property of certain objects in the grammar. Crucially, Roothood is *not* defined in terms of a position in a syntactic structure or within a "word". Thus, the term *Root* is employed in a more restricted sense than terms *stem* or *base*, which are often used (formally or informally) in morphological theory to describe the "basic" part of a word (i.e., the part to which affixes are added). Potential confusion of the Root with notions like the stem or base arises because in many cases, the Root is the most deeply embedded element in a complex word, so that it seems to serve (again, speaking informally) as a host for affixes. However, although these observations about the typical positions of Roots in complex forms are potentially important (since they implicate the distributional properties of Roots), the main point is that Roots are Roots intrinsically, wherever they appear.

A few examples will illustrate why it is important to be careful about what it means to be a Root. First, consider a complex form like *vapor-iz-ation*, in which the Root $\sqrt{\text{VAPOR}}$ is the most deeply embedded element in a complex head:

(30) *vaporization*

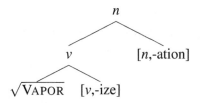

By virtue of its structural position in (30), the Root $\sqrt{\text{VAPOR}}$ happens to correspond to the informal notion of "host for further affixation" mentioned above.

In some other words, however, there is no Root in the technical sense, even though such words could conceivably have an element that is the "host" of affixes in the informal way of speaking. For example, the theory that is adopted in this book holds that *light verbs* are simply bundles of synsem features: i.e., varieties of *v*. Light verbs appear in structures that are Rootless in the way that is mentioned above. For illustration, we may employ the verb *go*, which is the realization of a functional head that can be referred to as v_{go}.

56 Morphemes and Features

In the word *goes*, which consists of v_{go}, T(ense), and the third person singular agreement marker *-s*, there is no Root in the sense defined in this book:

(31) *goes*

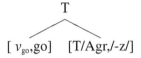

There is no Root $\sqrt{\text{GO}}$. Thus, the word in (31) (and others like it) consists only of functional morphemes; even if *go* appears to host the affix *-s*, this word is Rootless.

The idea that Roots are morphemes of a particular type—and that there may be verbs and other words that have no Root in them—connects directly with the theory of categorization outlined in section 2.3.2. Roots are category-neutral, such that the grammatical categories "noun", "verb" etc. are derivative of the functional vocabulary (types of *n*, types of *v*). By the Categorization Assumption, it is not possible to have a Root without a category-defining head. But there is no symmetrical requirement holding that categorizers must always occur with Roots.

2.4 Conclusions

The theory of morphology that is developed in this book is based on morphemes. This chapter has presented a first look at the two types of morphemes in the grammar, the functional morphemes and the Roots. They have some properties in common (they are both types of morphemes, and appear in syntactic structures), and some inherent properties that make them different from one another. These differences can be understood primarily in terms of how the two types of morpheme relate to different types of features.

Much of the material in this chapter looks at morphemes as objects in memory; i.e., at their underlying representations. In the more specific terms employed in chapter 1, this means in effect that we have a working theory of Syntactic Terminals: the list of elements that function as the building blocks of syntactic derivations.

In the discussion to come, the treatment of Roots that is outlined here will undergo little revision. With respect to the functional morphemes, there is much more to be said. To this point, functional morphemes have been treated as bundles of synsem features, with no phonological content. Starting with chapter 4, the phonological aspect of the theory of functional morphemes takes center stage, as the Vocabulary Insertion operation is defined and motivated.

Before looking at Vocabulary Insertion in detail, it will be useful to outline some additional assumptions concerning the structures in which morphemes appear. In terms of the architecture of the approach (recall chapter 1), functional morphemes receive their phonological form only at PF, *after* they have been combined into complex structures in the narrow syntactic part of the grammar. These complex structures, and the linear relations that are derived from them, are thus important parts of the theory of morphology; they are the subject of the next chapter.

Chapter 3
Structures and Linear Order

3.1 Introduction

When structures derived by the syntax are spelled out, they are subjected to a number of computations in each of the interface components. Collectively, the computations and representations that are found on the sound (and sign) interface are referred to as the PF component of the grammar.

As stressed in chapter 1, some PF computations are quite general, whereas other operations appear to be more specifically "morphological" in nature. In terms of this distinction, the material covered in this chapter is mostly of the more general variety. Specifically, I will look at some of the complex structures that are assembled out of morphemes, and how linear relations derived from these structures are represented. The guiding idea behind this overview is that it is in terms of the structural relations between morphemes and the linear relations derived from these that PF computations are defined.

A convenient starting point for this chapter is the architectural assumption that all complex objects are derived syntactically (recall chapter 1). A consequence of this view is that there is no architectural or modular division between "word formation" and "phrase formation". Rather, a single generative system is responsible for the construction of both types of objects.

One set of questions to be addressed concerns the nature of the complex objects that are derived from morphemes. Here, the focus is on the structures that are realized as what are ordinarily thought of as *words*, and the question of whether the word is a privileged object in the theory. As noted in chapter 1, the term *word* is often employed in an informal (i.e., non-technical) sense to refer to objects whose properties are normally taken to be of "morphological" interest. Somewhat more precisely, this use clusters around objects that show properties associated with phonological wordhood. Since the theoretical framework developed here is based on morphemes, and not words, one of the goals of this chapter is to outline the essential properties of the structures and linear relations in which morphemes appear, because it is in terms of these that the formal properties of complex objects must be stated.

With respect to the narrow syntactic part of the equation, it is assumed here that the syntax generates objects that are exclusively hierarchical in nature;

i.e., that syntactic structures do not encode linear order. The representation of linear order among syntactic objects is introduced in the PF component of the grammar.[1] The organization of the initial parts of this chapter reflects this view: after a preliminary look at some relevant structural notions in sections 3.2 and 3.3, I provide an overview of the main questions in the study of morpheme order in section 3.4. Section 3.5 then outlines some basic points about phonological wordhood, and how this notion relates to the theoretical objects identified in prior sections.

3.2 Structures

I assume a theory of constituent structure in which an important object for morphological concerns is the *complex head*. Complex heads are created by the affixation of one head to another. According to a familar view of this process, this affixation is a (head-)adjunction operation, produced by the operation of *head movement*. So, for example, head X can adjoin to head Y to yield the object in (1):

(1) Head Adjunction

The object shown in (1) is a hierarchical structure, one that also shows linear order for graphical convenience. In principle, the structure in (1) could be linearized in one of two ways, to produce either X-Y or Y-X; see section 3.4 below.[2]

Head movement (sometimes referred to as X^0-movement) has been examined in an extensive syntactic literature from the 1980s onwards; see, for example, Koopman (1984), Travis (1984), Chomsky (1986), and Baker (1988), as well as the notion of "Merger" from Marantz (1984). For the purposes of this work, it will be assumed that head movement is a syntactic operation. Not too much should be read into this assumption; it is possible to formulate the main results of this book in a framework that treats head movement as a PF operation (as suggested by Chomsky 2001) and not in the narrow syntax.

Adopting a standard view, in head movement the head X of projection XP moves upwards and adjoins to the head Y that takes XP as its sister.

Schematically, this process can be illustrated with reference to (2):

(2) Hypothetical Structure, Before Head Movement

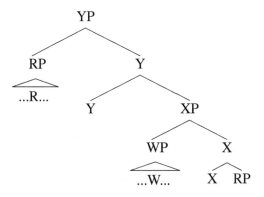

The result of moving X upwards and adjoining it to the head Y of YP is shown in (3); here X is shown in the higher position where it has adjoined to Y to form a complex head (here and below ~~strikethrough~~ is used for the lower copy of X):

(3) Hypothetical Structure, After Head Movement

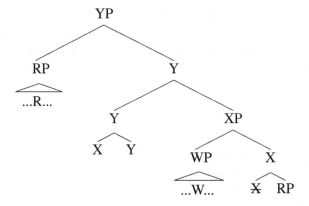

Head movement can apply recursively, so that if YP in (3) is the complement of a head Z, then the complex head [$_Y$ X Y] can undergo head movement and adjoin to Z to produce [$_Z$ [$_Y$ X Y] Z].

In many of the phenomena that are examined in this book, larger aspects of the syntactic structure are not relevant to the details of what happens inside the complex head [$_Y$ X Y] that is seen in (3). For this reason, in many case studies (particularly in later chapters) I will concentrate on complex heads like (1), and assume without further discussion that such heads are formed as shown in (2) and (3).

(4) Complex Head

These basic assumptions about head affixation suffice for many of the phenomena to be analyzed below; further assumptions about the clausal structures in which complex heads are created will be introduced only as necessary.

3.2.1 An Illustration

To this point it has been shown in relatively abstract terms how complex heads are derived in phrasal structures. Here, I provide a more concrete example of the role played by complex head structures in morphological analysis.

The examples in this section are drawn from the conjugation of verbs in Spanish; I adapt and develop aspects of the (much more detailed) treatment found in Arregi (1999) and Oltra-Massuet and Arregi (2005). As a first illustration, consider the present and imperfect (a kind of past tense) indicative forms of the verb *hablar* 'speak' in (5); these forms are from Latin American Spanish, where the second and third plural are identical in form:

(5) Spanish Verbs

p/n	present	imperfect
1s	hablo	hablaba
2s	hablas	hablabas
3s	habla	hablaba
1p	hablamos	hablábamos
2p	hablan	hablaban
3p	hablan	hablaban

The forms in (5) are not segmented. A first step in the analysis of these verbs is to develop a set of working hypotheses about how the forms are broken down into morphemes, one that takes into account both morphological (i.e. distributional) and syntacticosemantic (e.g., past tense forms have a T[+past] morpheme) considerations.

It is clear that a number of relatively simple observations can be made about the decomposition of the forms in (5). For instance, the imperfect forms contain a morpheme *-ba* that is not seen in the present tense forms; this is the marker of past (imperfective) tense in these verbs. It can be also seen that almost all of the verb forms in (5) contain a theme vowel *-a* immediately after the Root (recall the discussion of themes in section 2.3.5 in chapter 2), as well as an agreement morpheme after the tense morpheme. The tense morpheme is not realized overtly in the present tense, so with them agreement appears after the theme vowel.

Assuming that T(ense) can be either T[-past] (present) or T[+past], and assuming the person and number features [±1], [±2], and [±pl], the observations of the last paragraph lead to the hypothesis that Spanish contains the morphemes in (6), which are shown with their phonological exponents:

(6) Morphemes and Exponents Identified in (5)

    a. Theme Vowel: *-a*

    b. Tense Morphemes:
       T[-past], *-Ø*
       T[+past], *-ba*

    c. Agreement Morphemes:
       [+1,-2,-pl], *-o*; or *-Ø* in the imperfect
       [-1,+2,-pl], *-s*
       [-1,-2,-pl], *-Ø*
       [+1,-2,+pl] *-mos*
       [-1,+2,+pl], *-n*
       [-1,-2,+pl], *-n*

Note that certain morphemes have no overt realization. This is the case with T[-past], the first person Agr morpheme in the imperfect, and the third person singular Agr morpheme in both tenses. These are treated as having *-Ø* exponents.

Some further aspects of (6) will have to remain relatively vague at the moment. For example, the first person singular morpheme shows allomorphy, with the form *-o* in the present, but *-Ø* in the imperfect. An analysis of this effect can be given only after the Vocabulary Insertion operation has been introduced (see chapter 4). In addition, (6c) shows two distinct *-n* morphemes for second and third person plurals. As noted in chapter 1, though, this identity in form appears to be systematic (a syncretism), an important observation that needs to be accounted for in a comprehensive analysis. This kind of identity in form is analyzed in detail in chapter 5.

Beyond the complications with allomorphy and syncretism, there is at least one more minor deviation from the expected pattern seen in the forms above. In particular, there is no theme vowel in the first person singular present *hablo*. This effect can be treated as a phonological deletion (for clarity, the deleted vowel is shown in parentheses in the segmentation given below).

A segmentation of the forms in (5) that reflects the working analysis in (6) is shown in (8); for reference, the linear order of morphemes in these forms is given in (7):

(7) Linear Order: √R̄OOT-TH-T-Agr

(8) Spanish Verbs, segmented

p/n	present	imperfect
1s	habl-(a)-Ø-o	habl-a-ba-Ø
2s	habl-a-Ø-s	habl-a-ba-s
3s	habl-a-Ø-Ø	habl-a-ba-Ø
1p	habl-a-Ø-mos	habl-á-ba-mos
2p	habl-a-Ø-n	habl-a-ba-n
3p	habl-a-Ø-n	habl-a-ba-n

With respect to the primary aims of this chapter, the next question to be addressed is how the pieces identified in (8) (and, more generally, the linear sequence shown in (7)) relate to a complex head structure of the type introduced in the previous subsection. It can be assumed that the clause structure in which the forms in (8) are derived is that in (9), which contains a Root, a verbalizing morpheme *v*, and a Tense head; for purposes of illustration (and to emphasize the fact that (9) shows a clausal structure) I have put XP and WP phrases in the TP and *v*P specifier positions:

(9) Clause Structure Underlying Verbs in (8)

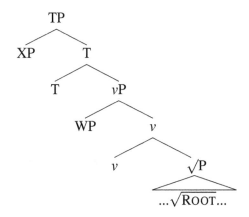

In this structure, the Root undergoes head movement and adjoins to *v*; subsequently, the [√ROOT *v*] complex itself is moved and adjoined to T. These movements result in the complex head in (10):

(10) Complex Head Structure Derived in (9)

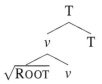

On the assumption that the T head is specified as [±past], (10) produces either present tense verbs ([-past]) or imperfective past tense verbs ([+past]). One further addition to (10) is required beyond this: an Agr (agreement) morpheme. I will assume that this type of morpheme is added to structures like (10) at PF, prior to Vocabulary Insertion, in order to meet language-specific well-formedness requirements.[3] Morphemes added at PF are called *dissociated* morphemes (or sometimes *ornamental* morphemes; see e.g. Embick (1997) and Embick and Noyer (2007)).

With the addition of Agr, which is adjoined to T, the complex head is as follows:

66   *Structures and Linear Order*

(11)   Structure with Agr Node

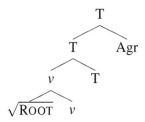

The functional morphemes in (11) undergo Vocabulary Insertion, which produces the forms seen in (8). The tree in (12) illustrates this analysis with first person plural imperfective *hablábamos* (for convenience I take the theme vowel to be the realization of v; see Oltra-Massuet (1999) and Oltra-Massuet and Arregi (2005) for a more detailed alternative to this, in which theme vowels are the realization of a dissociated morpheme attached outside of v):

(12)   Structure of Imperfect *habl-á-ba-mos*

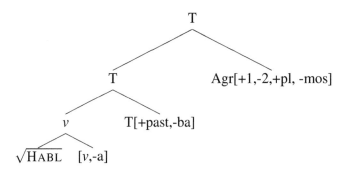

With different feature values for Tense and for the Agr node, the structure in (12) underlies all of the forms shown above.

3.2.2   Movement and Complex Heads: Summary

In the case studies that are presented in this book it will be assumed that complex head structures are created by an affixation operation that creates adjunction structures of the type employed above. In the typical case, such as in the analysis of the Spanish verb forms above, it will be assumed that the operation that derives the complex heads is head movement. While head movement is often implicated in the formation of complex heads, other operations have also been appealed to in this domain. For example, in a development of ideas from Marantz (1988), Embick and Noyer (2001) hypothesize that there are two PF affixation operations, *Lowering* and *Local Dislocation*, which are defined in terms of hierarchical and linear representations respectively; see Embick and Noyer (2007), Embick (2007a,b) for additional discussion.

Finally, although I have given an important role to head movement, the general contours of the theory presented here are compatible with a number of different auxiliary theories about how affixation works; it is possible to combine the architecture of chapter 1 with a theory in which head affixation is handled with another type of operation that is not head movement, or even a theory without head affixation.[4] While I will not explore alternatives to head affixation here, questions about the nature of syntactic affixation are currently being explored in a number of directions that are relevant to morphological concerns of the type addressed in this chapter.

3.3 Some Definitions: *M-Words* and *Subwords*

In the theory of affixation, there are privileged structural objects that are important for the central concerns of this book. These objects can be defined and illustrated with reference to the structure in (13), where a Root is adjoined to a head X, followed by subsequent movement to Y. This is the kind of structure that is typical of head movement, as discussed in the preceding section:

(13) Structure

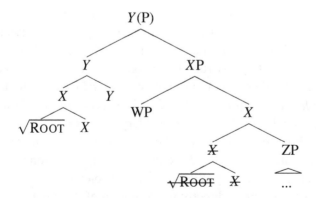

Embick and Noyer (2001) and Embick (2007b) argue that two objects in (13)

are special, in the sense that they are specifically referred to by PF rules. These are defined in (14):

(14) Definitions

  a. **M-Word:** (Potentially complex) head not dominated by a further head-projection.
  b. **Subword:** A terminal node; thus, a morpheme in the sense of chapter 2 (either a functional morpheme, or a Root).

Illustrating with reference to (13), the complex head (15) that contains the $\sqrt{\text{ROOT}}$, X, and Y is an M-Word:

(15) M-Word in (13)

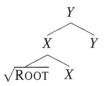

Within this object, the terminal nodes—the Root, X, and Y—are Subwords.

According to (14b), a Subword is a terminal. Subwords and syntactic terminals (i.e., morphemes) are equivalent in the normal case. The restriction to "normal" here reflects the fact that if some morphemes are added at PF (dissociated morphemes; recall the discussion of Agr(eement) in the Spanish example above), then there are some morphemes at PF that are Subwords, but not on the list of Syntactic Terminals.

Moving past the concerns of the syntax proper, Subwords are central to the theory of the morpheme for two reasons: first, because Subwords and morphemes are equivalent in most cases; and, second, because Subwords are the target of the Vocabulary Insertion operation. This computation is defined to provide phonological content to terminal nodes, and terminal nodes only: that is, Subwords, in the sense of (14b). This is a crucial claim of the theory presented in this book: it allows no Vocabulary Insertion at "intermediate" nodes, at the M-Word level, or at any of the other phrasal nodes that are represented in syntactic structures. The idea that Vocabulary Insertion is restricted to apply to terminals in this way is developed in chapter 4.

The M-Word corresponds directly to the notion of "complex head" employed above in section 3.2; in syntactic terms, it is equivalent to the H^{0max}

in Chomsky's (1995) theory of constituent structure. The significance of the M-Word for affixation is clear in situations in which the operation of head movement applies recursively. Consider, for example, a structure containing the heads X, Y, and Z, shown in (16) prior to head movement:

(16) Structure Before Head Movement

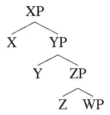

A first application of head movement in this structure adjoins Z to Y:

(17) Structure After Z-to-Y Movement

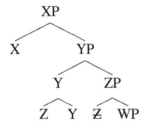

Subsequently, the (complex) Y may adjoin to X to yield a complex head containing X, Y, and Z:

(18) Structure After Y-to-X Movement

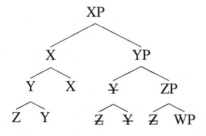

In standard versions of head movement, only the complex head [$_Y$ Z Y] may adjoin to X as shown in (18); it is not possible to move e.g. Z alone out of the complex head [_Y Z Y] and head-adjoin it to X.[5] Thus, the objects that are moved by head movement are M-Words in the sense defined in (14).

In addition to playing an important role in the composition of complex objects, the M-Word is also directly implicated in the linear relations that are established at PF (section 3.4), as well as in the mapping to domains of phonological interaction (section 3.5).

It is often the case that the definitions of M-Word and Subword do not overlap. For example, in the complex head used above to illustrate these notions (the one based on (13)), there is no Subword that is also an M-Word:

(19) M-Word in (13)

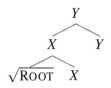

For much of the discussion of this book, where emphasis is placed on the analysis of complex heads, I will be looking at objects in which the M-Words and Subwords are distinct, as they are in (19). It is worth noting, though, that there are many configurations that contain objects that are simultaneously M-Words and Subwords according to (14). For example, in the DP *the cat* in (20), where a determiner head D[+def] takes a noun phrase complement, the D[+def] head is simultaneously an M-Word and a Subword:

(20) the cat

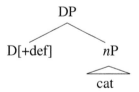

D[+def] is an M-Word because it is a head that is not dominated by further head material; and it is a Subword because it is a terminal element, i.e., a morpheme. By virtue of meeting both of these criteria, the D[+def] head is linearized as an M-Word (see the following section); it is also a Subword, and is therefore a target of Vocabulary Insertion. Further illustrations of how the M-Word/Subword distinction plays a role in PF processes can be found in Embick (2007b).

3.4 Linear Order

The preceding sections outline an approach to affixation that is centered on complex heads, and on the idea that two objects—M-Words and Subwords—are directly referred to by computations that are important for morphological concerns. The representations examined in the initial part of the discussion above are *hierarchical* structures. But hierarchical representations clearly do not exhaust all that there is to say about morphemes and their organization into complex forms: ultimately, because of the requirement that speech and sign be realized in real time, morphemes must also be put into a *linear* order. One of the key questions in morphology (and in other domains as well) concerns the respective roles of linear and hierarchical representations in accounting for grammatical generalizations. This section develops a working theory of linear relations between morphemes, in a way that accounts for certain systematic relations between linear order and hierarchical structure that are central to the syntax/morphology interface.

3.4.1 The Concatenation of M-Words and Subwords

Consider the complex head structure in (21):

(21) M-Word in (13)

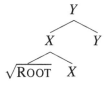

As a starting point for a more careful look at linear order, it is important to observe that the object in (21) contains two types of information. The first is the structural type examined in the last section: (21) represents the hierarchical structure of the complex head, in which the Root is the most deeply embedded object, the X head is less deeply embedded than the Root, and the Y head is the least embedded.

The second type of information conveyed by graphic representations like (21) is linear: it shows the complex head with the two morphemes X and Y linearized after the Root, i.e., what is written as $\sqrt{\text{ROOT}}$-X-Y in an exclusively linear notation. In the standard parlance of descriptive morphology, the scenario at hand is one in which X and Y are suffixes.

The syntax outputs hierarchical structures that are equivalent to (21), but which have no linear order. One way of thinking of this is that as far as hierarchy goes, $[_Y [_X \sqrt{\text{ROOT}}\ X]\ Y]$ and $[_Y Y\ [_X X\ \sqrt{\text{ROOT}}\ ]]$ are equivalent, in the sense that they represent exactly the same information; it is only the exigencies of (two-dimensional) graphic representation that forces them to be presented in one order or the other on the page. If it is assumed that syntactic derivations construct hierarchical structures that do not contain information about linear order, then it is necessary to say something about how hierarchical and linear representations relate to one another.

The standard way of talking about the relation between structure and linear order is to say that hierarchical structures determine a set of possible linearizations, such that structure and order are distinct, but systematically related to each other. Operationally, this means that a (set of) linearization procedures applies to the output of the syntax in the PF component. The details of the procedures that derive such representations will be left vague, since what I have to say about the linear order of morphemes is compatible with any number of linearization algorithms. The only constraint on linearization that I will assume is that hierarchical structure constrains possible linear orders in terms of a *No Tangling* condition (this is called *nontangling* in Partee et al. (1993)). The No Tangling condition on the linearization procedure says that certain linear orders of the morphemes in (21) are impossible; namely, the ones in (22):

(22) $\sqrt{\text{ROOT}}$-Y-X
X-Y-$\sqrt{\text{ROOT}}$

Speaking figuratively, these are impossible because they require the "crossing" (tangling) of branches of the syntactic tree; Y cannot be closer to the Root than X without crossing lines in this way.[6]

For the purposes of this book, it will be assumed that only No Tangling restricts the linearization of morphemes. Thus, linearization procedures are in principle capable of realizing a syntactic object $[X\ Y]$ as either X-Y or Y-X, depending on the language (and in some cases, the particular morphemes) in question.[7]

We are now in a position to look closely at exactly how two morphemes X and Y are connected linearly. It is quite likely that there are a number of different linear relations that are relevant for PF concerns in the broad sense, depending on what particular aspect of a representation is being analyzed (see Embick 2010b for some specific proposals concerning morphophonology). My interest in this chapter is on one specific type of linear relation: one that relates M-Words to M-Words, and Subwords to Subwords. The operator that does this encodes *concatenation*: a binary relation of immediate precedence. Notationally, the operator $\frown$ is used for concatenation, so that $X\frown Y$ is to be understood as *X immediately precedes Y*.

With reference to the structure in (21), if both X and Y are suffixes, then the linearization procedure generates the statements in (23), in which the Root is concatenated with X, and X with Y:

(23)   Concatenation Statements

$$\sqrt{\text{Root}}\frown X, X\frown Y$$

As mentioned in the introduction to this section, a key theme in understanding morphological locality is how linear and hierarchical notions of locality relate to one another. Conditions of locality that are defined in linear versus hieararchical terms make different predictions about when morphemes may potentially interact with each other. Crucially, it appears that linear locality is of central importance for several different PF computations: for example, in the PF affixation operation of Local Dislocation (see references in section 3.2.2 above), and in the locality conditions on contextual allomorphy (see chapter 7).

As far as notation is concerned, the concatenation operator will be used in many of the examples discussed below. However, it is often the case that this level of precision is not required. Thus, I will sometimes use the hyphen - to indicate morpheme order, particularly in forms discussed in the text and in tables.

3.4.2   Syntactic Structure and Morpheme Order

A topic that has generated a great deal of discussion in the literature on the syntax/morphology interface is how the order of morphemes inside words sometimes appears to "reflect" or "mirror" the order of syntactic projections in a clause. The latter terminology is employed by Baker (1985, 1988), where the mirroring effect is attributed to the so-called *Mirror Principle*.

74 *Structures and Linear Order*

The observation that morpheme order and syntactic structure relate to each other in this and other systematic ways is very important, particularly for the question of how morphemes are assembled into complex forms. As will be shown below, effects of this type do not call for an independent principle of the grammar per se. Rather, mirror effects—and, more generally, systematic connections between morphology and syntax—are an architectural consequence of a theory that constructs all complex objects syntactically.

An illustration of the mirroring effect is seen in (24), which employs Quechua examples drawn from Muysken (1981):

(24) a. *Maqa-naku-ya-chi-n*
 beat-RECIP-DUR-CAUS-3s

 'He is causing them to beat each other.'

 b. *Maqa-chi-naku-rka-n*
 beat-CAUS-RECIP-PL-3s

 'They let someone beat each other.'

Although the same causative (CAUS) and reciprocal (RECIP) morphemes appear in both of these sentences, the examples do not have the same interpretation. Rather, one is the causative of a reciprocal (24a), and the other is the reciprocal of a causative (24b) (see Muysken's work for detailed discussion). Crucially, the difference in interpretation is associated with a difference in morpheme order in a systematic way. In particular, the different *scopes* of the causative and reciprocal morphemes are reflected by different orders of these two morphemes; this is the observation that underlies the Mirror Principle.

As a first step towards understanding what mirror effects show us, it is necessary to review how the distinct interpretations of the words in (24) are produced. In (24a), a clause with reciprocal interpretation is subjected to causativization; and in (24b), a causative has reciprocal meaning added to it. This means that in (24a) the causative morpheme is structurally higher than the reciprocal morpheme (CAUS over RECIP), whereas in (24b) the reverse is true (RECIP over CAUS). Schematically (i.e., concentrating only on the causative morpheme and the reciprocal morpheme, and not the other morphemes in (24)), the phrasal structures that these two interpretations derive from are shown in (25); for notational convenience, I have used "CauseP" and "RecipP" for the phrasal projections of the two crucial heads:

(25) a. CAUS over RECIP

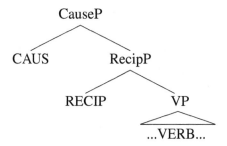

b. RECIP over CAUS

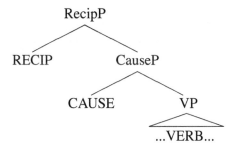

The standard version of head movement applied to (25a,b) produces the complex heads shown in (26a,b) respectively; these underlie the verbs in (24a,b):

(26) a. CAUS over RECIP

b. RECIP over CAUS

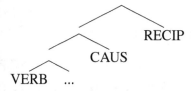

The key to understanding these examples is the order of the CAUS and RECIP morphemes. In Quechua, each of these affixes is linearized as a suffix. Thus, linearizing the tree in (26a) yields the order VERB-RECIP-CAUS, whereas for (26b) the order VERB-CAUS-RECIP is derived. The mirror effect is this: the phrasal syntax CAUS over RECIP over VERB (25a) is realized "morphologically" as VERB-RECIP-CAUS (26a), while RECIP over CAUS over VERB (25b) is realized "morphologically" as VERB-CAUSE-RECIP (26b). In each case, the linear order of morphemes in the complex heads in (26) is the "mirror image" of the order of the containing phrasal structures in (25): i.e., when RECIP dominates CAUS, the order of morphemes on the verb is CAUS-RECIP; and when CAUS dominates RECIP, the order is RECIP-CAUS.

Crucially, the mirror effect is derived as a consequence of constructing affixed words syntactically, with head movement. As discussed above, head movement moves a head to the immediately dominating head, and then moves the resulting complex to the next immediately dominating head, and so on. Starting with the different structures in (25), the locality conditions on head movement produce the different complex heads in (26), from which the different morpheme orders follow.

3.4.3 Structure and Order

Mirror orders are expected given how head movement works. But they are only part of the picture. In a theory that linearizes complex heads in a way that is contrained by No Tangling, transparent relations between syntax and morphology may also be found in scenarios that do not involve strict mirroring. That is, whether or not morpheme order actually mirrors the order of syntactic heads and projections depends on how the relevant morphemes are linearized within the M-Word; and this is something that is (by hypothesis) subject to cross-linguistic and perhaps (within a particular language) morpheme-specific variation. Thus, mirror orders are found in one possible way of linearizing a complex head, but they are not guaranteed to occur. There are other ways of realizing complex heads that do **not** involve strict mirror orders, but which are just as transparent as far as syntax/morphology connections are concerned.

Recall from section 3.4.1 that in a complex head like $[[\sqrt{\text{ROOT}}\ X]\ Y]$, either X or Y could be linearized either as a prefix or a suffix. Thus, it is possible to derive the orders $X\text{-}\sqrt{\text{ROOT}}\text{-}Y$ or $Y\text{-}\sqrt{\text{ROOT}}\text{-}X$—neither of these show a mirror effect, but both comply with No Tangling.

A wider range of possible linearizations can be illustrated with the structure in (27), which shows a Root and higher projections headed by X, Y, and Z:

(27) Structure

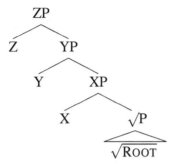

If the Root undergoes head movement to X, Y, and then Z, the resulting complex head (i.e., the complex head that is found at the Z position in the tree) has the structure in (28):

(28) Complex Head Formed in (27)

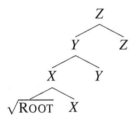

In terms of concatenation, a suffixal realization of (28) with $\sqrt{\text{ROOT}}$-X-Y-Z is produced with the following statements:

(29) $\sqrt{\text{ROOT}}\frown X, X\frown Y, Y\frown Z$

The mirror effect is in evidence in (29), since the morpheme order reflects the syntactic structure of the clause.

Thus far, the abstract example with X-Y-Z is, effectively, a review of what is illustrated in the Quechua examples in the preceding subsection. The move beyond strict "mirroring" is based on the observation that there are other possible ways of linearizing structures like (28). In particular, the linear orders that comply with No Tangling are those in (30):

(30) Possible Linearizations of (28)

    a. Root-X-Y-Z

    b. Z-Root-X-Y

    c. Z-Y-Root-X

    d. Y-Root-X-Z

    e. X-Root-Y-Z

    f. Y-X-Root-Z

    g. Z-X-Root-Y

    h. Z-Y-X-Root

In practice, of course, we would not expect a study of three morphemes X, Y, Z that often co-occur to find that all of these options are equally well-attested cross-linguistically. There are tendencies for languages to be either predominantly suffixal or predominantly prefixal, for example, which (presumably) make some of the "mixed" orders in (30) less likely to be found than the "uniform" orders (30a) and (30h). Nothing in the theory, though, prevents the mixed orders from existing.

At the same time, it would always be possible to introduce conditions beyond No Tangling into the theory, with the goal of restricting possible linearizations further. At present, however, I do not see compelling reasons for adopting any additional hypotheses of this type.

To summarize the discussion to this point, complex heads are syntactic objects, built in syntactic structures. Complex heads are linearized by a procedure that respects No Tangling, such that possible morpheme orders are restricted by the syntactic structures in which they appear.

As noted earlier, the phenomenon illustrated by the Quechua examples is often said to instantiate the *Mirror Principle*, put forward by Baker (1985, 1988), who hypothesizes that mirror orders are the result of an independent principle (i.e., the Mirror Principle) that exists as a *condition* on how syntactic structures and morphological representations relate to one another. As the discussion above is at pains to illustrate, however, it is not necessary to appeal to an independent principle of this type to account for systematic connections between syntax and morphology. What the Mirror Principle embodies is the *observation* that word-internal structure is directly related to syntactic structure (whether there is actual mirroring or not). The best-case scenario is that this observation would be accounted for by virtue of how complex forms are created, rather than by an independent principle that stipulates relationships between two distinct "word-creating" and "phrase-creating" systems. It is this level of *transparency* between syntax and morphology that is realized in a theory in which all complex forms are created in a single generative system, as they are on the approach adopted here.[8]

3.4.4 Bracketing and Order Mismatches

The generalizations that motivate a theory in which syntactic structure directly constrains possible morpheme orders are very strong empirically. However, while a syntactic approach accounts for great deal of what there is to be said about the conditions on morpheme order, there are certain phenomena that appear to create complications for this model of syntax and morphology. These complications arise when the order of morphemes (or the bracketing of morphemes) that is motivated on morphological or morphophonological grounds is not the same as what is expected on syntacticosemantic grounds. Terminologically, phenomena of this type are called syntax/morphology (or syntax/phonology) *mismatches*.

Some mismatches are quite familiar and have been the object of study in sizable literatures. For example, Chomsky and Halle (1968) highlight a type of mismatch between syntax and prosody that leads them to conclude that syntactic structures must be altered in limited ways in order to serve as the input to the phonology (see below). Or, to take a further example, the vast literature on cliticization (and, in many cases, the analysis of so-called "second position" clitics) addresses a kind of mismatch, because certain clitics surface in positions that are apparently unexpected from a purely syntactic point of view, for phonological or morphophonological reasons.

With reference to bracketing, another well-known type of mismatch can be illustrated with words like *unhappier*, which is an instance of what is referred to as a *bracketing paradox* (Pesetsky (1979,1985); see also Sproat (1985) and Marantz (1988)). Semantically, the comparative degree morpheme DEG (realized as *-er*) takes scope over *unhappy*. This is clear from the fact that *unhappier* means something like "more unhappy", not something like "not happier". Phonologically, though, synthetic *X-er* comparatives are only formed on short adjectives; and, while *unhappy* is too long to be affixed in this way, *happy* clearly is not, since *happier* is a grammatical word of English. Putting these observations together, it appears that the syntacticosemantic bracketing of *unhappier* is (31a), whereas the morphophonological bracketing is (31b):

(31) a. Syntacticosemantic:

[[un happy] er]

b. Morphophonological:

[un [happy er]]

The mismatch is found in the fact that the morphemes in words like *unhappier* appear to organized in different ways when different parts of the grammar are considered. Sproat and Marantz argue that the mismatch comes about because of the way in which hierarchical and linear relations differ. In particular, they argue that linear relations allow for free rebracketing, a position that has been explored in different directions in later work.[9]

Moving past bracketing, there are also apparent mismatches that implicate morpheme order. These are directly relevant to the discussion of sections 3.4.2 and 3.4.3 above, because they have been argued to be exceptions to (or to violate) the Mirror Principle. One argument to this effect is found in Hyman (2003), and is based on data from the Bantu language Chichewa. Chichewa has both causative (CAUS) and applicative (APPL) morphemes. According to Hyman's analysis, it is possible syntacticosemantically to form both the applicative of a causative, and the causative of an applicative (recall the reasoning that was employed in the discussion of Quechua in section 3.4.3). However, these two different interpretations are both realized with the same order of morphemes, CAUS-APPL *its-il* (Hyman 2003:248 and Hyman and Mchombo 1992; in these examples PROG is for "progressive", and FV is for "final vowel"):

(32) a. Applicative of Causative

*alenjé a-ku-líl-**íts**-**il**-a*   *mwaná ndodo*
hunters 3pl-PROG-cry-CAUS-APPL-FV child   sticks

'The hunters are making the child cry with sticks.'

b. Causative of Applicative

*alenjé a-ku-tákás-**its**-**il**-a*   *mkází mthíko*
hunters 3pl-PROG-stir-CAUS-APPL-FV woman spoon

'The hunters are making the woman stir with a spoon.'

The example in (32b) is a prima facie mismatch. If the most obvious syntacticosemantic analysis is correct (i.e. the analysis in which CAUS is above APPL), the morpheme order in should be APPL-CAUS, but it is not.

With respect to this type of mismatch in general, there are two main possibilities to be considered. One possibility is that the syntacticosemantic analysis that predicts the non-occurring morpheme order is simply false, and that the correct analysis does not produce a mismatch. For instance, Pylkkänen (2002) suggests that the "fixed" ordering of CAUS and APPL in Bantu has a syntacticosemantic basis. Because it maintains the simplest interaction between syntax and morphology, this first option represents the null hypothesis. As a general rule, it should thus be asked for any particular putative mismatch whether the mismatch is only apparent, and derivative of an incorrect synatico-semantic analysis. This might seem like it is placing a rather stringent set of requirements on morphological theory broadly speaking, since it requires close attention to syntactic and semantic detail; but this is a strength of the approach, not a weakness.

The second option is that the syntacticosemantic analysis is indeed correct, so that some part of the morphophonological representation is in fact distinct from the representation that is required for syntacticosemantic purposes. With much prior work in this area, I assume that true mismatches like this are the result of a small set of PF operations that apply to the output of the syntactic derivation to alter it in limited ways.

One of the primary tasks of this part of the syntax/morphology interface is to identify the set of PF operations that are responsible for these deviations from the nondefault case (see Embick and Noyer 2007 for an overview). This research program is a continuation of early work on the relationship between syntax and phonology like Chomsky and Halle (1968), where questions about mismatches are couched in terms of there being divergent notions of "surface structure" (one syntactic, one phonological) that are related to each other by rule. The nature of such rules is not at the center of Chomsky and Halle (1968), though, and it is only later that a broad range of syntax/phonology interactions are analyzed in their own right, in a large literature on prosodic phonology. Closer to the focus of this chapter, the general theme of how to constrain the divergences between the representation that is the output of the syntax and the representation(s) relevant for PF computation is a primary component of Marantz's (1984, 1988) work, which looks specifically at rebracketing and affixation operations in this light. Within the framework adopted in this book, it has been proposed that many mismatches are the result of PF movement operations; see Embick and Noyer (2001, 2007) and Embick (2007b) for overviews.

The main theme that unifies the approaches to mismatches cited above is the idea that syntactic structure and morphological structure are the same in the default case, with the exceptions to this general pattern calling for a restricted set of rules driven by language-specific PF requirements. This type of theory allows for systematic investigation of syntax/PF mismatches, while maintaining Interface Transparency in its strongest form possible. Indeed, a main research intuition behind Distributed Morphology is that while mismatches do exist, they do not compromise the general syntactic orientation of the theory, since the very fact that certain phenomena can be isolated as mismatches in the first place testifies to the robust transparency of syntax/morphology interactions more generally.

3.5 A Note on Structure and Phonological Wordhood

A final point for this chapter concerns the relationship between the morphemes and syntactic structures that are at the center of the theory on the one hand, and the intuitive notion of the *word* on the other.

In a theory that derives all complex objects syntactically, the term *word* is often used informally to pick out a number of objects that have a shared set of properties, properties that have some more or less direct relationship to the notion *phonological word*. Technically speaking, whether or not the phonological word is needed as part of the theory—i.e., whether it has ontological status in the approach, and is not just a convenient descriptive term—is an open question in phonological theory. However, for the purposes of the present discussion, I will assume that there is a notion of "word-level phonology" that is important for sound structure, because this will allow us to see how phonological domains relate to structural notions, i.e., to objects like Subwords and M-Words.[10]

The clearest connection to pursue along these lines identifies the M-Word as an object of phonological interest. M-Words almost invariably show the "close" types of phonological interaction that are associated with phonological wordhood. As a working hypothesis, it appears that the M-Word is special for phonological interaction, in the sense that it seems to correlate in the default case with the domain in which the word-level phonology takes place. Part of this special status could be analyzed by taking the M-Word to be where the non-cyclic phonology applies, for example (see Embick (2010b) for some preliminary discussion).[11]

The M-Word/phonological word correspondence is a good starting point for understanding how the informal notion of "word" can be understood structurally. There are many additional questions that arise when both smaller and larger phonological domains are considered.

In the case of smaller objects, asymmetries in the morphophonological behavior of certain (classes of) affixes, such as those associated with "Level 1" and "Level 2" affixes in English could in principle be analyzed in a number of different ways. For instance, this kind of difference might reflect important structural differences in how Subwords attach to their hosts, or perhaps whether certain morphemes are phase-defining or not; or it could be the case that phonological behavior like this results from individual exponents being specified as "cyclic" or "non-cyclic" in the phonological sense (cf. Halle and Vergnaud (1987)).

In the case of objects that are larger than the M-Word, questions about the trade-off between structures, morpheme-specific behavior, and locality domains are salient in a large literature on the phonology of cliticization (see e.g. Poser (1985), Booij and Rubach (1987), Hayes (1990), Halpern (1992), Odden (1993), and Embick (1995) for some different perspectives on this and some closely related matters). Beyond cliticization, the same sorts of questions about how structure relates to domains of phonological interaction arises for objects of larger sizes as well, in the area of research typically referred to as prosodic phonology, or the syntax/phonology interface. See Pak (2008) for an overview of the major research programs in this domain.

Programmatically, the idea at the center of this section is that domains of phonological interaction (whether the phonological word, or some other domain) are not primitives of the theory; rather, they are to be understood in terms of priviliged structural objects (as in the M-Word/phonological word hypothesis), or in terms of other parts of the theory (phase theory, the properties of exponents, and so on). For a sample of work looking more directly at some of the relevant phonological interactions in this framework, see e.g. Marvin (2002), Oltra-Massuet and Arregi (2005), Newell (2008), and Embick (2010b) for "word-internal" investigations, and for larger syntactic objects, Wagner (2005) and Pak (2008).

3.6 Conclusions

In a syntactic approach to morphology, morphemes are the terminal elements of syntactic derivations, and all complex forms are derived syntactically. In derived structures, an important role is played by the complex head, because complex heads result from the affixation operations that are of interest to morphological theory.

In this and the preceding chapters, two major components of the theory have been addressed. One, outlined in this chapter, is the idea that morphemes are assembled into larger objects in syntactic derivations. A consequence of this latter view is that the locality conditions that are relevant to morphological theory are either the locality conditions that apply to syntactic rules, or the locality conditions that derive from the linearization of syntactic objects. It is in this sense that the theory is fundamentally syntactic in orientation.

The second major idea, developed in chapter 2, is that the theory involves two types of morphemes, Roots and functional morphemes. Of these, at least the functional morphemes are represented without phonological features underlyingly. The computation that is responsible for adding phonological content to morphemes—Vocabulary Insertion—takes center stage in the chapters to come.

Chapter 4
Vocabulary Insertion: An Introduction

4.1 Fundamental Notions

The theory that is developed in this book is centered on two types of morphemes: Roots and functional morphemes. Functional morphemes are bundles of synsem features that do not possess phonological features underlyingly. Instead, they receive their phonological form in the PF component of the grammar, via the Vocabulary Insertion operation. This chapter begins a detailed examination of Vocabulary Insertion; this focus extends into chapters 5 and 6, where some additional topics—including the phenomenon of syncretism and its theoretical analysis—are examined.

As a starting point, it is convenient to begin with a review of some of the central points about morphemes and their phonological forms that are introduced in chapters 1 and 2. Recall that the grammar of every language contains a list that is referred to as the *Vocabulary* of that language. The members of this list are individual *Vocabulary Items*. According to the view that I will develop here, Vocabulary Items are objects, objects that are accessed and activated in the Vocabulary Insertion process.[1]

By definition, a Vocabulary Item is a pairing between a phonological *exponent* and a set of synsem features that determine the privileges of occurrence of that exponent. In essence, the synsem feature specification determines the morphemes to which a Vocabulary Item could in principle apply. A Vocabulary Item is schematized in (1), with its individual subparts labelled:

(1) Vocabulary Item

$$\underbrace{[\alpha\beta\gamma]}_{\text{synsem features}} \leftrightarrow \underbrace{/X/}_{\text{phonological exponent}}$$

So, for example, the familiar past tense *-ed* of English is the exponent of the Vocabulary Item in (2):

(2) T[+past] ↔ -ed

The effect of this Vocabulary Item is to give the phonological form *-ed* to the node T[+past]. So, for example, if the T[+past] node is combined with the

Root √PLAY and the categorizing head *v*, the result is a "past tense verb", as shown prior to Vocabulary Insertion in (3):

(3) past tense of *play*, prior to insertion

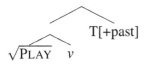

The Vocabulary Insertion operation applies to the terminal nodes in the structure in (3), and inserts the phonological exponent *-ed* into the position of the Tense node; the result is shown in (4), which also assumes that a *-Ø* exponent is inserted into the *v* head:

(4) past tense of *play*, after insertion

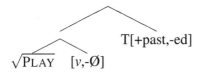

The treatment of Vocabulary Insertion in (3) and (4) is rudimentary in several ways. For example, it does not specify exactly how a functional morpheme like T[+past] comes to possess a phonological representation (i.e., /d/) by virtue of the application of (2). This detail has important consequences for some basic notions in morphological theory, as we will see below.

It also remains to be seen how Vocabulary Insertion can be used to analyze one of the central phenomena of interest in morphological theory: the phenomenon of *(contextual) allomorphy*. To a first approximation, allomorphy is found when a single object at the syntactic or semantic level of description—in the typical case, a single functional morpheme—appears with more than one phonological form, in a way that implicates more than one Vocabulary Item. Some well-known examples of this effect are found in the past tense system of English. While "regular" verbs like *play* show the *-ed* exponent for the functional morpheme T[+past], there are other verbs where this *-ed* is not found. Take, for example, the verb *bend*. The past tense of *bend* is not **bend-ed*; rather, it is *ben-t*, where the phonological exponent of the T[+past] morpheme is *-t*, not *-ed* (note in addition that the final /d/ of the Root is eliminated by a (morpho)phonological rule).

These simple observations about the phonological realization of T[+past] have a number of implications. A first is that the grammar of English must contain a Vocabulary Item that realizes T[+past] with the phonological exponent -*t*, in addition to the one with -*ed*. A second observation, which is very important when generalized, is that the Vocabulary Item with the -*t* exponent must apply with *bend*, but not with e.g. *play*; that is, we need a working theory of allomorphy that ensures the correct distribution of exponents. Relatedly, when the Vocabulary Item with the -*t* exponent applies with *bend*, it must prevent the Vocabulary Item in (2) from applying; so, the ungrammatical form **bend-ed* (and, for that matter, an ungrammatical form with two exponents like **ben-t-ed*) must not be derived. Taken together, these last observations comprise what are called *blocking effects*.

This chapter demonstrates how Vocabulary Insertion accounts for the observations outlined in the last paragraph, and develops a number of additional points that arise in the course of the discussion. As a preliminary step, section 4.2 implements Vocabulary Insertion formally with the idea that phonological exponents are substituted for a variable that is part of the representation of a functional morpheme. After this, section 4.3 introduces the idea that Vocabulary Items are ordered and compete for application to a given morpheme. This idea is crucial for the analysis of allomorphy; it is also essential to the (preliminary) treatment of blocking that is developed in section 4.4. This part of the discussion also introduces two additional ideas about Vocabulary Insertion: first, that it targets only terminal nodes (= morphemes; = Subwords), and no other structural objects; and, second, that it applies to a given node only once. Additional assumptions about the order of Vocabulary Insertion in complex structures are introduced in section 4.5. Finally, all of this material is synthesized in section 4.6, which works through some examples that illustrate and emphasize key points.

Before proceeding to specifics, a point is in order concerning the division of labor between this and the following chapter. This chapter provides a working model of how functional morphemes receive their phonological content. The emphasis is exclusively on *how* Vocabulary Insertion works, not on *why* something like Vocabulary Insertion is needed in the theory. The latter question is addressed in chapter 5, where I will look at a primary motivation for Vocabulary Insertion, which is the phenomenon of syncretism.

4.2 The Vocabulary Insertion Process in Detail

Ultimately, morphemes relate sound (or sign) and meaning. For functional morphemes, sound and meaning come together via Vocabulary Insertion. Thus, in a comprehensive theory of how phonological and synsem features are related by this operation, two basic sets of questions must be addressed.

The first type of question concerns the "insertion" part of Vocabulary Insertion, and asks what it means for a phonological exponent to be added to a terminal node. Specifically, there must be a theory of what happens when an object from the Vocabulary (a Vocabulary Item, which pairs synsem features with a phonological exponent) applies to a functional morpheme to yield a node that has a phonological representation.

The second question concerns the synsem features that are referred to in the insertion process, and what happens to such features when Vocabulary Insertion applies to the morpheme that possesses them. The question here is whether Vocabulary Insertion affects synsem features when phonological features are added (for example, by deleting them), or whether synsem features are unaffected by insertion, making them therefore potentially visible to subsequent computations. These questions are addressed in turn in the following subsections.

4.2.1 Adding Phonological Content

In the way that Vocabulary Insertion has been described to this point, the Vocabulary Item (5) applies to the node T[+past] with regular verbs like *play*:

(5) T[+past] ↔ -ed

The result is that its phonological exponent—the phonological matrix represented by *-ed* in (5)—appears in the position of that morpheme; (6) and (7) illustrate the pre- and post-insertion representations:

(6) *played*, before insertion   (7) *played*, after insertion

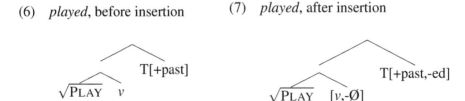

While the process sketched in (5)-(7) is accurate in its gross contours, many things remain to be said about the specifics of phonological instantiation.

To begin with, there are several different ways in which the procedure for adding phonological exponents to nodes can be formalized. As shown in (6) and (7), the process of Vocabulary Insertion is *additive*, in the sense that it introduces a new element—a phonological matrix—to the morpheme T[+past]; that is, it augments the T[+past] morpheme with material that it does not possess underlyingly.

Another possibility for the analysis of phonological realization, which is adopted here, is that Vocabulary Insertion is *replacive*. Halle (1990), for example, develops an approach that treats phonological realization in this way. In this theory, certain morphemes possess a place-holder Q as part of their underlying representation, rather than an actual phonological exponent. Thus, for example, the morpheme T[+past] is represented as T[+past,Q] prior to insertion. In the version of the replacement view that I will propose here, the Q element functions as a variable, such that the effect of Vocabulary Insertion is to replace Q with a phonological exponent, which can be seen as the value of the Q variable.

With this general picture in mind, the pre-insertion and post-insertion stages of the past tense example are as follows:

(8) Pre-insertion   (9) Post-insertion

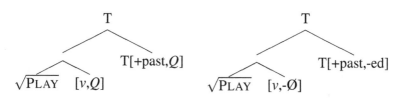

As part of a generalized theory with replacement, it will be assumed here that all functional morphemes possess a Q variable. Thus, all such morphemes have the form shown in (10), where α is a synsem feature:[2]

(10) functional morpheme, schematically:

   [α,Q]

The schematization of a functional morpheme in (10) shows only a single synsem feature α, but this is merely a matter of convenience. Functional morphemes are often bundles of multiple features, so that, for example, [α,β,Q] is a possible functional morpheme (recall chapter 2). Crucially, though, each functional morpheme contains only a single Q element. This latter assumption has important consequences which will be seen as the discussion proceeds.

As mentioned earlier, the Q element can be treated as a variable. The phonological realization part of Vocabulary Insertion can then be treated as the *substitution of a free variable*, in which the phonological exponent of the Vocabulary Item replaces Q. Using the notation [Q/X] for "phonological form /X/ is substituted for Q" in the expression to its left, this part of the Vocabulary Insertion process is shown in detail in (11) for the T[+past] example:

(11) Vocabulary Insertion in detail

   a. Functional morpheme: T[+past,Q]

   b. Vocabulary Item: T[+past] ↔ -ed

   c. Substitution: T[+past,Q] [Q/-ed] → T[+past,-ed]

The Q-analysis developed to this point provides a working account of the phonological realization of morphemes. However, it is partial, since it concentrates on the last steps of Vocabulary Insertion: that is, on the process by which a single Vocabulary Item gives phonological content to a morpheme. Several further components of Vocabulary Insertion—steps leading up to (11)—need to be clarified as well. In particular, (11) does not specify how the correct Vocabulary Item is active in such a way as to be consulted for the substitution operation. Being the active Vocabulary Item in a derivation requires a theory of how Vocabulary Items compete for application to a given node. This important topic is treated in section 4.3.

As a notational matter, it is not always necessary to show the Q-component of a morpheme. In much of the discussion in this book, the level of detail shown in (11) will be dispensed with in favor of simpler representations in which an abbreviated or "two-step" version of the Vocabulary Insertion process is used. This simpler type of representation will take the form of the initial discussion above, where a morpheme like T[+past] pre-insertion is represented as T[+past,-ed] post-insertion. The more detailed view of the Vocabulary Insertion process, which makes explicit reference to the Q variable and other steps outlined above, is made use of only when this additional level of detail is called for.

4.2.2 Vocabulary Insertion and Synsem Features

According to the view presented in chapter 2, functional morphemes consist of features from the Universal Feature Inventory (UFI). Abstractly, and with α, β for synsem features, a typical functional morpheme has the form in (12), which also shows the Q variable:

(12) $[\alpha, \beta, Q]$

Morphemes like the one shown in (12) function as terminal nodes in syntactic derivations, in the way described in the earlier chapters of this book. The features α and β are, by hypothesis, features that are interpreted semantically. Syntactic derivations containing morphemes like the one in (12) are spelled out, such that structures containing (12) are sent to the PF and LF interface components.

The synsem features of a morpheme are visible to computations at each interface. On the meaning side, features like α and β play a role in the procedure that constructs semantic representations from syntactic objects. In the PF component of the grammar, these features are visible to Vocabulary Insertion, and they determine which Vocabulary Item applies to give a morpheme its phonological form.

Having synsem features visible to the insertion process is a bare minimum. Beyond this, there is a further question about what happens to synsem features when Vocabulary Insertion occurs. More precisely, there are two options to consider here. The first is that synsem features are still present in a morpheme, after Vocabulary Insertion has applied. The second is that (at least some) synsem features are deleted when Vocabulary Insertion occurs.

In the representations that are employed in section 4.2.1 above, I adopted the first of these two views: Vocabulary Insertion adds phonological features to a morpheme, but it does not automatically delete that morpheme's synsem features when it does so. In the treatment of the past tense of *played*, for example, insertion of the *-ed* exponent does not trigger the deletion of [+past]:

(13) *played* again

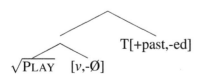

The non-deletion view will be adopted as the default case in the pages to come. The qualification to the default case reflects the fact that across-the-board non-deletion is probably an oversimplification; it is possible, for example, that there are some complex phenomena for which Vocabulary-driven deletion is required, as discussed in Noyer (1997) or Bobaljik (2000). However, for typical cases of Vocabulary Insertion non-deletion appears to be exactly what is needed; some empirical illustrations of this point are advanced in section 4.6.3 below.[3]

4.3 Ordering of Vocabulary Items

In the analysis of English past tense forms like *played* that is developed in the preceding section, only one Vocabulary Item is considered: the one that inserts *-ed*. However, it is often the case that there are multiple Vocabulary Items that could in principle apply to a particular functional morpheme, such that the winner is determined by a morpheme local to the morpheme undergoing insertion. This results in contextual allomorphy. For example, it can be seen in (14) that the T[+past] morpheme in English has *-t* and *-Ø* phonological forms in addition to the regular or default *-ed*:[4]

(14) T[+past] allomorphy in English

    a. *-ed*: play-ed, watch-ed, kiss-ed

    b. *-t*: ben-t, sen-t, lef-t

    c. *-Ø*: hit-Ø, quit-Ø, sang-Ø

Based on the facts in (14), it is clear that the Vocabulary of English must contain Vocabulary Items with *-t* and *-Ø* exponents in addition to the one with the *-ed* exponent. Provisional versions of these Vocabulary Items are shown in (15):

(15) Provisional Vocabulary Items for T[+past]

    a. T[+past] ↔ -ed

    b. T[+past] ↔ -t

    c. T[+past] ↔ -Ø

The reason that the Vocabulary Items in (15) are provisional is that, as things stand, they do not make correct predictions about the derivation of any particular past tense forms. Specifically, there is nothing in the Vocabulary Items in (15) that ensures that the past tense form of *leave* is *lef-t* (and not **leav-ed*), while the past tense form of *play* is *play-ed* (and not **play-Ø*), and so on. Clearly, then, the Vocabulary Items in (15) need to be modified in a way that produces the correct distribution of exponents.

The modifications that are required are of two types. The first type is representational: the Vocabulary Items in (15) must be augmented so that the non-defaults (those with the *-t* and *-Ø* exponents) apply only in the context of some verbs, and not across the board. This additional information is shown in the revised Vocabulary Items in (16a,b), where the notation /__X means "in the context of X":

(16) Modified Vocabulary Items

a. T[+past] ↔ -t/{√BEND, √LEAVE,...}__

b. T[+past] ↔ -Ø/{√HIT, √QUIT,...}__

c. T[+past] ↔ -ed

The modified Vocabulary Items in (16a,b) make reference to an element in the context of the T[+past] morpheme that is undergoing insertion. The Vocabulary Item in (16a), for instance, says (informally) that the functional morpheme T[+past] is realized with the phonological exponent *-t* when T[+past] occurs in the context of the Roots √BEND, etc., whereas (16b) specifies the same kind of supplemental condition for the *-Ø* exponent. The crucial point here is that it is an element in the *context* of the T[+past] node that plays a role in determining which Vocabulary Item is employed; it is with these contextual conditions that Vocabulary Insertion accounts for contextual allomorphy.

Another point of interest in (16) is that the "regular" Vocabulary Item in English (16c) does not have a contextual specification. This is what makes this item *-ed* a *default*: it needs no contextual information to apply. For this reason, it is this Vocabulary Item that is employed with nonce verbs (e.g. present tense *blick*, past *blick-ed*).

Specifying Vocabulary Items with contextual information is the first part of the analysis of contextual allomorphy. The second modification that is required concerns the relationship between the different Vocabulary Items that could in principle apply to the T[+past] node.

Vocabulary Insertion: An Introduction

Consider, for concreteness, the derivation of *left*. The structure that is the input to Vocabulary Insertion is shown in (17):

(17) *left*

An initial question is what principle determines which of the Vocabulary Items in (16) could potentially apply to the T[+past] node in the first place. A standard assumption is that Vocabulary Items must be featurally compatible with the nodes to which they apply. Informally, this means that a Vocabulary Item cannot apply to a node if the Vocabulary Item makes reference to features that are not on that node (this will be formulated more precisely below). So, for example, the Vocabulary Item [+pl] ↔ -*s* that inserts the regular plural exponent makes reference to features that are not part of the T[+past] morpheme. It is thus not a possible candidate for application to T[+past]. The same idea about feature compatibility extends to contextual conditions: a Vocabulary Item may not apply to a morpheme that does not have the correct contextual properties.

With these restrictions on Vocabulary Insertion, it is clear that there are two Vocabulary Items in (16) that could potentially apply to the T[+past] node in (17): the one with the -*t* exponent (16a) (which refers to √LEAVE), and the default Vocabulary Item with the exponent -*ed* (16c). The Vocabulary Item with -Ø is not a possible candidate for insertion when √LEAVE is present; the reason is that the Vocabulary Item with -Ø contains information (in the form of the list of Roots √HIT, etc.) that is not compatible with the T[+past] node undergoing insertion.

Of the two possible candidates for realizing T[+past] in the context of √LEAVE, the one with -*t* must be selected at the expense of the one with -*ed*. The way that this effect is achieved is by *ordering* these Vocabulary Items:

(18) *Ordering:* Vocabulary Items are ordered.

The introduction of *Ordering* is required because Vocabulary Items compete with each other to apply to a morpheme; and ordering provides a way of determining the winner of such competitions. In the particular example under discussion, ordering must ensure that the Vocabulary Item with -*t* wins out over the one with -*ed* in the context of √LEAVE.

A hypothesis that has been adopted in much work is that order among Vocabulary Items is defined by the familiar principle that specificity determines order of application, such that the Vocabulary Item most specified for insertion at a particular node applies in favor of less fully specified competitors. One way of ordering Vocabulary Items along these lines is given in the Subset Principle in (19), which also makes precise a version of the "compatibility" conditions that are alluded to in the text under (17):

(19) **Subset Principle:** The phonological exponent of a Vocabulary Item is inserted into a position if the item matches all or a subset of the features specified in the terminal morpheme. Insertion does not take place if the Vocabulary Item contains features not present in the morpheme. Where several Vocabulary Items meet the conditions for insertion, the item matching the greatest number of features specified in the terminal morpheme must be chosen. (Halle 1997)

With reference to the derivation of *left*, it is clear that the Vocabulary Item with the -*t* exponent is more specific than the Vocabulary Item with -*ed*. By convention, more specified Vocabulary Items appear higher on lists than less specified ones, as shown in (20):

(20) Vocabulary Items for T[+past], Ordered

   a. T[+past] ↔ -t/{√BEND, √LEAVE,...}__
   b. T[+past] ↔ -Ø/{√HIT, √QUIT,...}__
   c. T[+past] ↔ -ed

The Vocabulary Item with -Ø is also more specific than the -*ed* one, and is therefore ordered before it. Note, however, that the -*t* and -Ø Vocabulary Items are equally specific, in the sense that each refers to T[+past] and has a contextual condition. Because of this, one of them could not actually beat the other. However, this is irrelevant, since their lists are disjoint, so for any given verb, one will win. For notational convenience, in specificity "ties" of this type, one of the two Vocabulary Items will be listed above the other by fiat.

With the Vocabulary Items for T[+past] in English ordered as in (20), the analysis of *leave~lef-t/*leav-ed* can be completed. When the T[+past] morpheme in (17) is worked on, the Vocabulary is searched, and the most specific item that can apply to this node is the one that inserts the exponent -*t*. This derives *lef-t*. Thus, we can see form **leav-ed* is not derived, because the Vocabulary Item with -*t* beats the one with -*ed* in the context of $\sqrt{\text{LEAVE}}$.

The idea that Vocabulary Items are ordered and competing for application is an essential one, and its consequences arise at numerous places in this book, starting in section 4.4 immediately below.

With respect to the general theory of contextual allomorphy, a number of important questions remain to be addressed. Of these, two in particular come to the forefront. The first concerns what form a particular Vocabulary Item could take; i.e., what kind of information could be included in the contextual specifications that determine when a particular Vocabulary Item applies. The second type of question concerns locality, and the conditions under which one morpheme can see another for allomorphic purposes. These two questions are examined in detail in chapter 7.

As a final point, it should be noted that while Ordering plays a particularly important role in the analysis of contextual allomorphy above, it is important for other phenomena as well. As will be shown below in chapter 5, the Vocabulary of a language will sometimes contain two Vocabulary Items of the type shown in (21), where α and β are synsem features:

(21) a. $[\alpha,\beta] \leftrightarrow$ -x
b. $[\alpha] \leftrightarrow$ -y

In such a situation, functional morphemes that contain α and β will receive the phonological form -*x* from the item in (21a). On the other hand, any morpheme that contains $[\alpha]$ and not $[\beta]$ will be realized by (21b) and receive the phonological exponent -*y*. In the cases when a morpheme contains $[\alpha,\beta]$, (21a) wins the competition with (21b) because of specificity. However, the specificity is not induced by a contextual condition. Rather, the ordering arises because (21a) matches more features on the node undergoing insertion than (21b) does. Some concrete instances of (21) are considered below in chapter 5, after the notion of underspecification has been developed.

4.4 Vocabulary Insertion and Blocking: A First Look

In an informal way of speaking, *blocking effects* are found when (i) one form (or several) that might be expected to occur in a given context is not in fact found, and (ii) this failure can be related to the fact that some other form appears to take precedence over the non-existing one. The relevance of blocking to the past tense examples can be seen by observing that the ungrammaticality of the regular past *leav-ed of √LEAVE correlates with the grammaticality of *lef-t*.

Part of the explanation for why *lef-t* is grammatical while *leav-ed is not is implicated in the discussion of *competition for insertion* in the preceding section. Consider the structure in (22), along with the Vocabulary Items in (23):

(22) *left*

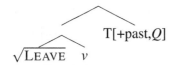

(23) Vocabulary Items for T[+past],

   a. T[+past] ↔ -t/{√BEND, √LEAVE,...}__
   b. T[+past] ↔ -Ø/{√HIT, √QUIT,...}__
   c. T[+past] ↔ -ed

By the Subset Principle (19), the most specific Vocabulary Item that can apply to T[+past] in (22) is the one with the *-t* exponent. This Vocabulary Item gives phonological content to the T[+past] node, producing *lef-t*.

There are two aspects of this analysis to consider further with respect to the notion of blocking. The first concerns the specifics of how the insertion of *-t* prevents the insertion of *-ed*; or, more precisely, how the application of the Vocabulary Item with the *-t* exponent prevents the application of the Vocabulary Item with the *-ed*. The second concerns the general question of what objects in the grammar Vocabulary Insertion applies to.

Beginning with the more specific question, it can be seen that Ordering will result in the Vocabulary Item with *-t* beating the one with *-ed*, so that we have *lef-t* instead of *leav-ed. But what insures that we do not see **both** of the past tense exponents *-t* and *-ed*, as in *lef-t-ed? Or two *-t* exponents, as in *lef-t-t, or three *-ed* exponents, as in *play-ed-ed-ed, and so on?

The basic answer to these questions is that these multiply-marked forms are ungrammatical because they are not derived by the grammar. The assumption that is responsible for ruling the "multiply marked" forms mentioned above is stated in (24) as *Uniqueness*:

(24)   *Uniqueness:* In a derivation, only one Vocabulary Item may apply to a morpheme.

In essence, Uniqueness is really just the assumption that each functional morpheme possesses a **single** Q variable that is the target of Vocabulary Insertion. Thus, when Vocabulary Insertion has applied once to a functional morpheme, the process is done as far as that particular node is concerned, as there are no further variables (i.e., Q positions) to be instantiated phonologically. Thus, **lef-t-ed* (or **play-ed-ed* etc.) are not derived, because there are no morphemes that the items in (23) could apply to after the T[+past] morpheme has been realized once.

The general question posed above concerns which objects are targets for Vocabulary Insertion. The answer is that it targets morphemes, as these are the only objects with Q variables. The idea that the morpheme is special in this way is stated here as *Terminal Insertion:*

(25)   *Terminal Insertion:* Insertion targets only morphemes (terminal nodes).

Understood in terms of the replacive view of Vocabulary Insertion that is adopted in this work, Terminal Insertion amounts to the claim that only functional morphemes have a Q position. Other objects in a complex structure, in particular, non-terminal nodes (i.e. intermediate or phrasal projections) do not have Q variables, and are not targets for Vocabulary Insertion. It follows from this view that competition for grammaticality of the type that produces blocking is restricted to morphemes, and morphemes only.

It is important for the theory that the blocking effect arises from a relationship between Vocabulary Items. Crucially, there is no blocking among words. So, it is not the case that the word *left* blocks the word **leaved*; rather, as we said above, the Vocabulary Item with *-t* wins over the one with *-ed* in the context of $\sqrt{\text{LEAVE}}$. The difference between morpheme-based blocking versus word-based blocking has a number of important implications. This and a number of other important themes are examined in greater detail in chapter 7, which looks further at blocking effects in the grammar.

4.5 The Order of Insertion in Complex Structures

Vocabulary Insertion often applies to morphemes that are part of a complex head. When this happens, some principle must determine the order in which Vocabulary Insertion applies to the different morphemes in the structure. A standard assumption in Distributed Morphology is that Vocabulary Insertion applies *from the inside out*. This means that Vocabulary Insertion applies first to the most deeply embedded structural position in a complex head and proceeds outwards, producing what is sometimes referred to as *cyclic* insertion.[5]

To illustrate, the complex head underlying the English past-tense verb *vapor-iz-ed* has the following structure:

(26) *vapor-iz-ed*

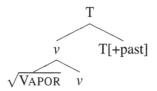

On the assumption that the Root has a phonological form underlyingly, Vocabulary Insertion applies first at the *v* node, inserting *-ize*:

(27) *vapor-iz-ed*

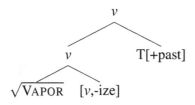

After this, Vocabulary Insertion applies at the T[+past] node, and inserts *-ed*:

(28) *vapor-iz-ed*

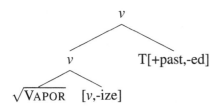

The assumption that Vocabulary Insertion operates in this inside-out or bottom-up fashion does not follow from any other assumptions that I have made to this point. Rather, it has been adopted as a working hypothesis in much work, in part because of how it connects with earlier theoretical models of cyclic effects in the grammar. Overall, it has proven to be quite successful in the interaction of morphology and phonology, where it makes strong predictions about patterns of allomorphy that appear to be largely correct (Halle and Marantz (1993), Bobaljik (2000), Embick (2010a)). See chapter 7 for some additional discussion.

4.6 Illustration: A Fragment from the Latin Conjugation

The analysis of a subset of the verbal forms of Classical Latin illustrates many of the key notions that are discussed in this chapter. (For expository simplicity, the representations used in this section dispense with Q positions.)

4.6.1 Preliminary Observations

As a starting point, (29) shows the Latin verb *laudāre* 'to praise' in three different tense forms, the present, imperfect, and perfect (all indicative):

(29) Three tenses for Latin *laudāre*

	present	**imperfect**	**perfect**
1s	laudō	laudābam	laudāvī
2s	laudās	laudābās	laudāvistī
3s	laudat	laudābat	laudāvit
1p	laudāmus	laudābāmus	laudāvimus
2p	laudātis	laudābātis	laudāvistis
3p	laudant	laudābant	laudāvērunt

Based on the synsem distinctions that are made in this system, there are a few observations to be made concerning the morphemes (and features) that play a role in the analysis of these verbs. The first is that the language distinguishes present from past tense. On this basis we can posit a feature [±past], which is negative in presents, and positive in imperfects. The status of [±past] in the perfect is slightly more complicated. Based on the fact that the language also has pluperfect forms (equivalent to English *I had praised*...), which clearly have T[+past], it can be assumed that the perfects in (29) are [-past].

A second point concerns aspectual specification. While there is a specific aspectual morpheme involved in the expression of perfect aspect, which is referred to henceforth as Asp[perf], there appears to be no such morpheme in non-perfect forms. For this reason, I will posit an Asp(ect) morpheme only with perfect tense verbs; presents and imperfects will have v and T, but no Asp. I will also assume that the feature [perf] is *unary* (either present or absent, not ±).

In addition to Tense (and Aspect), the verbs in (29) have Agr(eement) morphemes, with [±1], [±2] for person, and [±pl] for number. Finally, there is a theme vowel adjacent to the Root, which I assume to realize an arbitrary class feature [+I] for "first conjugation". For convenience, this will be treated as an exponent of *v*, but it would also be possible to treat it as a dissociated morpheme (see section 2.2.1 in chapter 2).

With this inventory of morphemes at hand, consider the segmentation of the forms in (29) shown in (30) (the vowels shown in parentheses are assumed to be present in the morphology but are deleted in the phonology):[6]

(30)   Three tenses for Latin *laudāre*

	present	**impferfect**	**perfect**
1s	laud-(ā)-ō	laud-ā-ba-m	laud-ā-v(i)-ī
2s	laud-ā-s	laud-ā-bā-s	laud-ā-vi-stī
3s	laud-a-t	laud-ā-ba-t	laud-ā-vi-t
1p	laud-ā-mus	laud-ā-bā-mus	laud-ā-vi-mus
2p	laud-ā-tis	laud-ā-bā-tis	laud-ā-vi-stis
3p	laud-a-nt	laud-ā-ba-nt	laud-ā-v(i)-ērunt

Structurally, the non-perfect (present and imperfect) forms are realizations of (31a), whereas the perfect forms are realizations of (31b):

(31)   a. non-perfects

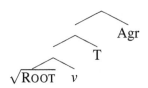

b. perfects

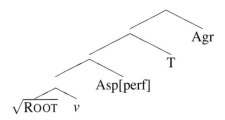

The forms that are segmented in (30) and the structures in (31) can be related to each other in a few steps. Beginning with v, Asp[perf], and T, a first set of exponents is as follows:

(32) Exponents of v, Asp[perf], and T

    a. v: -ā

    b. Asp[perf]: -vi

    c. Tense:

        i. Present, Perfect: -Ø (although see below)

        ii. Imperfect: -bā

For Agreement, the patterns are slightly more complicated. While some agreement morphemes are realized only in one form, namely those in (33a), the agreement morphemes in (33b) show contextual allomorphy:

(33) Agreement exponents

    a. No Allomorphy

        i. 3s: -t

        ii. 1p: -mus

    b. Allomorphy:

        i. 1s: -ō, -m, -ī

        ii. 2s: -s, -stī

        iii. 2p: -tis, -stis

        iv. 3p: -nt, -ērunt

Before analyzing the distribution of these exponents in terms of Vocabulary Insertion, one further set of forms will be considered; these are the Pluperfects, which are shown in (34)

(34) Pluperfect Indicative of *laudāre*

> **pluperfect**
> 1s laud-ā-ve-ra-m
> 2s laud-ā-ve-rā-s
> 3s laud-ā-ve-ra-t
> 1p laud-ā-ve-rā-mus
> 2p laud-ā-ve-rā-tis
> 3p laud-ā-ve-ra-nt

These forms introduce some additional facts that can be incorporated into the analysis. Working from the inside out, it can be seen that the Asp[perf] head is *-vi*, as it is in the perfects above in (30) (the vowel lowering that changes /vi/ to /ve/ can be assumed to be phonological; see e.g. Leumann et al. (1963)). In the position of Tense, the exponent *-rā* appears. Finally, outside of Tense, the Agreement morphemes are realized with the same exponents that appear in the Imperfect, as can be seen by comparing (34) with the imperfects in (30). Based on the last of these observations, it appears that insertion of the *-m* allomorph of first person singular agreement in (33b) is conditioned by T[+past].

4.6.2 Vocabulary Items

It is now possible to incorporate the observations about the different exponents above into an analysis that makes use of Vocabulary Items. The forms to be analyzed have the sequence of morphemes shown in (35), which is the linearization of the structures shown in (31) (Asp(ect) is parenthesized because it is present only with perfects):

(35) $\sqrt{\text{ROOT}}$-*v*-(Asp)-T-Agr

Working outwards from the Root, for the theme vowel and Asp[perf], the situation is simple given what has been examined above, as there is one Vocabulary Item for each of these:

(36) a. [+I] ↔ -ā
b. Asp[perf] ↔ -vi

In point of fact, this part of the analysis is simple only because I have restricted attention to one verb. When additional verbs are taken into account, it can be seen that there are more theme vowels in the language. In addition, there is contextual allomorphy for Asp[perf] with other verbs, a point which is examined in section 4.6.3 below.

For the Tense head, it was observed above that the T[+past] forms, the Imperfect and the Pluperfect, show distinct allomorphs: -bā and -rā respectively. An analysis of this effect is presented in (37), where the first Vocabulary Item makes reference to the presence of Asp[perf]:

(37) Vocabulary Items for T[+past]

T[+past] ↔ -rā/Asp[perf]__
T[+past] ↔ -bā

In the case of T[-past], which is found with Presents and Perfects, there is no overt realization of tense. Rather than treating this as the insertion of a -Ø, I will assume that this results from the deletion of T[-past], which is effected by the rule (38):[7]

(38) T[-past] ⟶ Ø

In part, this deletion rule is motivated by the fact that present tense T[-past] does not show an overt morphological realization in Latin verbs. Further motivation for deleting T[-past] in this way can be seen in the contextual sensitivities of Agr, which will become clear shortly when agreement allomorphy in the perfect is analyzed.

Turning to agreement, a first instance of allomorphy is found in the first person singular, where there are both -m and -ō realizations in the non-perfects. The former appears in the [+past] tenses, suggesting the following Vocabulary Items:[8]

(39) [+1,-2,-pl] ↔ -m/T[+past]__
[+1,-2,-pl] ↔ -ō

All of the other cases of allomorphy of Agr seen in (33) share one property: a special allomorph is inserted in Perfect forms. More precisely, the special forms appear in perfects, but not in pluperfects. This pattern can be seen clearly when all of the forms under discussion are considered together as in (40), where the agreement endings that are sensitive to the Asp[perf] are shown in bold:

(40) Four Tenses for Latin *laudāre*

	present	**imperfect**	**perfect**	**pluperfect**
1s	laud-(ā)-ō	laud-ā-ba-m	laud-ā-v(i)-ī	laud-ā-ve-ra-m
2s	laud-ā-s	laud-ā-bā-s	laud-ā-vi-**stī**	laud-ā-ve-rā-s
3s	laud-a-t	laud-ā-ba-t	laud-ā-vi-t	laud-ā-ve-ra-t
1p	laud-ā-mus	laud-ā-bā-mus	laud-ā-vi-mus	laud-ā-ve-rā-mus
2p	laud-ā-tis	laud-ā-bā-tis	laud-ā-vi-**stis**	laud-ā-ve-rā-tis
3p	laud-a-nt	laud-ā-ba-nt	laud-ā-v(i)-**ērunt**	laud-ā-ve-ra-nt

A straightforward way of accounting for the special forms seen in the perfect is by making the boldfaced allomorphs refer contextually to Asp[perf]. Recall that the structure of the perfect was assumed above to be the one shown in (41), with a T[-past] node:

(41) Structure of Perfect

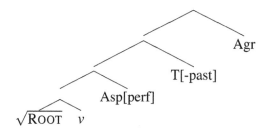

In (38) it was proposed that T[-pres] is deleted. In the case of the perfect forms, an effect of the deletion rule when it applies to (41) is that Agr is linearly adjacent to (i.e. concatenated with) Asp[perf], which makes the contextual condition local in a way that will be discussed in chapter 7. The special allomorphs in (40) can then be specified as shown in (42), which also includes the first person singular -*m* and the rest of the agreement Vocabulary Items required for Latin:

106 *Vocabulary Insertion: An Introduction*

(42)　Agreement Vocabulary Items

$$\begin{array}{lcll}
[+1,-2,-pl] & \leftrightarrow & \text{-ī} & /\text{Asp[perf]}\_\_ \\
[-1,+2,-pl] & \leftrightarrow & \text{-stī} & /\text{Asp[perf]}\_\_ \\
[-1,+2,+pl] & \leftrightarrow & \text{-stis} & /\text{Asp[perf]}\_\_ \\
[-1,-2,+pl] & \leftrightarrow & \text{-ērunt} & /\text{Asp[perf]}\_\_ \\
[+1,-2,-sg] & \leftrightarrow & \text{-m} & /\text{T[+past]}\_\_ \\
[+1,-2,-pl] & \leftrightarrow & \text{-ō} & \\
[+1,-2,+pl] & \leftrightarrow & \text{-mus} & \\
[-1,+2,-pl] & \leftrightarrow & \text{-s} & \\
[-1,+2,+pl] & \leftrightarrow & \text{-tis} & \\
[-1,-2,+pl] & \leftrightarrow & \text{-nt} & \\
\end{array}$$

The analysis in (42) illustrates the points about ordering of Vocabulary Items and competition for insertion that have been emphasized throughout this chapter. The more specific items—i.e., those that are contextually specified for reference to Asp[perf]—take precedence over the less specified items in perfects. Thus, for example, the second person singular agreement morpheme in the perfect (43) is realized as *-stī*, not as *-s*; (43) shows the structure with the T[-past] node deleted, and with the exponents in positions that they are realized in:

(43)　2s Perfect *laud-ā-vi-stī*

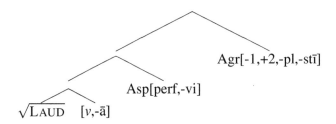

In this structure, the Vocabulary Item with *-stī* for [-1,+2,-pl] beats the one with *-s* because of the contextual specification that refers to Asp[perf]. In the pluperfect, though, the Agr morpheme is next to the T[+past] head, and *-s* is realized for second singular, not *-stī*, as shown in (44):

(44) 2s Pluperfect *laud-ā-ve-rā-s*

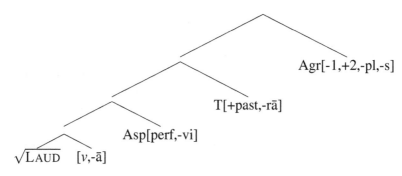

That is, because Agr[-1,+2,-pl] does not "see" Asp[perf] (in a way to be made precise in chapter 7), the Vocabulary Item that inserts *-stī* cannot be employed. Instead, the most specified item that can apply to this node is the one that inserts *-s*. As can be seen in (42), this is the default Vocabulary Item for second singular.

4.6.3 Non-Deletion of Features

With the analysis of section 4.6.2 at hand, an additional point may be made concerning the status of synsem features after Vocabulary Insertion. As a starting point, recall that (as per section 4.5) Vocabulary Insertion applies to the structures like (43) and (44) from the inside out; that is, first to the *v* position, then to Aspect and Tense when they are present, and finally to Agr. While this way of ordering Vocabulary Insertion is not crucial for the points emphasized immediately above in 4.6.2, it relates directly to the assumption made in 4.2.2 above, to the effect that synsem features are not automatically deleted when Vocabulary Insertion takes place.

As a first example of this point, consider the realization of T[+past], which is either *-rā* (when it occurs in the context of Asp[perf]) or *-bā* (in the Imperfect). The T[+past] head, which is realized in either of these two ways, has in turn an effect on the realization of Agr: Agr[+1,-2,-pl] is realized as *-m* in the context of T[+past], otherwise as *-ō* (see (39)). When these observations are put together, the importance of non-deletion of features becomes clear. On the assumption that Vocabulary Insertion proceeds from the inside out, as specified in section 4.5, the Agr node undergoes insertion *after* insertion takes place at the Tense node. If features are not deleted when Vocabulary Insertion takes place, there is no problem with having Agr[+1,-2,-pl] sensitive to T[+past].

On the other hand, if the synsem features of the T[+past] morpheme were deleted when Vocabulary Insertion applies, then it is predicted that outer morphemes may be sensitive only to the phonological features of inner nodes (i.e., their exponents). In the example at hand, this means that it would not be possible to state the distribution of first singular *-m* with reference to the local past tense feature. Rather, the contextual conditions on *-m* would have to refer to the two exponents *-rā* and *-bā* individually—missing a generalization—or some other means would have to be employed to state the correct distribution. In this example, then, it is clear that not deleting synsem features allows for a generalization about an outer Vocabulary Item's distribution to be handled in a straightforward manner; deleting features introduces complications.

This same point can be made with the agreement Vocabulary Items that make reference to Asp[perf] (those at the top of the list in (42)). To see this point, some additional verbs must be considered. The Root used in the examples above, $\sqrt{\text{LAUD}}$, shows a *-vi* allomorph of Asp[perf]. However, other verbs in Latin show different allomorphs for this head; in total, it takes three different forms, *-vi*, *si*, and *-i*, as shown in (45):

(45)   Allomorphs of Asp[perf]

   a. amā-vi-ī 'love'

   b. scrip-si-ī 'write'

   c. vēn-i-ī 'come'

Of these forms, the *-vi* allomorph is the default; the other two have to be contextually specified for lists of Roots that they are realized with (Embick 2000, 2010a).

Crucially, the same pattern of Agr allomorphy is found with all of these different allomorphs of Asp[perf]. Again, this pattern can be accounted for in a direct way if the relevant Vocabulary Items make reference to Asp[perf], as is the case in (42) above. However, if synsem features like Asp[perf] were deleted by insertion, the generalization about the distribution of the special perfect allomorphs would have to be stated in another, less general way.

In summary, the two phenomena just considered provide important illustrations of what kinds of information are available when Vocabulary Insertion occurs. In particular, it appears that a simper analysis of allomorphy patterns is possible when it is assumed that synsem features are *not* obligatorily deleted when Vocabulary Insertion occurs.

4.7 Summary

Functional morphemes do not possess phonological representations underlyingly. They are assembled into complex structures by the syntax and only receive phonological forms in the PF component of the grammar, when Vocabulary Insertion occurs. In the particular formalization of this operation that is assumed here, competition for insertion determines which Vocabulary Item is active for application to a morpheme, and the phonological exponent of that Vocabulary Item is substituted for the Q variable that is part of a functional morpheme. It is further assumed that (at least in the default case) the synsem features of a morpheme are not deleted when Vocabulary Insertion occurs.

The following three assumptions are part of this theory of Vocabulary Insertion:

1. ***Ordering:*** When multiple Vocabulary Items could potentially apply to a given morpheme, the winner is determined by ordering; specificity determines the order of Vocabulary Items.

2. ***Terminal Insertion:*** Vocabulary Insertion applies only to morphemes, not to any other type of object.

3. ***Uniqueness:*** Vocabulary Insertion applies only once to a given functional morpheme.

With this overview of Vocabulary Insertion now complete, the next chapter turns to an examination of syncretism, the phenomenon that provides the strongest motivation for treating sound/meaning connections in a realizational way.[9]

Chapter 5
Syncretism and (Under)specification

5.1 Introduction

The last chapter develops a theory of Vocabulary Insertion, the PF operation that supplies functional morphemes with phonological representations. As noted in chapter 1, the introduction of phonological material after the syntactic derivation in this way is sometimes referred to as *Late Insertion*. Theories with Late Insertion are commonly referred to as *realizational* theories, because they contain operations by which morphemes are *spelled out* or *realized* phonologically. As a final terminological point, the idea that morphemes do not possess phonological features as part of their underlying representation is referred to as the *Separation Hypothesis* (Beard (1966, 1995); see also Chomsky (1965)). The idea behind this term is that in realizational theories, the syntacticosemantic representation of the morpheme is separated from its (morpho)phonology.[1] This chapter works out further details of the theory of Vocabulary Insertion, with particular emphasis on syncretism, which provides the primary motivation for treating sound/meaning connections in this way.

A convenient starting point for the discussion is a review of how morphemes in realizational theories differ from "traditional" morphemes. The realizational approach advanced in this book agrees with many traditional approaches to morphology in holding that morphemes play a crucial role in establishing basic connections between meaning (synsem features, in the view advanced above) with sound (a phonological exponent). However, the present approach differs from traditional views of the morpheme in holding that sound and meaning come together via the process of Vocabulary Insertion, which applies to morphemes at PF.

In a traditional, non-realizational morpheme, sound and meaning are paired from the beginning. That is, a morpheme as an object in memory contains both synsem features (represented here with α) and phonological features (represented here with /X/); this view is presented schematically in (1):

(1) Traditional Morpheme (as Represented in Memory)

$[\alpha,/X/]$

There is, of course, no need for a Vocabulary Insertion operation in a theory in which all morphemes have the form schematized in (1). As a basic object, this type of morpheme already possesses both synsem and phonological features.

In a realizational theory, however, the meaning and sound components are not co-present in functional morphemes as primitives. Rather, as described in the last chapter, functional morphemes in memory consist of synsem features, with no phonological form. They are assigned a phonological form only after they have been combined into complex objects syntactically. Thus, this type of theory produces morphemes that connect sound and meaning; but, the sound/meaning connections arise only after morphemes have been combined by the syntax and are realized at PF through Vocabulary Insertion.

Viewed with reference to a theory that employs morphemes like (1), a realizational theory adds an additional computation (and an additional list) to the theory. Clearly, Vocabulary Insertion (and the Vocabulary) would not be required if sound and meaning were connected from the beginning in an object in memory. Thus, the motivation for Vocabulary Insertion must be clarified if the main claims of realizational morphology are to be understood.

As alluded to at various points earlier in this work, the motivation for Late Insertion is not *conceptual*, but empirical. In chapters 1 and 2, this point was made with reference to the idea that there are certain objects and types of information in the grammar that must be listed. There, it was pointed out that two lists—the list of Syntactic Terminals and the list(s) of idiosyncratic semantic information (the Encyclopedia, chapter 1)—are indispensable, in the sense that, in some form or other, all theories must contain a set of primitives, and must record idiosyncratic information about unpredictable interpretations. On the other hand, the Vocabulary is not motivated in the same obvious way that these other lists are. It is the assumption that functional morphemes do not possess phonological features that makes Vocabulary Insertion necessary. Whatever the status general conceptual concerns might have in the theory, in this domain they play a secondary place to empirical arguments for Late Insertion that come from the phenomenon of syncretism.

In short form, the argument for Late Insertion is that it allows for certain types of generalizations to be maximized by *minimizing* the number of Vocabulary Items in the grammar. The reasoning is as follows. A syncretism is found when distinct synsem features are realized in the same way phonologically. In the initial discussion in chapter 1 above, this phenomenon was illustrated with the inflection of verbs in Latin American Spanish. While such varieties of Spanish make a distinction between three persons (first, second, and third), and two numbers (singular and plural), there are not six distinct exponents found for the Agreement morpheme that is found on verbs. Instead, the second and third person plurals are realized with the same exponent, -*n*:

(2) Present Tense Forms of *hablar*, 'to speak'

p/n	form
1s	habl-o
2s	habla-s
3s	habla-Ø
1p	habla-mos
2p	habla-**n**
3p	habla-**n**

Two main claims of the current approach (along with other realizational theories) are (i) that the identity in form seen in second and third person agreement in (2) is systematic, not accidental; and (ii) that this systematicity must be encoded in the grammar, in a way that rules out the use of traditional morphemes like (1). In terms of the maximization of generalizations (and minimization of the Vocabulary), this means that the second and third person plural morphemes in (2) have to be analyzed with a single Vocabulary Item, not with two distinct Vocabulary Items.

The bulk of this chapter is devoted to an illustration of how Vocabulary Insertion is used in the analysis of syncretism. Along the way, some key concepts surrounding how morphemes are specified for features, and how, in particular, Vocabulary Items may be *under*specified, are introduced as well. Taken together, this chapter develops a working analysis of syncretism that is then applied to a number of examples in section 5.5.

5.2 Syncretism and Underspecification

The term *syncretism* is used differently in different descriptive and analytical traditions. In this book, it refers to situations in which distinct syntacticosemantic environments (i.e., distinct sets of synsem features bundled into a morpheme) show the same phonological exponent. This definition makes syncretism a morphological identity, and not just a phonological one; and the key idea that will be developed in this chapter is that syncretisms occur when the same Vocabulary Item applies to more than one functional morpheme.

Part of the motivation for defining syncretism in this way comes from the need to distinguish systematic identities in form—which I refer to as *(systematic) syncretisms*—from cases of *accidental homophony*, where phonological identity is accidental. For an example of the latter, the English (regular) plural morpheme has the phonology /z/ (*dog-s*), as does the third person singular agreement morpheme (*play-s*). But this identity in form appears to be an accident, and analyzing the language with two different Vocabulary Items that happen to have the phonological exponent /z/ does not miss significant generalizations (see section 5.4). On the other hand, when two feature bundles that are similar in synsem feature content and in distribution show the same exponent—as is the case with Spanish -*n* in section 5.1—generalizations are missed when two distinct Vocabulary Items with identical exponents are posited. A primary task of morphological theory is to give an account of the syncretisms that is able to explain how it is that the same phonological exponent appears in more than one synsem environment *in a way that is not accidental as far as the grammar is concerned.*

For present purposes it will be assumed that the lines between systematic syncretism and accidental homophony are clear in most cases, so that emphasis can be placed the analysis of the former. Nevertheless, the dividing line between syncretism and accidental homophony is an important and complex issue. Some additional thoughts on this point are advanced in the concluding section of chapter 6.

5.2.1 An Example: Hupa Agreement

Examples of syncretism are abundant in the languages of the world. As a concrete instance to analyze in detail, consider the prefixes for objects and subjects found in the Athabascan language Hupa (Golla (1970)).[2] Hupa verbs are affixed with a large number of morphemes, most of which are prefixes. Subject agreement exponents are shown boldfaced in (3):[3]

(3) Subjects

    a. *no:xoWtiW*

        no x^wi   **W**   tiW
        ADV   3s-OBJ 1s-SUBJ put

        'I put him down.'

b. *sinda*
   si **n** da
   STAT 2s-SUBJ sit
   'You are sitting.'

c. *kʸidiyaŋ*
   kʸi **di** yan
   OBJ 1p-SUBJ eat
   'We are eating.'

d. *Wohłcis*
   Wi **oh** ł cis
   1s-OBJ 2p-SUBJ CAUS see
   'You-pl see me.'

As can be seen in these examples, each of the four different person/number categories is associated with a distinct morphological form: first singular *W-*, second singular *n-*, first plural *di-*, and second plural *oh-*.

The Hupa verb also marks agreement with the object of the verb. In the case of object marking, though, there are only three distinct exponents found for the four person/number combinations under consideration. As (4c) shows, there is no distinction made between first person plural and second person plural objects:

(4) Objects

a. *yiWiwiłtehł*
   yi **Wi** wi ł teł
   ADV 1s-OBJ ASP CAUS carry
   'It carries me along.'

b. *niwiłtehł*
   ni wi ł teł
   2s-OBJ ASP CAUS carry
   'It carries you-sg along.'

c. *nohčiłca:n*
   noh či ł can
   1,2p-OBJ 3s-SUBJ CAUS see
   'He sees us/you-pl.'

In the light of (4) it is important to recall that subject agreement shows distinct morphological realizations for first person plural and second person plural subjects: *di-* versus *oh-*. From this contrast it can be seen that the language does in fact distinguish first from second person in the plural. That is to say, it is not the case that the language fails to make person distinctions in the plural at the level of synsem features. Rather, the point is that in the object agreement system, the distinction between first person and second person plurals is not manifested on the surface. Instead, the single exponent *noh-* appears whenever the object is either first plural or second plural.

Putting the facts in (3) and (4) together, the agreement prefixes in Hupa can be arranged as follows:

(5)   Subject and Object Exponents

	subject	**object**
1s	W-	Wi-
2s	n-	ni-
1p	di-	noh-
2p	oh-	noh-

Consider now the functional morphemes for Agreement, prior to insertion. Hupa distinguishes first from second person, and singular from plural. The analysis will therefore make use of the features [±1] and [±2] for person; [±pl] for number; and, finally [+subj] and [+obj]. Regarding these features, a few notes are in order.

First, technically speaking, only one binary feature is needed to distinguish first from second person. However, when third person arguments are analyzed, it is useful to have both [±1] and [±2], so that third person can be defined as [-1,-2]. For this reason (and for consistency with some of the other analyses developed in this book), I will employ two features.

A second point is that the features [+subj] and [+obj] stand proxy for a presumably more complicated feature system that is involved in representing the relevant grammatical notions. Thus, not too much should be read into this particular encoding.

As pointed out above, there is no incompatibility between the plural feature [+pl] and the person features that make up first and second person. Thus, it will be assumed that plural object morphemes contain both person and number features. The general principle that underlies this further assumption is that functional morphemes are *fully specified* for synsem features; this idea is made precise in section 5.3 below, where it is related to the general discussion of features in chapter 2.

With reference to the table in (5), full specification of functional morphemes means that verb forms in Hupa contain agreement morphemes with the feature combinations shown in (6); (6) corresponds exactly to (5), but shows only synsem features, not the exponents inserted by Vocabulary Insertion:

(6) Subject and Object Agreement Morphemes

	subject	object
1s	[+1,-2,-pl,+subj]	[+1,-2,-pl,+obj]
2s	[-1,+2,-pl,+subj]	[-1,+2,-pl,+obj]
1p	[+1,-2,+pl,+subj]	[+1,-2,+pl,+obj]
2p	[-1,+2,+pl,+subj]	[-1,+2,+pl,+obj]

The functional morphemes in (6) undergo Vocabulary Insertion in the individual derivations in which they are present. Concentrating on the different plural morphemes, the observation to be accounted for is as follows: while there are distinct feature bundles at the synsem level for first and second person plural objects, there is only a single phonological exponent associated with these two different functional morphemes.

5.2.2 Implementing an Analysis of Syncretism

As a first step towards an analysis of the syncretism in Hupa agreement, consider first just the functional morphemes with [+pl], shown in (7) with the exponents that they surface with in parentheses:

(7) Hupa Plural Morphemes

   a. [+1,-2,+pl,+subj] (= di-)
   b. [-1,+2,+pl,+subj] (= oh-)
   c. [+1,-2,+pl,+obj] (= noh-)
   d. [-1,+2,+pl,+obj] (= noh-)

There are three different phonological forms in (7). With this in mind, consider now the three Vocabulary Items in (8):

(8) Vocabulary Items

    a.   [+1,-2,+pl,+subj] ↔ di-
    b.   [-1,+2,+pl,+subj] ↔ oh-
    c.   [+pl,+obj] ↔ noh-

By (8), the first and second plural subject agreement morphemes (7a) and (7b) are realized via distinct Vocabulary Items, (8a) and (8b) respectively. However, realization of the [+obj] plurals is effected by a single Vocabulary Item, (8c). The fact that this Vocabulary Item must apply with the [+obj] morphemes follows from principles introduced in chapter 4. According to the theory of Vocabulary Insertion developed there, neither (8a,b) can apply to [+obj] morphemes, because they make reference to the feature [+subj]. Since neither of these Vocabulary Items in (8) can apply to (7c) or (7d), the most specific Vocabulary Item that can apply to each of these morphemes is (8c), which inserts *noh-*. Thus, the two distinct functional morphemes (7c,d) are realized with the same Vocabulary Item (8c); this is what it means to have a systematic syncretism in this theory.

An important component of the analysis based on (8) is that the Vocabulary Item (8c) does not refer to the features [±1] or [±2]. Rather, it refers only to the features [+pl] and [+obj]. Because it does not refer to person features, it is able to apply to both [+1,-2] object plurals *and* to [-1,+2] object plurals. In the type of situation just described, a Vocabulary Item is said to be *underspecified* with respect to the feature bundles to which it applies.

The general idea behind this kind of underspecification is that Vocabulary Items are able to apply to functional morphemes that contain a superset of the features that are mentioned in the Vocabulary Item (see section 5.3 below). In the particular case at hand, the effect of underspecifying the Vocabulary Item with the *noh-* exponent is that it is able to apply to both (7c) and (7d).

Underspecifying Vocabulary Items allows for syncretisms to be analyzed as systematic effects, and not as instances of accidental homophony. The identity in form in the first and second plural object agreement morphemes is systematic, since these two morphemes receive their phonological form from the single Vocabulary Item (8c). Put slightly differently, there is a single morphological object at the center of this analysis, one that allows the exponent *noh-* to appear in more than one plural morpheme.

5.2.3 Comparison

The analysis of syncretism developed above is motivated by the assumption that some identities in form are systematic, and that the grammar must encode this systematicity. In the particular example analyzed in 5.2.2., the identity in form in first and second person plural object markers arises because two distinct functional morphemes are realized by the same Vocabulary Item. A strong argument in favor of this analysis is that underspecifying Vocabulary Items is preferable to an alternative in which the distribution of *noh-* arises from two distinct Vocabulary Items, as shown in (9):

(9) Missing a Generalization: Two Vocabulary Items with *noh-*

$$[+1,-2,+pl,+obj] \leftrightarrow noh\text{-}$$
$$[-1,+2,+pl,+obj] \leftrightarrow noh\text{-}$$

The two Vocabulary Items in (9) are distinct objects, and the fact that they have an identical phonological exponent is an accident. Using two Vocabulary Items like the ones in (9) goes against the intuition that (all other things being equal) generalizations are maximized when the number of items in the Vocabulary is minimized. Recall moreover that in the case at hand, there is sufficient motivation for treating this identity in form as systematic, since the first person plural and second person plural object agreement morphemes show a considerable overlap in their feature content. This overlap in features speaks strongly against an analysis in terms of accidental homophony.[4]

We are now in a position to see why Distributed Morphology (and other realizational theories) have dispensed with traditional morphemes. In a theory that allows only traditional morphemes, with sound and meaning connected from the beginning, the only choice in analyzing Hupa object agreement would be to use the morphemes in (10):

(10) Traditional Morphemes

   a. [+1,-2,+pl,+obj,noh-]
   b. [-1,+2,+pl,+obj,noh-]

These are distinct objects, just like the Vocabulary Items in (9). There is no possibility of underspecifying sound with respect to meaning, since sound and meaning are combined in a single object from the beginning. Traditional morphemes are thus unable to account for syncretism in a systematic way.[5]

5.2.4 Some Additional Points

With this analysis of the syncretism in the plural object morphemes at hand, the analysis of Hupa Agreement can be completed with the addition of Vocabulary Items for the subject morphemes. In the subject system, there is no syncretism. Thus, the Vocabulary Items in (8) must be augmented with four additional Vocabulary Items, as shown in (11):

(11) Hupa Agreement Vocabulary Items

$$\begin{array}{rcl}
[+1,-pl,+subj] & \leftrightarrow & \text{W-} \\
[+1,-pl,+obj] & \leftrightarrow & \text{Wi-} \\
[+2,-pl,+subj] & \leftrightarrow & \text{n-} \\
[+2,-pl,+obj] & \leftrightarrow & \text{ni-} \\
[+1,+pl,+subj] & \leftrightarrow & \text{di-} \\
[+2,+pl,+subj] & \leftrightarrow & \text{oh-} \\
[+pl,+obj] & \leftrightarrow & \text{noh-}
\end{array}$$

With respect to the details of (11), two points are in order.

First, an innovation in (11), which is retained and examined throughout much of the subsequent discussion in this book, is that all of the Vocabulary Items are underspecified. The first person singular subject Vocabulary Item, for instance, does not make reference to the feature [-2]. The reason for this is that the correct results can be derived without making reference to this feature. The same is true of the other Vocabulary Items in (11). As a practical matter, it is often the case that Vocabulary Items are presented in this way, with the minimum number of features required to ensure their correct application. The empirical effects of this convention are not obvious in this particular kind of example, although there are cases where minimizing the specification of Vocabulary Items can have important consequences.[6]

Second, regarding the order of application, the order shown for the first six Vocabulary Items in (11) is more or less arbitrary, as the correct results are derived for any other order, as long as the Items are specified in this particular way. The only crucial point of ordering for the present analysis is that the Vocabulary Item inserting *noh-* must be underspecified in a way that allows it to be beaten in the case of [+subj] plural morphemes by the Items that insert *di-* and *oh-*.

The details about specification of Vocabulary Items, and the interaction of specification and ordering, are key themes that are revisited in the subsequent parts of this book (see in particular the case studies in section 5.5 below, as well as chapter 6).

With reference to the particular analysis in (11), many additional observations could be made along the general lines of inquiry outlined above. Many of these implicate the idea that the Vocabulary should be minimized when possible. To take a specific example, the first and second person singular exponents in the subject and object categories are remarkably similar: they differ only in the presence of a /i/ component in the object set (compare W-/Wi-, n-/ni-). If the presence of /i/ in the object set could be attributed to other factors (in particular, to the phonology), then it would be possible to reduce the number of Vocabulary Items in (11) further, with single Vocabulary Items for first person singular and second person singular.[7] In this revision, the Vocabulary Items inserting W- and n- are underspecified for the subject/object distinction, as shown in (12):

(12) Hupa Agreement Vocabulary Items, reduced more

$$[+1,+pl,+subj] \leftrightarrow di\text{-}$$
$$[+2,+pl,+subj] \leftrightarrow oh\text{-}$$
$$[+1,-pl] \leftrightarrow W\text{-}$$
$$[+2,-pl] \leftrightarrow n\text{-}$$
$$[+pl,+obj] \leftrightarrow noh\text{-}$$

The analysis in (12) maintains the intuition that the item inserting *noh-* is underspecified, and further reduces the number of Vocabulary Items in a way that improves on (11).

5.3 Specification

The main point of the last section is that a systematic analysis of syncretism is produced by underspecifying Vocabulary Items. The specific case of syncretism that is used to illustrate this point above, identity in Hupa first and second person plural object agreement morphemes, is derived with a Vocabulary Item that makes reference only to [+pl] and [+obj]. Because (i) this Vocabulary Item does not mention person features, and (ii) because it is not beaten by a more specific Vocabulary Item, it can apply to both [+1,+pl,+obj] and [+2,+pl,+obj] nodes.

One of the assumptions that makes this analysis possible concerns the representation of functional morphemes **prior** to insertion. In particular, it is assumed that while the first and second plural object agreement morphemes are not distinct phonologically, these nodes are distinct in terms of their synsem feature content. That is, a first person plural object morpheme is as in (13a), and a second person plural object morpheme is as in (13b):

(13) Plural Object Morphemes

   a. [+1,-2,+pl,+obj]
   b. [-1,+2,+pl,+obj]

Another way of putting this is to say that the identity in form arises as a result of the Vocabulary Insertion process, not because of something deeper.

The general principle at play here is a standard assumption of Distributed Morphology: the idea that functional morphemes are always fully specified for synsem features, whereas Vocabulary Items can potentially be underspecified. Terminologically, it can be said that functional morphemes show *Full Specification*, whereas Vocabulary Items may be subject to *Underspecification*. Full Specification is defined in (14), which is presented with a definition of Underspecification for purposes of comparison:

(14) **Full Specification:** Functional morphemes are fully specified for the synsem features that are active in the language.

(15) **Underspecification:** Vocabulary Items may make reference to a subset of the features of the nodes that they apply to.

Full Specification is an important idea in the theory. In order for Vocabulary Items to be underspecified, there must be something that is fully specified to do e.g. the syntactic and semantic work of features that are "ignored" when there are syncretisms.

Nevertheless, there is something inherently vague about Full Specification as it is defined in (14). The definition says that functional nodes in a language are fully specified for the synsem features that are active in a language. This leads, naturally, to the question how to determine for any particular language which synsem features are in fact active. The simple answer to this question is as follows: the features that are active in a language are those that are required for the syntax and semantics. Thus, the apparent vagueness of (14) is the result of the fact that any morphological analysis (that is, any analysis of a system in terms of Vocabulary Insertion) depends critically on syntactic and semantic theories of features.

For the reasons outlined immediately above, a comprehensive theory of Full Specification amounts to a theory of the features that are required for syntax and semantics. While a theory of this magnitude and scope cannot be presented here, some aspects of Full Specification are worth examining in more detail, as they prepare the way for some further comparisons and contrasts.

Recall for purposes of illustration that the distinct functional morphemes that are realized as *noh-* in Hupa are assumed to be those in (16):

(16) Plural Object Morphemes

    a. [+1,-2,+pl,+obj]

    b. [-1,+2,+pl,+obj]

Full Specification is the reason why the functional morphemes must be specified in this way. Informally, the idea is that first and second plural object morphemes are different objects as far as syntax (and semantics) are concerned. In spite of their surface morphological identity (i.e., they are realized by the same Vocabulary Item), they are different morphemes.

It is worth reflecting further on the motivation for positing the two distinct morphemes in (16). Here, some other facts about the language help.

One such fact is noted in section 5.2 above. In the subject agreement system, there are distinct exponents for all four combinations of person and number features; that is:

(17) Subject Agreement

p/n	exponent
1s	W-
2s	n-
1p	di-
2p	oh-

From this observation, it is clear (i) that the language distinguishes two persons (first and second) and two numbers (singular and plural); and (ii) that these features are fully cross-classified in functional morphemes. That is, the language contains at least one type of functional morphemes that combines e.g. [+1,-2,+pl] and [-1,+2,+pl], and so on.

It is important to stress that the language allows person and number features to be combined in the same functional morphemes, because this observation precludes some other conceivable approaches to the syncretism that is found in object morphemes. To see this, recall first that some languages fail to make synsem distinctions that are found in others. In the discussion of the Universal Feature Inventory in chapter 2, this was illustrated with reference to the fact that e.g. Classical Greek has morphemes that make for a *dual* number in addition to singular and plural, whereas e.g. English does not possess such dual morphemes. Given the fact that languages differ to some extent in terms of their functional morphemes, it is important to begin with the observation that Hupa does indeed allow person features like [±1] and [±2] and the number feature [±pl] to occur in a single morpheme. Without this type of evidence, we might simply conclude based on the object agreements that Hupa does not bundle person and number features together in the first place.

Continuing along these lines, there is additional evidence about the co-occurrence of person and number features that reinforces the conclusion that these features are bundled together throughout the grammar of Hupa. For example, they appear together in the system of free pronouns (Golla 1970:236):

(18) Hupa Pronouns

pronoun	**gloss**
We	'I'
nin	'you'
nehe	'we'
nohnɨ	'you-pl'

Taken together, the observations based on (17) and (18) indicate that Hupa morphemes contain both person and number features. Since there is no reason to believe that object morphemes should differ in this regard, Full Specification requires an analysis of object agreement with the functional morphemes in (16).

To this point, Full Specification has been viewed in a positive guise, i.e., as a way of motivating particular representations of functional morphemes. This perspective may be reversed, so that Full Specification is viewed negatively; i.e., in such a way that it rules out certain types of morphemes: namely, those that are simply "vague" with respect to a particular semantic dimension that is active in the language. Specifically, Full Specification (in conjunction with the observations above) rules out representations in which Hupa simply fails to make the distinction between first and second person plurals in the object system by not bundling person with object plural morphemes, as shown in (19):

(19) Putative Hupa Morpheme Ruled Out by Full Specification

[+pl,+obj]

This hypothetical morpheme is *vague* at the synsem level, in the sense that it does not contain person features. While it is a possible morpheme in some other languages (e.g., in a language that does not have active person features, or in one that does not bundle person and number features together), it is not part of the grammar of Hupa, for the reasons that are adduced above.[8]

In summary, Full Specification places restrictions on the representation of functional morphemes: it requires fully specified syntacticosemantic morphemes, and rules out "vague" morphemes that fail to make distinctions that are part of the grammar of a language. At the same time, Full Specification does not say exactly what the required features are; this is something that can only be determined in an analysis that takes into account syntax, semantics, and morphology.

Along these lines, in many of the case studies that are examined in later parts of this book it will become increasingly evident how the analysis of any system of complex morphological interactions based on Vocabulary Insertion depends crucially on assumptions about the nature of these different types of features (recall also the discussion of the UFI in chapter 2).

As a final point, it is important to stress that Full Specification places restrictions on the representation of morphemes *prior to any further operations that might apply to them*. As will be discussed below in chapter 6, it is possible to derive morphemes that look like (19) prior to Vocabulary Insertion with *Impoverishment* rules, which delete features at PF.

5.4 Syncretism versus Homophony

The identities in form that motivate Late Insertion are *systematic*; and the analytical tool of underspecification allows for syncretisms to be centered on a single Vocabulary Item.

The analysis of syncretism is central to morphological theory because, as noted earlier, it represents one of the major departures from the ideal "one meaning/one sound" state of affairs (recall that allomorphy, where a single functional morpheme is realized with many different Vocabulary Items, is the other major departure). Identity in form is, however, not always systematic. As mentioned earlier in this chapter, phonologically identical exponents are often found in distinct syntacticosemantic environments, but for reasons that are purely accidental. The illustration earlier in this chapter pointed to the exponent of third person singular agreement (shorthand: Agr[3sg]) in the English present tense, which is /-z/ (as in *He play-s*). The (default) exponent of the feature [+pl] on nouns is /-z/ as well (*two dog-s*). However, there is no reason to think that there is only one /-z/ involved here (more precisely: one Vocabulary Item with a /-z/ exponent), because Agr[3sg] and [+pl] do not have anything in common syntactically or semantically. It thus does not appear to be the case that significant generalizations would be missed by having two distinct Vocabulary Items, each of which has a /-z/ exponent.

The kind of identity in form just illustrated is called *(accidental) homophony*. In this particular instance the homophony is for functional morphemes; but accidental homophony is also found with Roots, as is discussed in chapter 2 with the Roots √BANK 'side of a river' and √BANK 'financial institution', which have identical phonological representations. As alluded to above, accidental homophony is analyzed with two different Vocabulary Items that happen to have the same phonological exponent. For the English Agr[3sg] and [+pl], the distinct Vocabulary Items are as follows:

(20) Accidental Homophony: Two Vocabulary Items
   a. Agr[3s] ↔ /-z/
   b. [+pl] ↔ /-z/

According to this treatment, the two Vocabulary Items in (20) are distinct entities; they have no more in common than any other pair of Vocabulary Items selected at random from the Vocabulary of the language, except for the fact that their exponents are identical.

There are, generally speaking, some salient differences between systematic syncretisms and accidental homophonies. To a first approximation, accidental homophonies are found when there is no shared synsem feature content in functional morphemes that have the same phonological form. In syncretism, on the other hand, there is typically shared feature content in the syncretizing environments.[9] For instance, in the case of Hupa *noh-*, the morphemes realized as *noh-* are both syntacticosemantically plural (i.e., share the synsem feature [+pl]). This may be contrasted with the English example in (20), where there is no syntacticosemantic basis for thinking of the [+pl] morpheme that attaches to nouns and the Agr[3sg] morpheme that attaches to verbs as having similar feature content.

Even with underspecification at our disposal, it would be extremely difficult to treat the Agr[3sg] and [+pl] morphemes as subject to insertion by the same Vocabulary Item. Thus, the best analysis is one in which there are two distinct Vocabulary Items in memory, as in (20); while accidental homophony should be minimized when possible (see chapter 6), there are many cases in which it is unavoidable.

5.5 Illustrations

This section provides some additional illustrations of how underspecification is used to derive syncretisms. The individual subsections below introduce fairly standard representations of features, in many cases from the domain of person and number, to connect with analyses considered earlier. In a few of the case studies, alternative analyses of the same phenomenon are considered. These alternatives take into account (i) different assumptions about feature inventories; (ii) different assumptions about how features are packaged into morphemes; and (iii) different possible ways of specifying Vocabulary Items to account for generalizations about syncretism. Considering alternatives in this manner is a way of making explicit the close connections between the Vocabulary and the theory of synsem features, two factors that play a role in every analysis in the theory.

5.5.1 Seychelles Creole Pronominals

Seychelles Creole is a French-based creole spoken in the Seychelles Islands (see Corne (1977)). The pronominals of the language show distinctions for person and number, and come in three morphosyntactic varieties, which I refer to as *subject*, *strong*, and *possessive*. As can be seen in the table in (21), a number of forms are underspecified with respect to the contexts in which they appear:

(21) Seychelles Creole Pronominals

p/n	subject	strong	possessive
1s	mõ	mua	mõ
2s	u	u	u
3s	i	li	sõ
1p	nu	nu	nu
2p	zot	zot	zot
3p	zot	zot	zot

The functional morphemes that are active in Seychelles Creole are as follows. In addition to [±1] and [±2] for person and the number feature [±pl], it can be assumed for convenience that the "strong" and "possessive" columns are defined by the features [+str] and [+poss] respectively. These features stand proxy for finer-grained morphosyntactically defined features (related to case, etc.) that do not play a crucial role in the main exposition. On the assumption that these features are cross-classified to yield fully specified functional morphemes, there are a number of observations to be made about the distribution of forms in (21). Overall, (21) shows eight distinct exponents. Of these, four appear in exactly one cell: *mua*, *i*, *li*, and *sõ*. There is no need to underspecify the Vocabulary Items that insert these exponents, since their distribution is such that each of them applies to only one functional morpheme. The remaining four exponents, though, first singular *mõ*, second singular *u*, first plural *nu*, and non-first person plural (or default plural) *zot* can be inserted into different morphemes to produce a variety of syncretisms. The Vocabulary Items that insert these exponents need to be underspecified in order to account for these distributions. Consider now (22):

(22) Vocabulary Items

a. [-1,-2,-pl,+poss] ↔ sõ
b. [-1,-2,-pl,+str] ↔ li
c. [-1,-2,-pl,+subj] ↔ i
d. [+1,-2,-pl,+str] ↔ mua
e. [+1,-pl] ↔ mõ
f. [+2,-pl] ↔ u
g. [+1,+pl] ↔ nu
h. [+pl] ↔ zot

There are a few crucial orderings in (22). For example, the Vocabulary Item (22d) specified with [+1,-2,-pl,+str] to insert *mua* must beat the item (22e) that inserts *mō*. In addition, the first person plural *nu* is inserted by (22g), which must beat (22h). Overall, the ordering of items in (22) reflects the general principle introduced in chapter 4, according to which Vocabulary Items specified for more features take precedence over less specified items.

5.5.2 Mongolic Possessors

The Mongolic language Oirat marks possessed nouns with suffixes that agree with the person and number of the possessor. The possessive morphemes are shown in (23), which is taken from Birtalan (2003:220):[10]

(23) Possessive Affixes

	singular	plural
1	-m	-mdn
2	-cn	-tn
3	-i	-i

The first and second person possessors show distinct forms in the singular and the plural; but third person possessors do not make this number distinction.

I will assume that in addition to person and number features, the possessive functional morphemes have a feature [+poss]. Thus, for example, the first singular possessor morpheme is [+1,-2,-pl,+poss], the second singular is [-1,+2,-pl,+poss], and so on. Although [+poss] does little in the analysis of (23), it assumes a more important role in a comparison to be made below.

The Vocabulary Items in (24) derive the distribution of exponents in (23):

(24) Oirat Possessive Vocabulary Items

    a.   [+1,+pl,+poss] ↔ -mdn
    b.   [+2,+pl, +poss] ↔ -tn
    c.   [+1,+poss] ↔ -m
    d.   [+2,+poss] ↔ -cn
    e.   [+poss] ↔ -i

The syncretism in third person forms arises because the Vocabulary Item (24e) with the *-i* exponent is not specified with number features. This aspect of (24e) works in combination with other properties of (24). In particular, the first four items are all specified positively for a person feature, either [+1] or [+2], and two of these items are also specified for number. These four items account for four of the feature combinations in (23), those that are first or second person. The remaining two morphemes to consider, those for the third person singular and plural, are not subject to insertion from any of (24a-d). Thus, these morphemes receive their phonological form from (24e), which is specified only for [+poss].

The analysis of Oirat in (24) assumes that the feature [+poss] is bundled with the person and number features of the possessor. In this language there is no obvious motivation for positing distinct person/number and possessor morphemes; but there are other Mongolic languages where this decomposition looks promising. Consider the possessor forms from Khalkha in (25):

(25) Khalkha possessors (Svantesson 2003)

	singular	plural
1	miny	maany
2	ciny	tany
3	ny	ny

Just as in the case of Oirat, there is no distinction made between singular and plural third person possessors. However, the exact manner in which underspecification produces this result might be slightly different in the two languages. It can be seen in the Khalkha forms in (25) that all of the possessive affixes end in -ny. A straightforward treatment of this pattern with a -ny exponent is possible if it is assumed that the forms in (25) are composite, with a person/number morpheme and a possessor morpheme:

(26) Decomposed Person/Number-Possessor

$[\pm 1, \pm 2, \pm pl]$ [+poss]

The -ny is then the exponent of a Vocabulary Item that refers to [+poss] alone:

(27) [+poss] ↔ -ny

And, completing the analysis, the Vocabulary Items for the person/number component are as follows:

(28) Person/Number Part of Khalkha Possessors

    a.   [+1,+pl]   ↔ maa
    b.   [+2,+pl]   ↔ ta
    c.   [+1]   ↔ mi
    d.   [+2]   ↔ ci
    e.   [ ]   ↔ Ø

In the analysis based on (27-28), the syncretism does not arise from underspecifying a Vocabulary Item with [+poss]. Rather, the Vocabulary Item (27) that realizes [+poss] applies to [+poss] in all of the forms in (25), on the assumption that these consist of the two morphemes shown in (26). Then, the syncretism arises in the person/number component of (26): in the case of third person morphemes, the most specific item in (28) that can apply is (28e). This Vocabulary Item inserts Ø for the person/number component both in third person singulars and third person plurals, producing the syncretism in the desired way: that is, Ø-*ny* for both third person singulars and third person plurals.

In sum, the analyses of possessor syncretism in both Oirat and Khalkha employs underspecified Vocabulary Items. However, the particular morphemes that are targeted by underspecified Vocabulary Items differs in a way that depends on further assumptions about how features are bundled into morphemes in the two languages. (As it stands, the analysis treats Oirat and Khalka with different structures; it would be possible to investigate the Khalka system further with a structure that contains a distinct number morpheme; I leave this and related moves to the reader.)

5.5.3 Barbareño Chumash Pronominals

The Barbareño variety of Chumash (formerly spoken in Southern California; Beeler (1976)) shows a syncretism in the realization of object pronominals that serves as a further illustration of underspecification. In addition, this example raises the question of how analyses might incorporate natural classes, in a way that is related directly to the theory of synsem features.

This language shows first, second, and third person pronominals, and a three-way number distinction (singular, dual, and plural). As shown in (29), the subject prefixes in the language show more overt distinctions for these feature combinations than the suffixal object pronominals do:[11]

(29) Barbareño Chumash Pronouns (Beeler 1976:255)

p/n	subj	obj
1s	k-	-it
2s	p-	-in
3s	s-	-ul
1d	k-iš-	-iyuw
2d	p-iš-	-iyuw
3d	s-iš-	-wun
1p	k-iy-	-iyuw
2p	p-iy-	-iyuw
3p	s-iy-	-wun

The subject series of pronouns shows a person ([±1], [±2]) morpheme, followed by number ([±sg], [±pl]). It will be assumed that the dual number is [-sg,-pl], although the crucial part of this is just the [-sg] part, as will be seen in a moment. In terms of their exponents, the subject pronouns are fully differentiated; in part because they show person and number realized in separate pieces, with *k-*, *p-*, and *s-* for first, second, and third person, and *-Ø*, *-iš*, and *-iy* for singular, dual, and plural, respectively.

Most of the action that is relevant to underspecification in (29) is in the object suffixes, and in the non-singulars in particular, since the singulars show distinct forms for the three persons and numbers. In the object system, first and second person duals and plurals are *-iyuw*, while third person duals and plurals are *-wun*. That is, the distinction between first and second persons is neutralized in the duals and plurals, i.e., the non-singulars. Moreover, these non-singulars (the [-sg] numbers) are themselves syncretized, so that duals and plurals are realized identically.

Since there are two exponents at play in the non-singular part of this system, there are in principle two ways of accounting for this part of (29). Either the Vocabulary Item that inserts *-wun* can be more specified than the one that inserts *-iyuw*, or vice versa.

Beginning with the former type of analysis, one way of accounting for the non-singular part of the objects in (29) is with the Vocabulary Items in (30):

(30) Barbareño Chumash Vocabulary Items

    a. [-1,-2,+obj,-sg] ↔ -wun
    b.   [+obj,-sg] ↔ -iyuw

These items produce the correct results. However, the analysis does so in a somewhat forced way. Rather than saying that *-iyuw* has a natural distribution, covering first and second person non-singulars, it instead makes reference to the third person [-1,-2] in the Vocabulary Item that inserts *-wun*. Given the general idea that natural classes should be stated positively whenever possible, it is worth looking at other analyses.[12]

An alternative to (30) is to take *-iyuw* as expressing a natural class, something that might be preferred on general grounds. To do this in the case at hand, an additional feature is required. As Noyer (1992) discusses, a natural class of "first or second person" cannot be stated directly using person features like [±1] and [±2]. He suggests a feature [±part] for "participant", whose value is positive for speech act participants (i.e., first and second person), and negative for non-participants (third person), and provides evidence that [±part] is important for natural-class behavior in morphology. Other ways of making the same distinction are conceivable (e.g., building on the idea that the third person is a "non person" in some sense that makes [-1,-2] a combination of features that cannot be referred to); but I will use [±part] here, since my primary focus is on how alternative underspecifications of Vocabulary Items can account for the distribution of forms in (29).[13]

The role of [±part] is easy to see in (29). The exponent *-iyuw* appears in first and second person duals and plurals. Thus, the Vocabulary Item that inserts it must be specified for [+part], and must be underspecified with respect to the dual versus plural number distinction. A way of analyzing the non-singular part of the system along these lines is shown in (31):

(31) Barbareño Chumash Vocabulary Items

    a.   [+part,+obj,-sg] ↔ -iyuw
    b.   [+obj,-sg] ↔ -wun

There are a number of different factors that have to be assessed in determining the differences between the analyses in (30) and (31). For example, if grammars are structured such that natural classes such as that defined by [+part] are always to be preferred over negative specifications like those provided by [-1,-2], then the analysis in (31) must be regarded as superior.[14]

Ultimately, the question of which of these analyses is to be preferred interacts with larger assumptions about feature theory. The main point of this illustration is to provide a further example of how underspecification produces syncretisms. Since both *-iyuw* and *-wun* are inserted into more than one functional morpheme, some type of underspecification is required independently of how the additional questions about features and natural classes are resolved.[15]

5.5.4 Anêm Possessive Suffixes

Anêm is a non-Austronesian language spoken in West New Britain, Papua New Guinea (see Thurston (1982)). The derivational and inflectional system of nouns in this language exhibits a number of intricate complexities, some of which will be touched on as the basic description of the data proceeds. Many of the more complex details are put to the side, however, so that emphasis can be placed on an analysis of part of the system in which underspecified Vocabulary Items are required.

Possessed nouns in Anêm consist of a Root morpheme, an unpredictable element which I will refer to as a *theme* (TH), and a possessor (POSS) affix that agrees with the person, number, and gender of the possessor:

(32)   Root-TH-POSS

Nouns are divided into four distinct classes, which differ in terms of the possessor allomorphs that they take. These are referred to as "class 1", "class 2", etc. here; and diacritic features [I], [II], etc. are employed for these classes in the analysis below. This treatment of the classes could be refined in various ways in a more comprehensive study of Anêm nouns, but it suffices for present purposes.

Singular possessed forms for nouns from the four different classes are shown in (33):

(33)   Nouns: *kom* 'water'; *gi* 'child'; *ti* 'leg'; *mîk* 'mat'

poss. p/n	class 1	class 2	class 3	class 4
1s	kom-Ø-i	gi-ŋ-e	ti-g-a	mîk-d-at
2s	kom-Ø-î	gi-ŋ-ê	ti-g-îr	mîk-d-ir
3s.masc.	kom-Ø-u	gi-ŋ-o	ti-g-î	mîk-d-it
3s.fem.	kom-Ø-îm	gi-ŋ-êm	ti-g-î	mîk-d-it

It can be seen in (33) that the possessor morphemes show class-determined allomorphy. There are different exponents for masculine and feminine third person possessors in classes 1 and 2, but not in classes 3 and 4.

Before looking at the third person possessors in greater detail, some points are in order concerning the class features that determine the realization of the distinct possessor allomorphs. The structure of possessed nouns is shown in (34); for the purposes of this analysis, it will be assumed that the theme is a realization of *n*:[16]

(34)   Structure of Possessed Noun

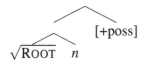

I will assume that class features of the Root appear on the *n* morpheme, where they condition the insertion of the different possessor allomorphs; it can be assumed that the features are copied to *n* via concord.[17]

With respect to the latter, the [+poss] morphemes shown in (34) are specified for features of the possessor, which are derived from combinations of [±1], [±2] for person, [±pl] for number, and [±fem] for gender. So, for example, the first person singular possessed form of *gi* 'child' is as follows:

(35)   Structure of 1s Possessed *gi* 'child'

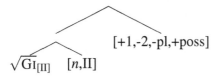

Although there is clearly much to be said about the relationships between Roots, theme classes, and possessive allomorphy (not to mention further possible connections with gender and number), the role of underspecified Vocabulary Items in the possessive morphology is relatively straightforward. As can be seen in (33), classes 1 and 2 show distinct exponents for third person masculine and third person feminine possessors, but in classes 3 and 4 there is a single third person possessor exponent in each class. In terms of Full Specification, then, it is clear that distinctions for the gender of the possessor are present on all [+poss] morphemes prior to Vocabulary Insertion. Thus, the syncretism in classes 3 and 4 can and must be attributed to the underspecification of Vocabulary Items.

Concentrating on the third person (i.e. [-1,-2]) part of the system, the following Vocabulary Items produce the correct results:

(36) Third Person Possessor Vocabulary Items

[+fem,+poss]	↔	-îm	/[I]__
[+fem,+poss]	↔	-êm	/[II]__
[-fem,+poss]	↔	-u	/[I]__
[-fem,+poss]	↔	-o	/[II]__
[+poss]	↔	-î	/[III]__
[+poss]	↔	-it	/[IV]__

Each Vocabulary Item in (36) bears a contextual specification for class. The point to note is that class 1 and class 2 are associated with distinct Vocabulary Items for [+fem] and [-fem], so that there are two distinct items for each of these classes. On the other hand, classes three and four are referred to only by one Vocabulary Item each in (36). As a result, there is only one item that can apply to both [+fem] and [-fem] possessor morphemes in these classes; and this produces the syncretism in (33).

In this case, unlike what we have seen in prior examples, the syncretism involves Vocabulary Items that have a contextual specification for noun class features. In this way, the syncretism is restricted to a particular subset of nouns of the language. Underspecifying Vocabulary Items produces the correct results for these nouns. However, for other contextually determined syncretisms, additional mechanisms are required; see chapter 6.

5.6 Conclusions

The primary goal of this chapter was to show how Vocabulary Insertion can be used for the analysis of syncretisms. A key assumption is that Vocabulary Items may be underspecified with respect to the functional morphemes that they apply to. Because of this, it is sometimes the case that a single Vocabulary Item can apply to multiple, distinct functional morphemes in a language. When this happens, the resulting surface identities in form are treated as systematic effects in the grammar. They are systematic because they are derived from the same Vocabulary Item. Without using Vocabulary Items (more generally, without a realizational approach to morphology), a straightforward analysis of syncretisms is not possible.

Underspecified Vocabulary Items are the key to understanding how syncretism is analyzed in Distributed Morphology. As mentioned at various points above, though, there are some phenomena which appear to require additional mechanisms that work together with underspecification. These additional complications, and some of the mechanisms that have been proposed to deal with them, are the topic of the next chapter.

Chapter 6
Further Topics in the Analysis of Syncretism

6.1 Introduction

The discussion to this point demonstrates how underspecified Vocabulary Items are used to analyze systematic syncretisms. In the terms that are employed at the beginning of the last chapter, underspecification allows for generalizations about sound/meaning connections to be maximized by providing a way of minimizing the Vocabulary.

Underspecification is a central and indispensable component of the theory. However, some phenomena in the domain of syncretism seem to call for additional mechanisms. That is, there are limits to the types of generalizations that can be accounted for with underspecified Vocabulary Items alone, and it has therefore been proposed that the theory must be augmented by an additional type of rule that works together with underspecification in ways that will be made precise below. Rules of this type, which are the main focus of this chapter, are called *Impoverishment rules*. These are rules that (to a first approximation) delete specific features of a morpheme in certain contexts, prior to Vocabulary Insertion at that morpheme.

Broadly speaking, there are two classes of phenomena that are relevant to the feature deletion that is effected by Impoverishment rules. Both of these build on the way in which underspecification works.

The first class of phenomena is found in contexts in which a less specified Vocabulary Item appears to win a competition against a more specified one. This is the kind of effect that can be treated with Impoverishment, since eliminating some of the features of a morpheme prior to insertion produces exactly this result. This property of Impoverishment can be exploited both in very specific contexts in which a relatively less specified Vocabulary Item is employed, and in complex systems in which a particular Vocabulary Item seems to have a very broad or "elsewhere" distribution. These points are developed in section 6.2.

The second class of phenomena connected with Impoverishment rules is found with general patterns of syncretism. In particular, Impoverishment makes it possible to encode a type of identity in form that goes *deeper* than the properties of individual Vocabulary Items, something that is impossible with underspecified Vocabulary Items alone. Generalizations of this type are the topic of section 6.3.

6.2 Impoverishment

By definition, an Impoverishment rule is a rule that deletes a feature in a particular context. Early approaches using rules of this type are found in Bonet (1991, 1995) and Noyer (1992), and a number of later theories have explored different formulations and applications of Impoverishment (see Embick and Noyer (2007) and references cited there).

Schematically, a morpheme consisting of features $[\alpha,\beta]$ could be subject to the Impoverishment rule (1), which deletes $[\alpha]$ in the context K:

(1) Impoverishment Rule:

$[\alpha] \longrightarrow \emptyset/\_\_\text{K}$

Impoverishment rules apply to a morpheme at PF, before that morpheme undergoes Vocabulary Insertion. For concreteness, it can also be assumed that Impoverishment rules apply before the Vocabulary Insertion process begins across the board (i.e., that all Impoverishment rules precede all Vocabulary Insertion).

The effects of Impoverishment rules are primarily seen in the Vocabulary Insertion process: in particular, Vocabulary Items that make reference to Impoverished (i.e. deleted) features cannot be employed. For example, Vocabulary Insertion applying to the morpheme in (1) targets a node that bears only the feature $[\beta]$, since $[\alpha]$ is deleted by the Impoverishment rule. Thus, any Vocabulary Item that makes reference to $[\alpha]$ cannot be employed in the context K.

As mentioned earlier, one of the main motivations for Impoverishment comes from cases in which underspecification alone does not correctly determine Vocabulary Insertion. In many of the examples studied in this chapter, this occurs when a distinction that is made in one part of a language's morphology is neutralized in another context or set of contexts. For example, as will be seen below in section 6.3.2, Latin nouns show distinct forms for ablative and dative cases in the singular, but are invariably identical in the plural. When this kind of context-specific effect is found, an Impoverishment rule is used to delete a feature in the relevant environments, so that (i) a Vocabulary

Item that makes reference to that feature cannot apply, with the result that (ii) a less specified Vocabulary Item does apply.

The contexts in which an Impoverishment rule is specified to occur can in principle be very specific, or very general. The illustrations in this section concentrate on the first, specific application of Impoverishment rules. The more general application is the topic of section 6.3.

6.2.1 Spurious *se* in Spanish

Bonet (1991, 1995) provides an important illustration of Impoverishment in an analysis of the "spurious *se*" effect in Spanish clitics. As a first step towards illustrating the phenomenon (and its analysis), it can be seen in the examples in (2) that Spanish possesses a third person singular masculine accusative clitic *lo*, and a third person dative clitic *le* (clitics are shown boldfaced; the examples here and below are repeated from Bonet's work):

(2) a. *El premio,* **lo** *dieron a Pedro ayer.*
    the prize   3.ACC gave.3p to Pedro yesterday
    'They gave the prize to Pedro yesterday.'

  b. *A Pedro,* **le** *dieron el premio ayer.*
    to Pedro 3-DAT gave.3p the prize yesterday
    'They gave the prize to Pedro yesterday.'

The examples in (2) show the third person accusative and dative clitics in isolation. The important observation at the center of Bonet's analysis is that these two clitics cannot co-occur; rather, in the equivalent of (2) with two clitic pronouns—one for the theme argument and one for the recipient—neither **le lo* or **lo le* surfaces; instead, the sequence *se lo* is found:

(3) *A Pedro, el premio,* **se lo** *dieron.*
    to Pedro the prize SE 3-ACC gave.3p
    'They gave the prize to Pedro.'

The second clitic, *lo*, is what is expected for the masculine accusative (recall (2a)). The first clitic, *se*, is glossed simply as SE. This clitic has a complicated distribution in Spanish (and, in fact, in other Romance languages as well). It occurs in reflexive clauses, certain anticausatives (unaccusative intransitives), and in a number of other contexts. This broad distribution (along with other facts about Spanish discussed by Bonet and others) suggest that it is the default in the system of Spanish clitics. This aspect of SE plays an important role in Bonet's analysis, as will be seen immediately below.

Bonet's observation is that while the behavior of the clitics in (3) is opaque, since the expected outcome *le lo* is not found, it is also not arbitrary: rather, the expected and more specified dative clitic is realized instead with the default clitic *se*. The realization of an independently existing default in this context suggests that clitic realization constitutes a closed system. It is exactly with this kind of phenomenon that Impoverishment can work together with underspecified Vocabulary Items to derive the correct results, because Impoverishment can be used to force the application of a less specified Vocabulary Item within the clitic system.

A number of different analyses employing Impoverishment to derive the spurious *se* effect appear in the literature; all share the same essential insight, which is that contextual deletion of features of the dative clitic results in the application of a highly underspecified (default) Vocabulary Item. To take one particular analysis for purposes of illustration, in the treatment that is developed in Halle and Marantz (1994), Spanish clitics are analyzed as internally complex, as shown in (4):

(4) Spanish Clitics (from Halle and Marantz 1994)

    a. First Person: *m-e* (singular); *n-o-s* (plural)
       [same for accusative, dative, and reflexive]

    b. Second Person: *t-e* (singular); *o-s* (plural)
       [same for accusative, dative, and reflexive]

    c. Third Person

case	number	masc.	fem.
acc	sg	l-o	l-a
	pl	l-o-s	l-a-s
dat	sg	l-e	l-e
	pl	l-e-s	l-e-s
REFL	sg	s-e	s-e
	pl	s-e	s-e

The category of REFL clitics in (4c) contains the clitic SE (on this analysis, *s-e*), which has the elsewhere distribution in the clitic system. Concentrating on the third person part of this system, Halle and Marantz suggest that the *l-* component of the various third person clitics can only be inserted in the context of a [+case] feature. The *s-* of the reflexive, on the other hand, is the default. This is shown in the Vocabulary in (5), which looks only at third person forms:

(5)　Partial Vocabulary for Spanish Clitics

$[_{cl}$ +case$] \leftrightarrow $ l
$[_{cl}$] $\leftrightarrow $ s

With the Vocabulary Items in (5), the spurious *se* phenomenon is then analyzed with the contextual deletion of dative case features, here abbreviated [+dat]:

(6)　[+dat] $\longrightarrow$ Ø/__ [+acc]

This rule deletes the [+dat] feature in the context of [+acc]. With the Vocabulary in (5), the result of the Impoverishment rule applying is that *l* cannot be inserted, since its Vocabulary Item makes reference to case features; thus, the default *s* is found.

Impoverishment accounts for the special behavior of particular clitic combinations in a way that directly accounts for the intuition that the action occurs within a closed system, in which contextual deletion results in the application of a less-specified Vocabulary Item.

6.2.2　Norwegian Adjectives

A second illustration of how Impoverishment results in the insertion of a default is provided by the inflection of Norwegian adjectives (see Sauerland (1995)). This case study also highlights some important questions about how the need for Impoverishment interacts with the specification of Vocabulary Items.

Adjectives in Norwegian, like in other Germanic languages, are "strong" or "weak" in their agreement patterns, depending on the context that they appear in. These contexts are abbreviated with the features [weak] and [strong] (for now these features suffice to distinguish the relevant contexts; see below for further discussion).

Morphologically speaking, the strong adjectives allow for four possible feature combinations, crossing [±pl] for number and [±neut] for gender, with the exponents shown in (7):

(7) Norwegian Strong Adjectives

	-neut	+neut
-pl	-Ø	-t
+pl	-e	-e

The singular shows sensitivity to [±neut], with -Ø for [-neut] and -*t* for [+neut]. The plural is not sensitive to [±neut], and shows only -*e*.

As far as just these forms go, the Vocabulary Items in (8) can be employed to derive the correct forms. The only point that is worthy of further attention is that (8) treats -*e* as a default, not as the exponent of a Vocabulary Item specified for [+pl]. The reasons for doing this will become clear below.

(8) Vocabulary Items

$[_{adj}$+neut,-pl$]$ ↔ -t
$[_{adj}$-neut,-pl$]$ ↔ -Ø
$[_{adj}$ $]$ ↔ -e

Moving past the strong adjectives, an important observation about the system of adjective agreement as a whole is that the inflection of weak adjectives involves only one exponent, -*e*:

(9) Norwegian Weak Adjectives

	-neut	+neut
-pl	-e	-e
+pl	-e	-e

In light of (7) and (9), it is clear that the Vocabulary Item with -*e* is a typical default: it applies in a range of environments that is not a natural class, covering both the weak/strong distinction, singulars and plurals, and neuters and non-neuters. However, simply allowing the Vocabulary Items in (8) to apply in the weak context does not generate the correct results, even if -*e* is underspecified in the way that is shown in (8). The reason for this is that the -*t* and -Ø Vocabulary Items should win out over -*e* in weak non-neuter and neuter singulars, just as they do with the strong adjectives. Thus, in the analysis developed to this point (i.e., (8)), it is predicted that strong and weak adjectives should show exactly the same pattern of exponents, contrary to fact.

Looking at (7) and (9), it can be observed that the distinction between [±neut] values plays a role in the realization of singulars in (7), but no role in (9). Mechanically, what needs to happen for (9) to be derived is that the Vocabulary Items with -*t* and -*Ø* exponents must not apply in the weak context, so that the default Vocabulary Item, with -*e*, is used.

The Impoverishment rule (10) causes this to happen by deleting [±neut] in the weak environment:

(10) [±neut] ⟶ Ø/___[weak]

In the weak context, the feature [±neut] is deleted by (10), whatever its value. As a result, neither of the first two Vocabulary Items in (8) can be employed in that context, because each of these makes reference to one of the values of [±neut]. Thus, the only Vocabulary Item from (8) that can apply in weak contexts is the default, with the result that -*e* occurs across the board.

To this point, the reasoning follows Sauerland's (1995) discussion in using Impoverishment to derive the distribution of -*e* in the weak adjectives. The need to use Impoverishment in this example depends, however, on some further assumptions on what features the Vocabulary Items are specified for.

Impoverishment deletes gender in the weak contexts, with the result that neither of the first two Vocabulary Items in (8) can be used there. Consider now what would happen if, rather than referring to [weak] in an Impoverishment rule like (10), the analysis referred to [strong] in the Vocabulary Items inserting -*t* and -*Ø*. The analysis would then be as in (11), which assumes that [strong] is a feature on the node undergoing insertion:

(11) Vocabulary Items

$[_{adj}$+neut,-pl,strong] ↔ -t
$[_{adj}$-neut,-pl,strong] ↔ -Ø
$[_{adj}$] ↔ -e

This alternative analysis also derives the correct distribution of exponents. The first two Vocabulary Items cannot be used in weak contexts, because they refer directly to the feature [strong]. This analysis employs underspecification alone, and does not require Impoverishment.

146   *Further Topics in the Analysis of Syncretism*

In summary, both analyses developed above derive the correct results. For comparing them, what is at issue is whether or not it is possible for Vocabulary Items to refer directly to the feature [strong]. The distribution of weak versus strong forms in Germanic is a complex issue, one that implicates the interaction of syntactic structures with morphosyntactic features in ways that warrant careful investigation. For immediate purposes, what is important is how the two analyses discussed above illustrate how Impoverishment interacts with other assumptions about the features that are referred to in Vocabulary Items: for some phenomena, the need for Impoverishment is mitigated when alternative specifications for Vocabulary Items are considered.

6.2.3   Default Vocabulary Items

It is not uncommon to find default (i.e. highly underspecified) Vocabulary Items applying in complex morphological systems. The analysis of defaults follows the general principles outlined at the beginning of this section: in some cases, a default distribution can be analyzed with underspecification alone; but in other cases, the distribution of defaults appears to require Impoverishment rules as well. These phenomena will be illustrated in turn.

6.2.3.1   Ugaritic

An analysis that involves underspecification alone is found in Noyer's (1997) treatment of the prefix conjugation of Ugaritic, an ancient Semitic language (see Pardee (1997) for an overview). Ugaritic distinguishes three persons, two genders (masculine and feminine), and three numbers (singular, dual, and plural). The inflection of the verbs in what is called the prefix conjugation is shown in (12) for the root $\sqrt{\text{KTB}}$; variation is shown with two exponents separated by a slash, (e.g. *y/t-*), vowels are omitted, and parenthesized forms are dubious. The prefix to focus on is boldfaced *t-*.

The patterns exhibited by these forms are complex because of variation in certain parts of this conjugation (see Noyer (1992) and references cited there). For present purposes, however, the central observation concerns the distribution of the *t-* exponent. On Noyer's analysis, the Vocabulary Item with *t-* is the default for the Agreement node; its optionality with *y-* in some parts of the system is analyzed as an extension of the distribution of the default.

(12) Ugaritic Prefix Conjugation (adapted from Pardee 1997:139)

p/n/g	form
1s	ʔ-ktb
2s.masc.	**t**-ktb
2s.fem.	**t**-ktb-n
3s.masc.	y-ktb
3s.fem.	**t**-ktb
1d	(n-ktb)
2d.masc.	**t**-ktb-(n)
2d.fem.	N/A
3d.masc.	y/**t**-ktb-(n)
3d.fem.	**t**-ktb-(n)
1p	n-ktb
2p.masc.	**t**-ktb-(n)
2p.fem.	(**t**-ktb-n)
3p.masc.	y/**t**-ktb
3p.fem.	(**t**-ktb-n)

Consider the analysis of (12) shown in (13):

(13) Vocabulary Items: Ugaritic

$$[_{Agr}-1,-2,+masc,-pl] \leftrightarrow y-$$
$$[_{Agr}+1,+pl] \leftrightarrow n-$$
$$[_{Agr}+1] \leftrightarrow ʔ-$$
$$[_{Agr}\ ] \leftrightarrow t-$$

The intuition behind this analysis is as follows. First, all of the verbs in the prefix conjugation are prefixed with an Agr(eement) morpheme, which has features for person, number, and gender. Second, while there are a few Vocabulary Items that realize specific feature combinations, as can be seen in (13) for those that insert *y-*, *n-* and *ʔ-*, the Vocabulary Item with *t-* realizes the rest; that is, it applies in a non-natural set of environments, the defining property of a default or elsewhere form.

6.2.3.2 Polish

Halle and Marantz (2008) analyzes the complex system of nominal case inflections in Polish (cf. Cameron-Faulker and Carstairs-McCarthy (2000)). Their treatment is limited to the inflection of masculine singular nouns, which can be divided into a number of distinct inflectional classes (**1, 2,** ... below) depending on the set of case affixes that they appear with:

(14) Summary of Affixes

case/class	1	2	3	4	5	6	7
nom	–	–	–	–	–	–	–
gen	-a	-a	-a	-a	-a	-u	-u
dat	-owi	-owi	-u	-u	-owi	-owi	-owi
inst	-em	-em	-em	-em	-em	-em	-em
loc	-e	-u	-e	-u	-u	-e	-u
voc	-e	-u	-e	-e	-e	-e	-u

The aspect of (14) that is directly relevant to the discussion of defaults is exhibited by the *-u* exponent, which can be seen in the genitive, dative, locative, and vocative rows. In Halle and Marantz's analysis, the Vocabulary Item with *-u* is the default for realizing cases, as shown in (15).[1]

(15) Vocabulary Items for Polish (Halle and Marantz 2008:68)

[nom] ↔ -Ø
[gen] ↔ -a
[dat] ↔ -owi
[inst] ↔ -em
[loc] ↔ -e
[voc] ↔ -e
[ ] ↔ -u

Clearly this analysis must be augmented, since, as it stands, it makes incorrect predictions. In particular, the genitive *-a* must not occur in classes 6 or 7; dative *-owi* must not occur with classes 3 or 4; locative *-e* must not occur with classes 2, 4, 5, or 7; and vocative *-e* must not occur with classes 2 or 7. Crucially, in all of the contexts in which one of these otherwise expected case exponents is not found, *-u* surfaces.

To account for these effects, Halle and Marantz propose a set of Impoverishment rules that are sensitive to the class that a noun belongs to. These rules, which are shown in (16), have the effect of deleting particular case features in the context of a noun from the listed class:[2]

(16) Impoverishment Rules

   a. [gen] ⟶ ∅/{6,7}__
   b. [dat] ⟶ ∅/{3,4}__
   c. [loc] ⟶ ∅/{2,4,5,7}__
   d. [voc] ⟶ ∅/{2,7}__

These rules apply prior to Vocabulary Insertion, and delete case features in the manner specified. As a result, the most specific Vocabulary Item that can apply to the Impoverished case nodes is the default in the system, which inserts -*u*. In this way, Impoverishment and underspecification work together to derive the default distribution of the -*u* exponent.

6.3 Impoverishment and Patterns of Syncretism

As discussed at length in chapter 5, underspecified Vocabulary Items allow syncretisms to be analyzed as non-accidental, because they provide a mechanism by which the same Vocabulary Item (and hence the same phonological exponent) can apply to different functional morphemes. In the last section, it was demonstrated that Impoverishment rules can be used in conjunction with underspecification to force relatively unspecified or default Vocabulary Items to apply in particular contexts. This section looks at an additional type of effect that Impoverishment rules can be used for.

Because Impoverishment rules apply before Vocabulary Insertion, they can be employed to account for patterns of syncretism that go *deeper* than the specification of Vocabulary Items. What it means to be 'deep' in the relevant sense will be illustrated in two steps. First, I will give a schematic overview of the type of pattern at issue in 6.3.1. Then, in sections 6.3.2-6.3.5, specific examples from different languages are adduced in a series of case studies.

6.3.1 Illustration in the Abstract

With underspecified Vocabulary Items, it is possible to say that functional morphemes $[+\alpha,+\beta]$ and $[+\alpha,-\beta]$ receive the same phonological expression -X, as shown in (17):

(17) $[+\alpha] \leftrightarrow$ -X/__ Context 1

An important aspect of (17) is the specification that the Vocabulary Item inserting -X applies in Context 1. The reason for this is that many languages show patterns in which, in another context (call it Context 2), the same functional morphemes are realized identically, *but with a different phonological exponent* than in Context 1. So, for example, in this Context 2, the Vocabulary Item in (18) would produce a syncretism for the morphemes $[+\alpha,+\beta]$ and $[+\alpha,-\beta]$, but with the form -Y, not -X:

(18) $[+\alpha] \leftrightarrow$ -Y/__ Context 2

The general pattern here is that $[+\alpha,+\beta]$ and $[+\alpha,-\beta]$ show the same form in multiple contexts, in a way that seems to go beyond the individual Vocabulary Items in (17) and (18); in particular, $[+\alpha]$ nodes are realized in a way that ignores values of $[\pm\beta]$, in more than one Vocabulary Item. While the Vocabulary Items (17) and (18) are capable of stating the correct distribution of exponents in this hypothetical scenario, an analysis employing these items does not directly encode the generalization that $[\pm\beta]$ is systematically ignored when it appears with $[+\alpha]$ in Contexts 1 and 2. Rather, an analysis with (17) and (18) alone makes it an accident of the Vocabulary that $[\pm\beta]$ is not referred to in these Vocabulary Items. As the number of Vocabulary Items that make no reference to $[\pm\beta]$ increases, this begins to look more and more unfortunate. What is needed is a way of saying that $[\pm\beta]$ cannot be referred to in any of the Vocabulary Items that apply to $[+\alpha]$ morphemes; that is, that the distinction between $[\pm\beta]$ is systematically *neutralized* when this feature occurs with $[+\alpha]$.

Since Impoverishment rules delete features, they are able to account for contextual neutralization straightforwardly. In particular, the rule (19) can be employed to delete $[\pm\beta]$ in the context of $[+\alpha]$:

(19) $[\pm\beta] \longrightarrow \emptyset/[+\alpha,\_\_]$

The rule (19) has the effect of neutralizing the distinction between $[+\beta]$ and $[-\beta]$ in functional morphemes with $[+\alpha]$ prior to Vocabulary Insertion.

Thus, the fact that $[\pm\beta]$ cannot be referred to in Vocabulary Insertion at $[+\alpha]$ morphemes is accounted for directly. Syncretism for $[+\alpha,\pm\beta]$ in multiple environments (and with more than one surface realization) then follows from the fact that $[\pm\beta]$ cannot be referred to by Vocabulary Items applying to $[+\alpha]$ morphemes. In short, it is not simply an accident of the Vocabulary that the two Vocabulary Items (17) and (18) fail to refer to values of $[\pm\beta]$; rather, the rule in (19) directly accounts for the generalization that the language systematically eliminates $[\pm\beta]$, in a way that has consequences for a number of distinct Vocabulary Items.

In the following sections, some concrete examples of this use of Impoverishment are examined.

6.3.2 Latin Dative and Ablative Plurals

The inflection of Latin nouns provides an example of the deeper type of formal identity introduced above. Nouns in the language are inflected for five cases: nominative, genitive, dative, accusative, and ablative (an additional vocative case is ignored in this example); they also show a distinction between singular and plural numbers. The nominals are organized into five declension classes, given here as I-V; the declension to which a Root belongs is an arbitrary property of that Root. The case and number forms of five nouns from the different declensions is shown in (20) (the noun are *mēnsa* 'table'; *hortus* 'garden'; *cōnsul* 'consul'; *frūctus* 'fruit'; *rēs* 'thing'):[3]

(20) Declension of Five Latin Nouns

case	I	II	III	IV	V
sg. nom	mēns-a	hort-us	cōnsul	frūct-us	rē-s
gen	mēns-ae	hort-ī	cōnsul-is	frūct-ūs	re-ī
dat	mēns-ae	hort-ō	cōnsul-ī	frūct-uī	re-ī
acc	mēns-am	hort-um	cōnsul-em	frūct-um	re-m
abl	mēns-ā	hort-ō	cōnsul-e	frūct-ū	rē
pl. nom	mēns-ae	hort-ī	cōnsul-ēs	frūct-ūs	rē-s
gen	mēns-ārum	hort-ōrum	cōnsul-um	frūct-uum	rē-rum
dat	*mēns-īs*	*hort-īs*	*cōnsul-ibus*	*frūct-ibus*	*rē-bus*
acc	mēns-ās	hort-ōs	cōnsul-ēs	frūct-ūs	rē-s
abl	*mēns-īs*	*hort-īs*	*cōnsul-ibus*	*frūct-ibus*	*rē-bus*

The segmentation shown in (20) is conservative and somewhat coarse, in the sense that it posits a single suffix that could itself be potentially decomposed further into a thematic vowel, along with affixes for case and number (see e.g. Halle and Vaux (1998) and Calabrese (2008)). For the purposes of this example, I will not attempt a more detailed segmentation, since the point that is to be made about Impoverishment does not require this.

There are a large number of identities in form in (20). The one that I will focus on is found in the plurals. There, it can be seen that the ablative plural and dative plural forms are identical in all five declensions. Moreover, the identity in form does not involve a single Vocabulary Item. There is declension-specific allomorphy at play in (20), with Declensions I and II showing *-īs* for the dative and ablative plurals, and Declensions III-V showing *-(i)bus*. This pattern provides a concrete example of what was schematized in 6.3.1: every noun in the language shows identical dative and ablative plurals, in a way that implicates more than one Vocabulary Item.

Some additional assumptions about the representation of case are required before it can be seen exactly how Impoverishment can be used to analyze the dative/ablative plural generalization. In a familiar way of analyzing the morphology of case, individual cases like "nominative", "accusative", etc. are not the names of individual features in the grammar. Rather, these names stand proxy for different combinations of features. In works like Halle (1997) and Halle and Vaux (1998), the feature system in (21) is employed for case decomposition (here I show only those cases that are found in Latin):

(21) Latin Case Decomposition (Halle 1997)

	nom	**acc**	**gen**	**dat**	**abl**
obl(ique)	-	-	+	+	+
str(uctural)	+	+	+	+	-
sup(erior)	+	-	-	+	+

The features [±obl], [±str], and [±sup] are defined morphosyntactically (see the works cited for details). In terms of (21), there is a single feature value that distinguishes dative case morphemes from ablative case morphemes: dative is [+obl,+str,+sup], while ablative is [+obl,-str,+sup].

To derive dative/ablative syncretism in the plural, the following Impoverishment rule can be used:

(22) Impoverishment:

[±str] ⟶ Ø/[__ +obl,+sup,+pl]

This rule operates prior to Vocabulary Insertion to remove the feature [±str], but only when [+obl], [+sup], and [+pl] are present. Both dative plural morphemes (23a) and ablative plural morphemes (23b) are subject to this rule. Since [±str] is the only feature that distinguishes ablative from dative, the effect of (22) is to make these two case morphemes identical prior to Vocabulary Insertion, as shown in (23):

(23) Morphemes

   a. Dative Plural: [+obl,+str,+sup,+pl]
   b. Ablative Plural: [+obl,-str,+sup,+pl]
   c. Post-Impoverishment: [+obl,+sup,+pl]

Because dative and ablative plural morphemes are made identical prior to Vocabulary Insertion by (22), no Vocabulary Items can treat them differently. They thus always have the same form, even if the Vocabulary Items that realize them differ in a way that depends on noun class. Concretely, the following Vocabulary Items could be employed to realize the plurals in (20):

(24) Vocabulary Items

   [+obl,+sup,+pl] ↔ -īs   /I,II__
   [+obl,+sup,+pl] ↔ -(i)bus   /III, IV, V__

There are, as mentioned above, ways of refining this analysis to take into account further decomposition of the case/number morphemes. There are also different possibilities for treating the declension-specific behavior encoded in (24). But whatever form(s) such refinements take, the central insight behind the analysis sketched above is that the deep pattern of formal identity arises because dative and ablative plural morphemes are made identical prior to Vocabulary Insertion through Impoverishment.

6.3.3 Second/Third Plurals in Latin American Spanish

For a second illustration, I return to the example from Latin American Spanish that is used to illustrate syncretism in chapter 1. Recall that there is a general neutralization of the second and third persons in the plural, as shown in (25a) for three tenses, the present, imperfect, and preterite (all indicative) for the verb *hablar* 'speak'; (25b) shows Peninsular Spanish for comparison:

(25) Three Tenses for Latin American and Peninsular Spanish

   a. Latin American

p/n	present	imperfect	preterite
1s	hablo	hablaba	hablé
2s	hablas	hablabas	hablaste
3s	habla	hablaba	habló
1p	hablamos	hablábamos	hablamos
2p	***hablan***	***hablaban***	***hablaron***
3p	***hablan***	***hablaban***	***hablaron***

   b. Peninsular

p/n	present	imperfect	preterite
1s	hablo	hablaba	hablé
2s	hablas	hablabas	hablaste
3s	habla	hablaba	habló
1p	hablamos	hablábamos	hablamos
2p	habláis	hablabais	hablasteis
3p	hablan	hablaban	hablaron

The second/third person plural syncretism is completely general in the verbal system of Latin American Spanish; it is found in every verb tense and mood. In fact, as discussed by Harris (1998), the patterns seen in the verb forms in (25a) are part of a larger generalization about the language, in that the distinction between second person and third person is eliminated in other plural contexts (pronouns, etc.) as well.

To account for this pattern (and for the fact that the forms that result pattern with third person forms), Harris posits an Impoverishment rule that deletes second person features in the context of [+pl], along the lines of (26):

(26) Impoverishment Rule for Latin American Spanish

$[\pm 2] \rightarrow \emptyset / [\_, +pl]$

The effect of this rule is to make second person plural morphemes [-1,+2,+pl] and third person plural morphemes [-1,-2,+pl] identical prior to Vocabulary

Insertion: both become [-1,+pl] after Impoverishment. Thus, the Vocabulary of Spanish cannot make any reference to values of [±2] when Vocabulary Insertion occurs, with the result that second and third person forms will always be identical.

6.3.4 Syncretisms in Macedonian Verbs

The inflection of verbs in the South Slavic language Macedonian provides a further example of the role that Impoverishment may play in the analysis of syncretism; the discussion here is based on Bobaljik (2002).

The forms in (27) for the verb *padn* 'fall' are for the present, past imperfective, and aorist (a type of past perfective) tenses. Two comments are in order concerning the segmentation of forms shown in (27). First, for simplicity, the present tense morpheme, always -Ø, is not shown. In addition, I have taken the liberty of including a parenthesized theme vowel -(e)- in 1s and 3p presents, which is not present in the surface forms (*padnam* and *padnat*); this deletion can be assumed to be phonological:

(27) Macedonian Verb Forms

p/n	present	past impf.	aorist
1s	padn-(e)-am	padn-e-v-Ø	padn-a-v-Ø
2s	padn-e-š	***padn-e-Ø-še***	***padn-a-Ø-Ø***
3s	padn-e-Ø	***padn-e-Ø-še***	***padn-a-Ø-Ø***
1p	padn-e-me	padn-e-v-me	padn-a-v-me
2p	padn-e-te	padn-e-v-te	padn-a-v-te
3p	padn-(e)-at	padn-e-Ø-a	padn-a-Ø-a

I will assume that these forms are derived in structures consisting of a Root, a Theme position TH, a Tense node, and an Agreement morpheme:

(28) Structure for Macedonian Verb Forms

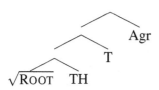

Regarding aspect, I will assume that the imperfects are T[+past], while the aorists are T[+past, perf], with [perf] a unary feature.[4]

The important pattern is found in the second and third person singulars in the past tenses: they are identical, both in terms of how Agreement and Tense are realized. Moreover, the identities in form go beyond the properties of particular Vocabulary Items, as they are found in both the past imperfective and in the aorist. These facts make the system a prime candidate for an analysis with Impoverishment.

Starting with agreement, the second singular Agr morphemes start as (29a), whereas the third singular Agr is as in (29b):

(29) Macedonian Agreement Morphemes

    a. [-1,+2,-pl] (2nd person singular)

    b. [-1,-2,-pl] (3rd person singular)

If an Impoverishment rule deletes the second person feature in past tense singulars, then, as Bobaljik points out, the different identities in form in (27) can be accounted for straightforwardly. The Impoverishment rule that effects this deletion can be formulated as follows:

(30) Impoverishment:

    [±2] $\longrightarrow$ Ø/[+past], [__,-pl]

The result of this rule is that, prior to Vocabulary Insertion, the two morphemes in (29) become identical: [-1,-pl].

With respect to agreement, no distinction between second and third persons can be made in Vocabulary Items that apply to the Agr node itself. Thus, the same Vocabulary Items will apply to second and third person singulars in the past, with -še inserted in the imperfect, and -Ø in the aorist:

(31) Vocabulary Items for 2nd/3rd Singulars

    [-1,-pl] $\leftrightarrow$ -Ø/T[+past,perf]__
    [-1,-pl] $\leftrightarrow$ -še/T[+past]__

An important part of this analysis is that deleting the [±2] feature does not make second person morphemes behave like e.g. first person morphemes; this is not possible, because (29a) does not possess the feature [+1]. Thus the "direction" of the neutralization, in which second persons come to be essentially like third persons, is accounted for with the deletion rule.

This latter aspect of the Impoverishment analysis is important when a second effect in (27) is considered: the allomorphy of the past tense morpheme, which alternates between -*v* and -*Ø*. The former allomorph is found in first person singulars, first person plurals, and second person plurals, and the latter in second and third singulars, and third plurals as well. All other things being equal, this pattern looks somewhat complicated. However, recall that the rule in (30) has the effect of making second and third person singulars identical prior to Vocabulary Insertion. With this in mind, it can be seen that -*Ø* occurs in the "third person" parts of this system: that is, those that do not have [+1] or [+2]. Recall that second person singulars count as a third person in this sense because the Impoverishment rule (30) deletes the [+2] feature.

Putting these observations together, the Vocabulary Items for Tense can be specified as follows, where the idea is that the -*v* allomorph is inserted when [+1] or [+2] (that is, the non-third person categories) are present:[5]

(32) T[+past] ↔ -v/__[+1], [+2]

  T[+past] ↔ -*Ø*

In this analysis, the distribution of Tense exponents is also directly affected by the deletion of [±2]: Impoverishment makes insertion at Agr identical for second and third person singulars in the past, and also makes it impossible to distinguish between second and third singulars for processes that are contextually sensitive to features on the Agr node, such as insertion at Tense. As a result, the Vocabulary Item with -*v* cannot be used with second singulars, and -*Ø* is inserted.

6.3.5 Person and Number in Amele

The New Guinea language Amele, described and analyzed in Roberts (1987), provides an example of a pattern of syncretism that appears to be quite broad in the system. This language shows singular, dual, and plural numbers. The main pattern of interest is that second and third persons are not distinct in non-singulars. Thus, second person duals and third person duals are identical, as are second person plurals and third person plurals. However, second and third person duals are still distinct from second and third person plurals.

The identity in form in non-first-person non-singulars appears throughout the verbal system of Amele. It involves a number of distinct realizations of the relevant person/number combination, as can be seen in (33), which shows a subset of the tenses of the language. In these forms, the agreement morphemes are underlined; note that in some tenses, the tense/aspect morphemes follow agreement (e.g. present, pasts I, II, and III), while in others (represented by the past habitual here) they precede it:[6]

(33)   Some Tenses of the Amele Verb

p/n	present	past I	past II	past III	past hab.
1s	fi-gi-na	fi-g-a	fi-g-an	fe-em	fo-l-ig
2s	fa-ga-na	fa-g-a	fa-g-an	fe-em	fo-lo-g
3s	fe-na	fe-i-a	fe-i-an	fe-n	fo-lo-i
1d	fo-wo-na	fo-w-a	fo-w-an	fo-h	fo-lo-u
2d	*fe-si-na*	*fe-si-a*	*fe-si-an*	*fe-sin*	*fo-lo-si*
3d	*fe-si-na*	*fe-si-a*	*fe-si-an*	*fe-sin*	*fo-lo-si*
1p	fo-qo-na	fo-q-a	fo-q-an	fo-m	fo-lo-b
2p	*fe-gi-na*	*fe-ig-a*	*fe-ig-an*	*fe-in*	*fo-lo-ig*
3p	*fe-gi-na*	*fe-ig-a*	*fe-ig-an*	*fe-in*	*fo-lo-ig*

The same syncretisms are found in other parts of the language as well; for example, in free pronouns and in pronominal (direct) object clitics:

(34)   Pronominals and Clitics

p/n	pronoun	clitic
1s	ija	-it
2s	hina	-ih
3s	uqa	-ud
1d	ele	-il
2d	*ale*	*-al*
3d	*ale*	*-al*
1p	ege	-ig
2p	*age*	*-ad*
3p	*age*	*-ad*

The pronouns are actually internally complex in the non-singulars, consisting of an element *a* followed by an exponent for number, *-le* for dual, *-ge* for plural, that occurs elsewhere in the language. The second and third persons are identical in duals and plurals, exactly as in the verbal agreement above.

As in the examples studied earlier in this section, it is possible to account for this general pattern of identity with Impoverishment. In the case at hand, the Impoverishment rule must eliminate the distinction between second and third person in the non-singular numbers. This can be done with the rule (35):

(35) Impoverishment:

$$[\pm 2] \longrightarrow \emptyset / [\_\_, -sg]$$

The effects of this rule are shown in (36), which shows morphemes for the different person/number combinations in (33) prior to and after Impoverishment (– – is shown for singulars because the rule does not apply to them):

(36) Amele Person/Number Morphemes

	before	after
1s	[+1,-2,+sg,-pl]	– –
1d	[+1,-2,-sg,-pl]	[+1,-sg,-pl]
1p	[+1,-2,-sg,+pl]	[+1,-sg,+pl]
2s	[-1,+2,+sg,-pl]	– –
2d	[-1,+2,-sg,-pl]	[-1,-sg,-pl]
2p	[-1,+2,-sg,+pl]	[-1,-sg,+pl]
3s	[-1,-2,+sg,-pl]	– –
3d	[-1,-2,-sg,-pl]	[-1,-sg,-pl]
3p	[-1,-2,-sg,+pl]	[-1,-sg,+pl]

As can be seen in the "after" column of (36), the first person non-singulars are [+1], and distinct from second and third person non-singulars. Within the second and third persons, there is no distinction for person. There is, however, a distinction for number (dual versus plural), so that the difference between duals and plurals can be referred to when Vocabulary Insertion applies.

Impoverishment clearly plays an important role in the analysis of this syncretism. Relying on underspecification alone, it would be possible to derive the correct forms, but the generalization that second and third persons are the same in a number of places in the language would not be accounted for.

The pattern in Amele highlights a further question about the role of Impoverishment in the grammar. The question is based on the observation that there does not seem to be any place in the grammar of Amele in which either second and third person duals, or second and third person plurals actually *are* distinguished from each other morphologically. Unlike e.g. Macedonian, where second and third person singular forms are distinct elsewhere in the verbal system, there appears to be no indication anywhere in the morphology of Amele that the relevant feature combinations are realized distinctly.

These observations raise the question of whether another analysis should be considered for "across the board" neutralizations of this type. The Impoverishment analysis holds that Amele person and number features are specified as in the **before** column of (36), and Impoverished at PF to yield the **after** before Vocabulary Insertion occurs. A more radical alternative would be to say that the language simply does not distinguish person in non-first person non-singulars, at the level of its inventory of functional morphemes. According to this view, the language does not possess functional morphemes with the full cross-combination of person/number features in the first place; rather, its morpheme inventory consists of the **after** column in (36) (more precisely: the inventory would consist of the singulars from the **before** column and the non-singulars from the **after** column). This can be called an *inventory* analysis.

Whether or not the inventory analysis is to be preferred over Impoverishment depends on other assumptions about how languages bundle features into morphemes in the first place. To start with, something would have to be said about the semantic interpretation of morphemes that do not have [±2], and which are therefore "vague". Beyond this, if there were a general principle to the effect that languages default to a full combination of features in their basic inventory of morphemes, then this would be an argument in favor of maintaining the first theory proposed above, with full feature combination plus subsequent Impoverishment. On the other hand, if there is a general principle to the effect that morphemes are only posited when their feature combination is realized uniquely somewhere in the language, then this might provide motivation for the inventory analysis. As both of these principles seem to have something in their favor, it is not clear whether there is an obvious preference, at least at this level of abstraction. And, importantly, the two analyses under consideration both derive the surface identity of forms, though in different ways; this makes it difficult to see what types of empirical evidence could be used to distinguish them from each other.

In summary, Amele shows a very systematic pattern of identity in form that could be treated either with a completely general Impoverishment rule, or with an inventory of morphemes that does not combine [±2] with non-singular number features in the first place. It remains to be seen in future work which of these two types of analyses is correct for "across the board" patterns of syncretism like this.

6.4 Underspecification and Impoverishment

Impoverishment rules delete features prior to Vocabulary Insertion, with the result that Vocabulary Items that make reference to the deleted features may not be employed. In this way, Impoverishment works together with underspecification (and the assumption that Vocabulary Items are ordered) to expand the distribution of less specified or default Vocabulary Items.

In some of the examples considered above, and those in section 6.3 in particular, the precise relationship between Impoverishment and underspecified Vocabulary Items was examined closely. A main point of those case studies was to show that an analysis that employs underspecified Vocabulary Items alone produces the correct results, but in a way that relies on accidents of the Vocabulary. The argument was that in order to successfully explain "deep" patterns of syncretism, it is necessary to employ Impoverishment. On the theme of when Impoverishment is required beyond underspecification, it is also instructive to re-examine basic syncretisms of the type analyzed in chapter 5. Take, for instance, the example from Hupa object agreement:

(37) Hupa Subject and Object Agreement Morphemes

	subject	object
1s	[+1,-2,-pl,+subj]	[+1,-2,-pl,+obj]
2s	[-1,+2,-pl,+subj]	[-1,+2,-pl,+obj]
1p	[+1,-2,+pl,+subj]	[+1,-2,+pl,+obj]
2p	[-1,+2,+pl,+subj]	[-1,+2,+pl,+obj]

(38) Hupa Agreement Vocabulary Items

[+1,+pl,+subj]	↔	di-
[+2,+pl,+subj]	↔	oh-
[+1,-pl]	↔	W-
[+2,-pl]	↔	n-
[+pl,+obj]	↔	noh-

The question to consider in light of this chapter is why this system is not treated with an Impoverishment rule that eliminates the distinction between first and second person plural in the object system; that is:

(39) $[\pm 1/\pm 2] \longrightarrow \emptyset/[\_\_,+\text{pl},+\text{obj}]$

With underspecification alone, as in (38), the analysis says that person is not referred to in the Vocabulary Item that applies to object plurals. In an analysis with the Impoverishment rule (39), the further component is that it is part of the grammar that Vocabulary Items could not refer to person features in object plurals, because of deletion; this appears to be a stronger claim (see Noyer (1998) for some pertinent discussion of the latter point).

The typical perspective, adopted here, is that Impoverishment is not needed in examples like the Hupa one; rather, Impoverishment rules are posited only when necessary. This necessity can, as we saw earlier in the chapter, take one of two forms: it can be found either (i) when Impoverishment is needed to make a less specified Vocabulary Item apply (section 6.2); or (ii) when Impoverishment is needed to account for a generalization that is deeper than the Vocabulary (section 6.3). Since neither of these conditions is met with Hupa object plurals, the analysis with underspecification alone is to be preferred.

There is in fact a way of testing the predictions of the "underspecification only" versus Impoverishment analyses. I will first present the predictions abstractly, and then turn to actual examples.

Schematically, and using the features $[\pm\alpha,\pm\beta]$, and assuming in addition that both $[+\alpha]$ morphemes are realized in the same way as -X, the effect to concentrate on is as follows. When underspecification alone is used, the value of $[\pm\beta]$ can be ignored for Vocabulary Insertion in the way shown in (40), which realizes both $[+\alpha,+\beta]$ and $[+\alpha,-\beta]$ with the exponent -X:

(40) $[+\alpha] \leftrightarrow \text{-X}$

Consider now what would happen in a language in which the morpheme with $[\pm\alpha,\pm\beta]$ is preceded or followed by a morpheme with the feature $[+\gamma]$. According to the underspecification-only approach, the difference between $[+\beta]$ and $[-\beta]$ is visible to the γ-morpheme, even if $[\pm\beta]$ is not referred to in the Vocabulary Item (40). Thus, it would be possible for $[+\gamma]$ to show contextual allomorphy in a way that refers to $[\pm\beta]$, even though $[\pm\beta]$ is not referred to in the Vocabulary Item (40) itself. The relevant Vocabulary Items for $[+\gamma]$ are shown in (41) (I have put the __ both before and after $[\pm\beta]$, since in principle the effect could happen in either position):

(41) Hypothetical Vocabulary Items

$[+\gamma] \leftrightarrow$ /-Z/ /__[+\beta]__
$[+\gamma] \leftrightarrow$ /-Y/ /__[-\beta]__

In other words, with underspecification alone it is possible that a feature that is not referred to in the Vocabulary Item that applies to its morpheme might still have a contextual effect on another morpheme's realization.

On the other hand, the scenario outlined in (40) and (41) is not compatible with an Impoverishment analysis of $[\pm\beta]$. In such a treatment, the feature $[\pm\beta]$ is deleted by (42):

(42) $[\pm\beta] \longrightarrow \emptyset/[+\alpha,\_\_]$

Thus, this analysis predicts that $[\pm\beta]$ should have no effect on morphological realization, whether in the morpheme in which $[\pm\beta]$ originates, or in nearby morphemes.

With this schematization at hand, we may consider a few concrete examples that illustrate the empirical predictions of the different approaches.

One pertinent case study is provided by the Macedonian verbs considered above in section 6.3.4. The relevant verb forms are repeated in (43), and the structure that they are realized in is shown in (44):

(43) Macedonian Verb Forms

p/n	past imperfective	aorist
1s	padn-e-v-Ø	padn-a-v-Ø
2s	padn-e-Ø-še	padn-a-Ø-Ø
3s	padn-e-Ø-še	padn-a-Ø-Ø
1p	padn-e-v-me	padn-a-v-me
2p	padn-e-v-te	padn-a-v-te
3p	padn-e-Ø-a	padn-a-Ø-a

(44) Macedonian Past Tense: Root-TH-T-Agr

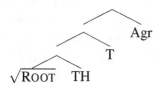

Recall with respect to (43) that the imperfect and aorist are both past tenses, with the former having T[+past], and the latter T[+past,perf].

The facts in (43) were discussed in section 6.3.4 with reference to two effects: the realization of the Tense morpheme, which alternates between -*v* and -Ø; and the syncretism of second and third person singulars. The main point of section 6.3.4 was to show that a single Impoverishment rule that deletes [±2] in the context of T[+past] produces both of the effects of interest. It accounts for the second/third person singular syncretism, in a way that is implemented with the Vocabulary Items in (45); and, by eliminating [±2], there is also an effect on the Vocabulary Items that realize Tense shown in (46), by causing -Ø to be inserted with second person singulars, and not the expected -*v*:

(45)   Vocabulary Items for 2nd/3rd Singulars

   [-1,-pl] ↔ -Ø/T[+past,perf]__
   [-1,-pl] ↔ -še/T[+past]__

(46)   T[+past] ↔ -v/__[+1], [+2]
   T[+past] ↔ -Ø

The allomorphy in second and third singulars is sensitive to the distinction between imperfects and aorists, which are [T+past] and [T+past,perf] respectively. The Tense morpheme is realized identically in imperfects and aorists, with the Vocabulary Items in (46). These Vocabulary Items are underspecified with respect to the Tense morpheme's features, in that they do not make reference to [perf]. However, the realization of the Agr node **does** make reference to [perf], as seen in (45). If all syncretisms were treated wth Impoverishment, it is predicted that insertion at Agr could not make reference to [perf] in this way, contrary to what is required in (45). We thus have an empirical argument for using only underspecification (and not Impoverishment) in the analysis of typical syncretisms.

A similar phenomenon is seen in German verbs, which show a process of vowel fronting called *Umlaut*. In (47) I have given the present tense forms of two German verbs: *laufen* 'to run', which undergoes Umlaut (orthographically, V̈); and *kaufen* 'to buy', which does not. The verbs like *laufen* that show Umlaut are subject to this process only in certain person/number combinations:

(47) Two German Verbs

	laufen	**kaufen**
1s	lauf-e	kauf-e
2s	*läuf-st*	kauf-st
3s	*läuf-t*	kauf-t
1p	lauf-en	kauf-en
2p	lauf-t	kauf-t
3p	lauf-en	kauf-en

The second and third person singular forms are Umlauted. As I mentioned above, Umlaut is a morphophonological rule: one that is triggered by certain morphemes, and which applies only to certain hosts (in this example, $\sqrt{\text{LAUF}}$ but not $\sqrt{\text{KAUF}}$) (cf. Wiese (1996) and Embick and Halle (2005)). In verbs, Umlaut is triggered by second and third singular morphemes ([-1,+2,-pl] and [-1,-2,-pl]), but not by other Agr morphemes.

The realization of the suffixal Agr morpheme in these verbs shows a syncretism that is important for the main argument of this section. In the third person singular and the second person plural, Agr is realized as -*t*. If this pattern is treated with underspecification alone, there is no issue with the distribution of Umlaut in (47): it is possible to say that an underspecified Vocabulary Item inserts -*t* into these two morphemes, but that the Umlaut rule is triggered only by second and third person singular Agr, and not by second plural. That is, second person plural is still different from third singular (and second singular) in a way that can be seen by the Umlaut rule, even though the third singular and second plural morphemes are both realized with -*t*. On the other hand, if Impoverishment were required for all syncretisms, it would not be possible to account for the different behaviors of Vocabulary Insertion and Umlaut in a straightforward way. The distinction between the Agr morphemes realized as -*t* would have to be neutralized by Impoverishment prior to Vocabulary Insertion. This would work as far as the insertion of -*t* goes, but it would then not be possible to refer to the different feature values for the triggering of Umlaut; 3s and 2p Agr should either both trigger Umlaut or both not do so, contrary to fact.

In summary, examples like those considered just above argue that underspecified Vocabulary Items alone are responsible for simple syncretisms, and that Impoverishment is only used in a particular set of circumstances, as discussed earlier in the chapter.

6.5 General Conclusions: Syncretism and Vocabulary Insertion

Vocabulary Insertion, which is at the heart of the theory of the morpheme developed in this book, is motivated empirically by the existence of syncretism in natural language. By providing a way of underspecifying phonology with respect to syntax and semantics, the theory is able to account for syncretism in a systematic (i.e. non-accidental) way. In concluding this look at Vocabulary Insertion, there are two additional points to be addressed: one general, and one specific.

On the more general level, the idea that syncretisms should be analyzed with underspecified Vocabulary Items is, in effect, a manifestation of a general economy principle along the lines of (48):

(48) MINIMIZE VOCABULARY: Analyze the system with the fewest Vocabulary Items possible.

There are other ways of framing this principle that are more or less equivalent for present purposes (e.g. in Embick 2003 it is called "Avoid Accidental Homophony"); something along these lines is assumed in all work that tries to account for syncretism systematically. In the theoretical framework that is advanced in this book, the principle in (48) is not part of the grammar per se. Rather, it is employed by the learner in the course of the acquisition process, where it functions as the learner's default hypothesis; one that can be overridden in the event that no systematic analysis of an identity in form is possible (in which case there is homophony).

On the more specific front, it is important that the identities in form that I have called *systematic* syncretisms are treated in the theory as fundamentally distinct from accidental homophony. However, having a way of representing syncretism and homophony distinctly in the grammar does not mean that it is always clear whether a particular identity in form is analyzed in the grammars of speakers in one way versus the other. As emphasized at various points earlier in the book, some of the boundary conditions for the theory of syncretism come from the theory of synsem features, such that the analysis of whether a particular pattern of formal identity is systematic or accidental must be linked closely to syntax and semantics. As a result, the theory of syncretisms and the theory of synsem feature-types rely crucially on one another, or, at the least, are mutually informative. This is an essential property of the theory: it reinforces the point that the theory of morphology is responsible for connections with several distinct subparts of the grammar, and, in fact, cannot be pursued meaningfully without direct reference to these other facets of language.

In practice, the distributional facts from a language will not always provide definitive evidence in favor of syncretism or accidental homophony. Ultimately, identifying whether speakers treat a particular identity in form as systematic or as accidental raises the types of questions that call for unification of theoretical and experimental (psycho- and neuro-linguistic) lines of inquiry (cf. Poeppel and Embick (2005), Embick (2010b)). It is quite likely that for many borderline or contentious identities in form, arguments based on distributions of exponents are simply not going to be decisive in one direction or the other. Moreover, it is also possible that different speakers of the same language sometimes analyze surface identities in form in different ways. However, experimental investigation of grammatical representation and use has made clear steps towards identifying differential responses to polysemy versus homophony (see e.g. Beretta et al. (2005) and Pylkkänen et al. (2006)), and it is to be hoped that the techniques used in these studies can be extended to give insight into the questions of syncretism versus homophony raised here.

Chapter 7
Contextual Allomorphy, and Blocking

7.1 Introduction and Review

A key component of the theory of Vocabulary Insertion is that Vocabulary Items *compete* for application to a given node. As illustrated at many points in the preceding chapters, competition is resolved by ordering, such that the Vocabulary Item that is most specified for application to a given morpheme wins.

With these points in mind, it may be seen by way of review that past tense verbs in English can be accounted for with the Vocabulary Items in (1) applying to the structure in (2):

(1) Vocabulary Items for T[+past]

    a. T[+past] ↔ -t/{√BEND, √LEAVE,...}__

    b. T[+past] ↔ -Ø/{√HIT, √QUIT,...}__

    c. T[+past] ↔ -ed

(2) Structure for the Past Tense

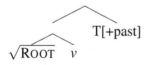

When a "non-default" Vocabulary Item like the ones that insert -Ø or -t is employed, there are two different effects to focus on.

The first concerns the fact that T[+past] has a special pronunciation in the context of certain Roots. Something must guarantee that this contextual effect works properly. Speaking informally, the T[+past] morpheme must "see" the Root in order for the proper Vocabulary Item to apply. While this effect has been implemented by placing a contextual condition on certain Vocabulary Items, we have yet to develop a general theory of when morphemes are able to see each other in the relevant way. Importantly, it appears that there are locality conditions that restrict when this happens. Together, the conditions under which a morpheme may or may not see another morpheme in its context comprise the theory of *contextual allomorphy*.

The second effect of interest in analyses like (1) is that the Vocabulary Items with special exponents like -Ø and -*t* prevent the regular past tense form from occurring, such that both "overregularized" **bend-ed* and "doubly marked" **ben-t-ed* are ungrammatical. These effects are referred to as *blocking effects*; and an important part of Distributed Morphology is the proposal that Vocabulary Insertion as defined in this work produces the types of blocking effects that are found in language.

Contextual allomorphy and blocking are central components of morphological theory. The rest of this chapter looks at each of these in turn, starting with an overview of different types of allomorphic conditioning in section 7.2. Section 7.3 then outlines the principal aspects of a theory of contextual allomorphy, with particular emphasis on the locality conditions that constrain allomorphic interactions, and the predictions that derive from the assumption that Vocabulary Insertion proceeds from the inside out. Section 7.4 examines blocking effects in the grammar, and develops the idea that blocking is limited to interactions at the level of the morpheme; i.e., to interactions among Vocabulary Items. Along with this discussion, I examine non-affixal morphological alternations, like the one in *sing/sang*, from the perspective of a morpheme-based theory of blocking. Section 7.5 concludes.

7.2 Types of Allomorphic Conditioning

A number of the analyses presented in earlier chapters use contextual conditions on Vocabulary Items to analyze allomorphy. In this section I will present an overview of the different types of contextual allomorphy that are found in natural language. These are defined in terms of whether morphemes look inwards or outwards to the element that conditions allomorphy (section 7.2.1), and in terms of whether the trigger of the effect is "grammatical" (a list of Roots, or functional morphemes) or phonological (section 7.2.2).

As a preliminary to this overview, it is necessary to look at a more general range of phenomena, as a means of understanding the status of contextual allomorphy in the theory of morphological (and morphophonological) alternations. The term *allomorphy* is sometimes used to refer to **any** variations in phonological shape that morphemes undergo when they are combined. Viewed from the theoretical perspective developed here, this general descriptive definition covers what are treated with two distinct mechanisms: one that is phonological, and one that is morphological (see below). In this work, *allomorphy* is used to refer to only the second of these two senses—that is, to cases in which more than one Vocabulary Item realizes a given morpheme, as in the case of the English past tense example considered above in (1). When it is necessary to emphasize that a given alternation is morphological, the term *(suppletive) contextual allomorphy* is employed.

As noted in the last paragraph, suppletive contextual allomorphy is only one type of morphological alternation; there is also a phonological way in which morphemes change their form. A simple example suffices to illustrate what is at issue in the distinction between the morphological and phonological alternations. Consider the fact that the English plural /-z/, which is the default realization of the plural morpheme [+pl], does not always surface as /z/; rather, it surfaces in the forms shown in (3):

(3) dog-s (/z/)
    cat-s (/s/)
    church-es (/əz/)

As it turns out, the distribution of the different surface forms of the plural morpheme in English is phonologically determined. If the underlying form of the exponent of the default plural is assumed to be /z/, then the surface forms /s/ and /əz/ can be derived via phonological rules. In this (standard) analysis of this alternation in form, there is one object at the morphological level of analysis (the Vocabulary Item with the exponent /z/), and three different surface realizations at the phonological level of analysis:

(4) English Plural (regular)

   a. phonological underlying form of exponent: /z/
   b. phonological surface forms: /z/, /s/, /əz/

One way of thinking about (4) is that it reduces the number of Vocabulary Items stored in memory. That is, there is no need to posit Vocabulary Items with the exponents /s/ and /əz/, because it is straightforward to derive these surface forms from a single Vocabulary Item, in the way described above.

The situation with the alternations seen in (3) contrasts with (suppletive) contextual allomorphy of the plural morpheme in e.g. *ox*, which has the plural *ox-en*. This fact about [+pl] has to be memorized; it is not phonologically triggered, since e.g. *box* takes the default plural (*box-es*). Importantly, there is no reason to think that *-en* should be derived from /-z/ in the phonology (or vice versa). Rather, it appears that *-en* is part of a separate Vocabulary Item; the same considerations apply to the *-Ø* realization of plural seen in *moose* etc., so that we have the Vocabulary Items in (5):

(5) Vocabulary Items for English Plurals

$$[+pl] \leftrightarrow -en/\{\sqrt{OX}, \sqrt{CHILD}, ...\}\_\_$$
$$[+pl] \leftrightarrow -\emptyset/\{\sqrt{FISH}, \sqrt{MOOSE}, ...\}\_\_$$
$$[+pl] \leftrightarrow /-z/$$

Thus, in this morphological type of alternation, there are multiple objects at the morphological level of analysis—viz., the Vocabulary Items in (1) or (5)—making this alternation an instance of allomorphy (i.e., suppletive contextual allomorphy), as the term is employed in this book.

To summarize, it will be said that the plural morpheme [+pl] has three *allomorphs*, which are the exponents of the Vocabulary Items in (5). For the differences in form that we saw with /-z/ when it attaches to different hosts, as illustrated in (4), it may be said that there are different *surface realizations* of the /-z/ exponent of plural.

7.2.1 Inwards versus Outwards

A first question to ask about the conditions constraining contextual allomorphy concerns the relative structural positions under which morphemes can see each other. Early work on this topic, in particular Carstairs (1987), identified both *inwards sensitive* and *outwards sensitive* cases of allomorphic conditioning. By definition, a morpheme shows inwards sensitive allomorphy when its form is determined by a morpheme that is structurally inside of it. In (6), for example, Y looks inwards at X:

(6) Complex Head

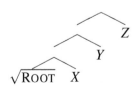

Inwards sensitive allomorphy is quite common, and is seen in many of the examples considered both in this chapter and in earlier chapters.

Outwards sensitivity in (6) involves e.g. *Y* looking at *Z*, since *Z* is structurally outside of *Y*; it is not as well known, but has been found in a number of languages. Carstairs (1987) discusses an example of outwards sensitive allomorphy in Hungarian, where the plural morpheme is realized as *-(V)k* in unpossessed forms, but as *-((j)a)i-* when there is a following possessive morpheme (each of these exponents can be subsequently altered phonologically in various ways, hence the parentheses):

(7) Hungarian Plural/Possessive (Carstairs 1987:165)

singular	**singular-1s poss.**	**plural**	**plural-1s poss.**	**gloss**
ruha	ruhá-m	ruhá-k	ruha-ái-m	'dress'
kalap	kalap-om	kalap-ok	kalap-jai-m	'hat'
ház	ház-am	ház-ak	ház-ai-m	'house'

The nouns consist of Noun-[+pl] in the simple plurals, and Noun-[+pl]-[+poss] in the possessed plurals. If the Vocabulary of Hungarian contains the following Vocabulary Items, the correct results are derived:

(8) [+pl] ↔ -((j)a)i-/__[+poss]
     [+pl] ↔ -(V)k-

Thus far, we have seen examples of morphemes looking both inwards and outwards for contextual allomorphy. The Vocabulary Insertion mechanism provides a way of accounting for these effects, but more remains to be said about potential asymmetries between looking inwards and looking outwards. In particular, it will be shown in section 7.3 below that the assumption that insertion proceeds from the inside out—which was introduced in chapter 4— makes predictions about the types of information that can be referred to in inwards sensitive versus outwards sensitive allomorphy.

7.2.2 Grammatical versus Phonological Conditioning

Descriptively speaking, there are two different kinds of triggers for contextual allomorphy: *grammatical* triggers and *phonological* triggers:

(9) a. ***Grammatically conditioned allomorphy:*** The contextual factor that triggers allomorphy is a specific set of grammatical elements (i.e., a set of Roots, or morphemes, or features).

   b. ***Phonologically conditioned allomorphy***: The contextual factor that triggers allomorphy is a phonological representation.

Grammatically conditioned allomorphy is seen in all of the instances of contextual allomorphy that have been considered to this point. For example, when English T[+past] is realized as *-t* in the context of $\sqrt{\text{LEAVE}}$, this is because the Vocabulary Item inserting *-t* makes reference to that Root. In this particular example, it is clear that the conditioning factor is grammatical (referring to a particular Root) and not phonological because other Roots that are effectively identical phonologically, such as $\sqrt{\text{GRIEVE}}$, do not take the *-t* allomorph (*grieve/griev-ed*). The same point was made above with the plural example, where nouns that rhyme with e.g. $\sqrt{\text{OX}}$ and $\sqrt{\text{MOOSE}}$ do not take the *-en* and *-Ø* allomorphs of [+pl]: e.g. *box/box-es, juice/juic-es*.

Moving past (9a) to (9b), many languages of the world have morphemes that exhibit phonologically conditioned contextual allomorphy. The importance of this phenomenon is highlighted in works by Carstairs (1988, 1990) and, more recently, Paster (2006) and Embick (2010a). One example of this phenomenon is found in Korean, where what is called the "nominative" suffix shows the forms *-i* and *-ka*, depending on whether the host that it attaches to ends with a consonant or a vowel respectively (see e.g. Lapointe (1999)):

(10)   Korean Nominative Suffix

allomorph	context	example	gloss
-i	/C__	pap-i	'cooked rice'
-ka	/V__	ai-ka	'child'

In this kind of allomorphy, it is not necessary to list the Roots that take the *-i* allomorph (or those that take the *-ka* allomorph) in the relevant Vocabulary Items. Rather, the Vocabulary Items are specified so as to make reference to the triggering phonological factor, as shown in (11):

(11)   Korean Nominative

[nom] ↔ -i   /C__
[nom] ↔ -ka /V__

The kind of distribution illustrated in (10) and analyzed with the Vocabulary Items in (11) is not uncommon. For example, the language Seri, spoken in Mexico, shows the same kind of C/V conditioning for its passive prefix (Marlett and Stemberger (1983)):

(12) Seri Passive Prefix

allomorph	context	example	gloss
p-	/__V	-p-eši	'be defeated'
a:?-	/__C	-a:?-kašni	'be bitten'

Haitian Creole shows something that looks quite similar with its definite morpheme (Klein (2003)):

(13) Haitian Creole Definite

a. *-a* after V

noun	noun-def	gloss
tu	tu-a	'hole'
papje	papje-a	'paper'
papa	papa-a	'father'
lapli	lapli-a	'rain'
chẽ	chẽ-ã	'dog'

b. *-la* after C

noun	noun-def	gloss
liv	liv-la	'book'
pitit	pitit-la	'child'
ãj	ãj-la	'angel'
kay	kay-la	'house'

This particular distribution is interesting from the perspective of theories of phonology/morphology interaction, because the C-initial allomorph is selected after C-final stems, while V-final stems take the V-initial allomorph; see Klein (2003), Paster (2006), Bonet et al. (2007) and Embick (2010a) for some discussion.

While the examples above show allomorphy conditioned by segmental properties, other types of phonological representation are implicated in phonologically conditioned allomorphy as well. For example, many languages are described as showing allomorphy that is conditioned by metrical structure; see Paster (2006) for examples.

The existence of phonologically conditioned allomorphy shows that certain Vocabulary Items must be able to make reference to phonological representations. Thus, phonological representations are visible during Vocabulary Insertion to at least this extent; it is not possible to completely separate morphology and phonology.

7.2.3 Contextual Allomorphy and (Morpho)phonology

Before looking in detail at the theory of contextual allomorphy, some comments are in order concerning the dividing lines between morphological alternations (i.e., allomorphy in the sense used here) and phonological alternations. In the introductory comments at the beginning of this section I distinguished suppletive contextual allomorphy (which involves multiple Vocabulary Items) from alternations in which the exponent of a single Vocabulary Item is changed phonologically. In the latter case, which was illustrated with the various pronunciations of the English plural morpheme /-z/, it was said that the single Vocabulary Item [pl] ↔ /-z/ had an exponent with multiple surface realizations (/z/, /s/, and /əz/).

In many cases, it is clear in which of these two ways a particular alternation should be analyzed. Sometimes, though, either type of solution seems plausible. For example, the third person singular possessive morpheme in Turkish has the form *-sı* after vowels, and *-ı* after consonants, as shown in (14) (see Lewis (1967), Carstairs (1987), Kornfilt (1997), and Paster (2006)):

(14) Turkish Possessor Allomorphy

a. *-ı* after C

bedel-i 'its price'
ikiz-i 'its twin'
alet-i 'its tool'

b. *-sı* (after V)

fire-si 'its attrition'
elma-sı 'its apple'
arı-sı 'its bee'

This looks more or less like the cases of phonologically conditioned allomorphy seen in the different examples in section 7.2.2 above. At the same time, since the two surface realizations of third person singular possessor are similar, in the sense that they overlap considerably in their phonological content, it is conceivable that they could derive from a single exponent. Under the first scenario, contextual allomorphy, the Vocabulary of Turkish would contain the two different Vocabulary Items in (15):

(15)　[-1,-2,+poss] ↔ -sɪ/V__
　　　[-1,-2,+poss] ↔ -ɪ/C__

According to the second type of analysis, there needs to be only a single Vocabulary Item:

(16)　[-1,-2,+poss] ↔ -sɪ/V__

Then, in the phonology, a rule that deletes the /s/ component of this morpheme must apply when it is adjacent to a consonant (alternatively, a Vocabulary Item with the exponent *-ɪ* could be posited, with the /s/ inserted phonologically).

　　Each of these two analyses derives the correct results. In the absence of other assumptions, it is not clear which is correct. For example, if minimizing the size of the Vocabulary is paramount, then the second analysis would be superior to the first. This (morpho)phonological analysis could receive some further support from the fact that Turkish has a large number of morphemes that show the deletion of an initial consonant when they are preceded by a consonant (see e.g. Lewis (1967) and Kornfilt (1997)). However, the deletion rule must be restricted so that it applies to certain morphemes, and not others. While the third singular possessive alternates between *-sɪ* and *-ɪ*, other superficially similar morphemes do not; for instance, conditional *-se* always surfaces in that form, and does not alternate with *-e* (Lewis (1967:130)). Thus, if there were reasons for holding that morphologically conditioned phonological rules are to be avoided whenever possible, then it would be preferable to posit two Vocabulary Items along the lines of (15).

　　The general kind of question raised by the facts of Turkish examined immediately above—allomorphy versus (morpho)phonology—arises in a number of languages and has been a disputed topic for many years (see e.g. Kiparsky (1996) and Embick (2010b) for general perspectives). As can be seen in even this preliminary discussion, a number of language-specific and general theoretical considerations must ultimately play a role in determining whether a particular alternation should be treated via Vocabulary Insertion, or as part of the (morpho)phonology. As with other grey areas discussed above (e.g., the dividing lines between syncretism and accidental homophony; recall section 6.5 in chapter 6), I will assume for present purposes that for many phenomena the type of analysis to be pursued is clear, and continue with the development of a theory of contextual allomorphy. Although this focus means that morphophonology will mostly be put to the side, some important themes in that domain are addressed in greater detail below in section 7.5, with reference to non-affixal morphology and its relation to the morpheme-based theory developed in this book.

7.3 Conditions on Contextual Allomorphy

The primary question for a theory of contextual allomorphy is under what conditions a morpheme could be affected by a morpheme in its context. To this point, we have developed a theory in which Vocabulary Items implement contextual allomorphy by representing the form that a morpheme X takes in the context of a morpheme Y by referring to Y as a contextual condition:

(17)　$X \leftrightarrow$ -x/__Y

With reference to this schematization, the question is what conditions of locality must be respected in order for X and Y to see each other.

As an introduction to this area of research, I will present an overview of the theory of allomorphy that is developed in Embick (2010a), which brings together some different threads from the literature. A major theme of that work is the idea that patterns of allomorphy arise from the interaction of two distinct types of locality conditions. In particular, it is proposed that contextual allomorphy requires both (C1), a type of locality that derives from the syntactic theory of phases and cyclic spell out; and (C2), a PF-specific requirement of linear adjacency:

(C1) *Cyclic Locality:* Two morphemes can see each other for allomorphic purposes only if they are active in the same phase-cyclic domain.

(C2) *Concatenation (linear adjacency):* A morpheme X can see a morpheme Y for allomorphy only when X is concatenated with Y: $X ⌢ Y$ or $Y ⌢ X$.

In addition to (C1) and (C2), the idea that insertion in complex structures occurs from the inside out, which was introduced in chapter 4, places further constraints on contextual allomorphy. This is stated as (C3):

(C3) *Insertion proceeds from the inside-out:* Vocabulary Insertion works from the inside out.

The "deepest" of the conditions (C1)-(C3) is (C1), which holds that morphemes can interact at PF only if they are active in the same phase cycle of spell out, assuming a syntactic theory of phases along the lines of Chomsky (2000, 2001). If (C1) is correct, then at least this part of morphology is sensitive to locality domains that are defined by syntactic computation. On the other hand, (C2) is relatively superficial by comparison, since it invokes linear order, which, by hypothesis, does not play a role in syntactic computation.

In the remainder of this section, the effects of (C1)-(C3) are outlined and illustrated.

7.3.1 Cyclic Domains

The idea that syntactic derivations operate in terms of cyclic (sub)domains is a leading idea in much theoretical work; in its most recent incarnation, the cyclic domains are referred to as *phases*, as in the work of Chomsky (2000, 2001). The idea that morphological phenomena should be sensitive to phases is advanced in works like Marantz (2001, 2007), Marvin (2002), Arad (2005), and Newell (2008) with reference to different morphophonological and semantic phenomena. This section reviews a theory of phases that is developed specifically with the concerns of allomorphy in mind in Embick (2010a).

A representative observation for understanding why phases might be important for allomorphy comes from Chomsky's (1970) discussion of different types of nominalization in English (for a general overview, see Alexiadou et al. (2007)). In terms of the theory that is assumed in this book, nouns are formed with nominalizing n heads. The forms that are taken by n heads seem to show important patterns; in particular, as seen in (18) n shows a number of distinct allomorphs when it is Root-attached as in (19), in what are called "derived nominals", or just "nouns", but appears as *-ing* across the board in gerunds, where, according to a standard syntactic analysis, the Root is categorized by v before being nominalized, as shown in (20) (the gerund structure is simplified in the sense that it does not consider other heads that might occur between *v* and *n*):

(18) Realization of *n* Heads

derived nominal	gerund
marri-age	marry-ing
destruct-ion	destroy-ing
refus-al	refus-ing
confus-ion	confus-ing
⋮	⋮

(19) Derived Nominal (noun) (20) Gerund (simplified)

The intuition to be implemented is that patterns of this type are phase effects; to a first approximation, if the head *n* is in the same cyclic domain with the Root in derived nominals like (19), but in a distinct domain from the Root when there is an intervening *v* as in (20), then important parts of the theory of allomorphy can be made to follow from the more general theory of how complex objects are built and spelled out.

The precise way in which phases operate is complex and requires a number of further assumptions about syntactic derivations. According to a hypothesis that is developed in different forms in Marantz (2001, 2007), Embick and Marantz (2008), and Embick (2010a), the *category-defining* heads *n*, *v*, *a*, etc. play a special role in cyclic derivation by triggering spell out and by defining the domains that are spelled out (these heads are introduced in section 2.3.4 in chapter 2). For this reason, these heads are sometimes referred to as *cyclic heads*.

The pattern illustrated with English nouns in (18) suggests that a cyclic head cannot see a Root across another cyclic head. However, other types of morphemes that appear outside of a cyclic head—i.e., different *non-cyclic* morphemes—**do** appear to be able to see the Root across a phase head. The example of past tense allomorphy in English, which has been considered extensively in earlier examples, is of this type, since the T[+past] morpheme can see individual Roots in spite of the intervening *v* head:

(21) Past Tense Verb

```
        v         T[+past]
     ╱      ╲
   √ROOT    v
```

(22) Vocabulary Items: T[+past]

T[+past] ↔ -t/__ {√LEAVE, √BEND, ...}
T[+past] ↔ -Ø/__ {√HIT, √SING, ...}
T[+past] ↔ -d

Putting these points together, there appear to be two generalizations for the cyclic part of the theory to account for:

Generalization 1: A cyclic head *y* outside of cyclic head *x cannot* see a Root or other morphemes in the complement of *x*, in e.g. [[√ROOT *x*] *y*].

Generalization 2: A non-cyclic head *Y can* see a Root (or other morphemes in the complement of cyclic *x* in [[√ROOT *x*] *Y*].

The theory of phases that is developed in Embick (2010a) accounts for these generalizations in a way that begins with two initial assumptions. The first specifies *under what conditions* a cyclic domain is sent to the interfaces; the second specifies *what constitutes* a cyclic domain that is spelled out:

Assumption 1: When a cyclic head is merged, it is a trigger that causes cyclic domains in the complement of that head to be spelled out. So, if *x* is a cyclic head, *x*'s cyclic domain is spelled out only when higher cyclic *y* is merged.

Assumption 2: The domains that are spelled out are defined around cyclic heads and their attendant material. A domain defined by cyclic *x* includes (i) *x* itself; and (ii) non-cyclic heads between *x* and the cyclic trigger *y*; it **does not** include the cyclic *y* that triggers spell out of *x*.

Assumptions 1 and 2 work together to produce a theory of when morphemes are *active* (co-present) in the same cyclic domain. Recall that the intuition is that when two morphemes are active in the same domain they can potentially see each other for allomorphic purposes (as with n and the Root in derived nominals); but when they are not both active in the same domain, they should not be visible to each other for contextual allomorphy (as in the case of gerunds). Another way of stating this is that certain objects must become *inactive* in the phase cyclic sense; this is stated in the *Activity Corollary* in (23):

(23) Activity Corollary: In [[.... x] y], where x and y are both cyclic, material in the complement of x is not *active* in the PF cycle in which y is spelled out.

Illustrating with cyclic x and y, and non-cyclic Y, the *Activity Corollary* says that all of the heads in (24) and (25) are active in the same cycle of spell out:

(24)   "Root-attached" x (25)   With Non-Cyclic Y

On the other hand, in (26), the cycle in which the Root and x are active does not contain y, so that when y is spelled out, the Root is inactive:

(26)   Outer Cyclic y

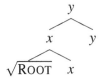

With the schemas (24)-(26) at hand, it can now be seen how the cyclic part of the theory accounts for the important contrasts seen above: that between n in derived nominals versus gerunds (which falls under Generalization 1), and that between n in gerunds versus T[+past] in verbs (which falls under Generalization 2). Starting with the first comparison, n and the Root are clearly active in the same cycle in derived nominals, where *n* is Root-attached. In gerunds, though, *n* is merged after *v* has already categorized the Root; thus, when *n* is merged it triggers the cylic domain defined by *v* in its complement. The *n* head is only operated on in a later cycle (when some other cyclic head, e.g. D, triggers its spell out). Crucially, in that later cycle *n* cannot see the Root for allomorphic purposes, because the Root is not active in that cycle.

By contrast, T[+past], which is a non-cyclic morpheme, is spelled out as part of the domain defined by *v* (cf. Assumption 2 above). Thus, the Root and T[+past] are active in the same cycle of spell out, so that they are visible to each other for allomorphic purposes.

An important aspect of the derived nominal versus gerund contrast examined above is that *n* heads apparently cannot see the Root in gerunds, even though the Root and the *n* morpheme are linearly next to each other in the surface string (since the *v* morpheme has no overt realization). This observation is particularly striking when we consider that linear adjacency appears to play an important role in the theory of allomorphy. This is the topic of the next subsection.

7.3.2 Concatenation

It will be assumed here that the linearization mechanisms that apply to syntactic structures at PF (cf. chapter 3) produce statements of concatenation which order terminal nodes. For the purposes of looking at the effects of linear relations on contextual allomorphy, it suffices to begin with an example like (27a), and the idea that if a structure like (27a) is linearized with X and Y as suffixes, the concatenation statements in (27b) are derived:

(27)   Structure and Linearization

    a. Tree

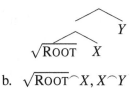

    b. $\sqrt{\text{ROOT}}\frown X, X\frown Y$

In terms of statements like those in (27b), (C2) says that Vocabulary Items can refer only to morphemes that are concatenated with the morpheme undergoing insertion. With this in mind, Vocabulary Items can be represented so that they explicitly contain information about concatenation. For instance, in the "outwards looking" allomorphy of the Hungarian plural morpheme considered in section 7.2, the Vocabulary Items are as follows, with concatenation shown:

(28) [+pl] ↔ -((j)a)i-/__⌢[+poss]
    [+pl] ↔ -(V)k-

The intuition behind (C2) is that a PF-specific linear condition restricts possible interactions among morphemes. That is, the deep cyclic condition (C1) defines a set of morphemes that could in principle interact at PF, and this interacts with the PF-specific condition (C2), which places a further condition on which morphemes can see each other within that cyclic domain.

The condition (C2) operates in ways that interact with further assumptions about linear order, particularly as it concerns silent morphemes. As emphasized at various points in earlier chapters, it appears that many morphemes in different languages have no overt phonological realization. In the most typical way of treating this effect, a Vocabulary Item is specified with a null (i.e. -∅) exponent. With respect to locality defined in terms of concatenation in particular, it appears that many morphemes with no overt realization have a special status. Consider, for example, the English past tense, which has been examined at various places earlier in the book. The Vocabulary Items that realize the past tense morpheme are shown in (29), modified now so that concatenation is represented:

(29) Vocabulary Items for Past Tense
    a. T[+past] ↔ -t/{√BEND, √LEAVE,...}⌢__
    b. T[+past] ↔ -∅/{√HIT, √QUIT,...}⌢__
    c. T[+past] ↔ -ed

The concatenation of T[+past] with particular Roots is the point of interest in (29). According to assumptions about the categorization of Roots introduced in chapter 2, the structure of a past tense form involves a *v* head in addition to the T[+past] morpheme and the Root, as shown in (30) for the Root √LEAVE:

(30) Past Tense of √LEAVE

On the assumption that *v* is a suffix in English (this is where *v* with overt exponents appears, in e.g. *dark-en* or *vapor-ize*), the concatenation statements derived from (30) are those in (31):

(31) Concatenation Statements from (30) :

√LEAVE⌢*v*, *v*⌢T[+past]

The issue here, which is discussed in Embick (2003, 2010a,b), is that the Root and the T[+past] morpheme see each other for allomorphic purposes in spite of the presence of the (by (31), linearly intervening) *v* morpheme.

Morphemes like the *v* in (31) seem to become transparent only when they have no overt exponent. Thus, one way of analyzing what happens in (31) is to say that (at least some) morphemes that have a -Ø exponent are deleted, or *Pruned*. There are some different ways of thinking about how this Pruning process might be formulated. For instance, if (certain) morphemes are specified to be Pruned immediately after they are realized as -Ø, they will be removed from concatenation statements. In the case of (31), Pruning *v* in this way will make √LEAVE and T[+past] immediately adjacent, which is what is required for contextual allomorphy by (C2). However, rather than deleting morphemes after they are realized as -Ø, it is also possible that Pruning applies in much more general ways to particular types of morphemes (something like this is implemented in section 4.6 in chapter 4). Which zero morphemes are transparent in the way described above, and how the Pruning of such morphemes should be formalized, are at present open questions.

With the basics of concatenation and its role in allomorphy at hand, I turn in the next pages to two related dimensions of (C2). The first involves an illustration of the linear locality effect enforced by this condition. The second point concerns the idea that allomorphy is restricted linearly in such a way that syntactic constituency is ignored; that is, concatenation (and therefore contextual allomorphy) ignores syntactic brackets.

7.3.2.1 Linear Locality

By (C2), morphemes can interact for allomorphy only when they are concatenated. Thus, it should be possible to find cases in which (i) a morpheme Y shows contextual allomorphy conditioned by a concatenated morpheme X, but where (ii) Y does not alternate allomorphically when it is separated from X by a linearly intervening morpheme Z. That is, contextual allomorphy should show linear intervention effects.

An example of this type is provided by the Latin perfect tense system; the discussion here draws on Embick (2010a); see also Carstairs(-McCarthy) (1987, 2001, 2003), Adger et al. (2003) and Lieber (1992). (Some initial points about this part of the Latin verb system are analyzed in section 4.6 in chapter 4, but the discussion of this section is self-contained.)

Latin verbs that are marked for perfect aspect come in several types that are differentiated by their Tense (present, past, future) and Mood (indicative, subjunctive) specifications. For instance, in addition to the (simple) perfect forms in (32), there are the pluperfect indicative, perfect subjunctive, pluperfect subjunctive, and future perfect forms in (33); to keep the exposition simple, (32) and (33) do not segment the theme vowel:

(32) Perfect Indicative Forms

p/n	form
1s	laudā-v(i)-ī
2s	laudā-v(i)-**stī**
3s	laudā-vi-t
1p	laudā-vi-mus
2p	laudā-vi-**stis**
3p	laudā-v(i)-**ērunt**

(33) Additional Perfect Forms of *laudō* 'praise'

p/n	plup. ind.	perf. subj.	plup. subj.	fut. perf
1s	laudā-ve-ra-m	laudā-ve-ri-m	laudā-vi-s-se-m	laudā-ve-r(i)-ō
2s	laudā-ve-rā-s	laudā-ve-rĭ-s	laudā-vi-s-sē-s	laudā-ve-rĭ-s
3s	laudā-ve-ra-t	laudā-ve-ri-t	laudā-vi-s-se-t	laudā-ve-ri-t
1p	laudā-ve-rā-mus	laudā-ve-rī-mus	laudā-vi-s-sē-mus	laudā-ve-rĭ-mus
2p	laudā-ve-rā-tis	laudā-ve-rĭ-tis	laudā-vi-s-sē-tis	laudā-ve-rĭ-tis
3p	laudā-ve-ra-nt	laudā-ve-ri-nt	laudā-vi-s-se-nt	laudā-ve-ri-nt

Syntacticosemantically, it will be assumed that perfect tenses consist of a Root with *v*, Asp[perf], Tense, and Agr morphemes, as shown in (34):

(34)   Structure:

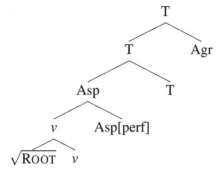

I will also assume that Tense comes in three varieties, which, in combination with the Asp[perf] feature, yield (present) perfects, pluperfects, and future perfects:

(35)   Features of T:

T[-past] = (present) perfect
T[+past] = pluperfect
T[+fut] = future perfect

For subjunctive forms, it will be assumed that Tense bears a feature [subj]; this part of the analysis could be modified in different ways, but they are irrelevant to the main point of this section. This feature combines with those in (35) to produce perfect subjunctives and pluperfect subjunctives in addition to the three types of indicative perfect that are listed in (35).

The order of morphemes in Latin perfect forms is as shown in (36):

(36)   Root-TH-Asp[perf]-Tense/Mood-Agr

In the system of forms to be considered, the realization of person/number Agreement morphemes provides the point of central interest for the themes of this section. An important observation to be explained is that the Agr exponents that are boldfaced in (32) occur only in perfect indicatives. They do not occur anywhere else in the verbal system; in particular, they are not found in the other perfect tenses in (33).

To understand the implications of this observation, consider (37), in which the forms from (33) are repeated:

(37) Additional Perfect Forms of *laudō* 'praise'

p/n	plup. ind.	perf. subj.	plup. subj.	fut. perf
1s	laudā-ve-<u>ra</u>-m	laudā-ve-<u>ri</u>-m	laudā-vi-<u>s-se</u>-m	laudā-ve-r(i)-ō
2s	laudā-ve-<u>rā</u>-s	laudā-ve-<u>rĭ</u>-s	laudā-vi-<u>s-sē</u>-s	laudā-ve-<u>rĭ</u>-s
3s	laudā-ve-<u>ra</u>-t	laudā-ve-<u>ri</u>-t	laudā-vi-<u>s-se</u>-t	laudā-ve-<u>ri</u>-t
1p	laudā-ve-<u>rā</u>-mus	laudā-ve-<u>rī</u>-mus	laudā-vi-<u>s-sē</u>-mus	laudā-ve-<u>rĭ</u>-mus
2p	laudā-ve-<u>rā</u>-tis	laudā-ve-<u>rĭ</u>-tis	laudā-vi-<u>s-sē</u>-tis	laudā-ve-<u>rĭ</u>-tis
3p	laudā-ve-<u>ra</u>-nt	laudā-ve-<u>ri</u>-nt	laudā-vi-<u>s-se</u>-nt	laudā-ve-<u>ri</u>-nt

The underlined morphemes in (37) are exponents of Tense/Mood, which immediately follows Asp[perf].

The generalization that can be seen in (32) and (37) is that when there is an overt exponent of Tense, as there is in each of the tenses in (37), the special Agr exponents do not appear. Rather, the forms with overt Tense/Mood exponents show Agr forms that are found elsewhere in the verbal system (i.e., in non-perfects). More specifically, the perfect-specific Agr forms are found only when Tense is not overt, i.e., when they are linearly adjacent to Asp[perf], on the assumption that T[-pres] is Pruned (cf. section 4.6 in chapter 4). That is:

(38) Generalizations

   a. Asp[perf]⌢Agr → perfect-specific allomorphs of Agr possible
   b. Tense⌢Agr → perfect-specific allomorphs of Agr not found

Taken together, the generalizations in (38) manifest (C2), with (38b) being the linear intervention effect described abstractly at the beginning of this section.

The analysis of this part of Latin is based on Vocabulary Items that bear contextual conditions stated in terms of concatenation. In particular, the special, perfect-specific Vocabulary Items apply only when Agr is concatenated with Asp[perf], as shown in (39):[1]

(39) Vocabulary Items: A Fragment of Agr in Latin

[+1,-2,-pl]	↔	-ī	/Asp[perf]⌢__
[-1,+2,-pl]	↔	-stī	/Asp[perf]⌢__
[-1,+2,+pl]	↔	-stis	/Asp[perf]⌢__
[-1,-2,+pl]	↔	-ērunt	/Asp[perf]⌢__
[+1,-2,-pl]	↔	-m	/T[+past]⌢__
[+1,-2,-pl]	↔	-ō	
[-1,+2,-pl]	↔	-s	
[-1,+2,+pl]	↔	-tis	
[-1,-2,+pl]	↔	-nt	

Using second singular agreement for illustration, the situation is as follows. In a perfect indicative, Pruning eliminates T[-past], and the Agr morpheme is concatenated with Asp[perf]. The most specific item that can be used is the second one in (39), which applies and inserts -*istī*. In the other perfect tenses in (37), the Tense/Mood morpheme is realized overtly, and not Pruned. The Agr morpheme is thus not concatenated with Asp[perf]. The most specific item that can be used to realize it is the less specified one for second person, which inserts -*s*.

To conclude, this example shows how contextual allomorphy between Agr and Asp[perf] is found only when these morphemes are concatenated. The conditions under which contextual allomorphs are found—and, importantly, the conditions under which they are *not* found—are expected in a theory with (C2).

7.3.2.2 Concatenation and Syntactic Structure

A second important aspect of (C2) concerns the relationship between the linear relations it refers to on the one hand, and structurally defined relations of locality (e.g. sisterhood) on the other. In particular, by (C2), morphemes can see each other for contextual allomorphy in a way that ignores syntactic brackets.

Most, if not all, of the examples of contextual allomorphy that have been analyzed earlier illustrate this point. To take a specific case that has figured in many of the illustrations earlier, consider the fact that the English past tense shows Root-specific allomorphy. This means that the T[+past] node must be able to see the Root (= be concatenated with the Root when Vocabulary Insertion occurs), when the underlying structure is that in (40):

(40) Past Tense Structure

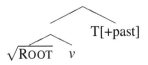

In other words, T[+past] can see the Root even though the Root is part of a constituent that excludes T[+past]; i.e., in spite of the fact that there is an intervening syntactic bracket.

In a theory with (C2), the Root and T[+past] can see each other in the linear representation derived from (40) because concatenation, as a linear notion, is not sensitive to syntactic brackets (recall also that the *v* in this example is Pruned).

The example (40) does not involve very many brackets between T[+past] and the Root; especially when we take the Pruning of *v* is taken into account. However, it is possible to make the point that contextual allomorphy ignores syntactic brackets with other relatively straightforward examples. For example, consider the verb *understand*, and its past tense *understood*; the structure of the latter is shown (41):

(41) *understood*

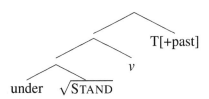

Here, T[+past] must be able to see √STAND in order for the -∅ exponent of T[+past] to be inserted (moreover T[+past] must be visible to the Root in order for the Root to be changed morphophonologically from *stand* to *stood*). These morphemes see each other because they are concatenated. The fact that there is a further syntactic bracket in (41) relative to (40) (i.e., in the constituent [under √STAND]) has no effect on allomorphy, as predicted in a theory with (C2).

With reference to examples of this type, it is important to consider alternatives to treating contextual allomorphy as subject to linear locality. If, for example, contextual allomorphy operated in terms of a structural notion like sisterhood, the fact that the past tense of *understand* is *understood* is not expected. Since √STAND is part of a constituent that excludes the T[+past] morpheme, contextual allomorphy defined in terms of constituency would predict, all other things being equal, the form **understand-ed*. (Depending on other assumptions, such a theory might also predict **stand-ed* for the case of the past tense of *stand* as well.) Though relatively simple, these observations drive home the importance of treating contextual allomorphy in terms of a linear condition like (C2).

7.3.3 Inside-Out Insertion

As discussed in section 4.5 in chapter 4, it is standardly assumed in Distributed Morphology that Vocabulary Insertion operates from the inside out in complex structures. This assumption is stated as (C3) above, because ordering insertion in this way has consequences for contextual allomorphy.

By way of review, the proposal in (C3) is that in a structure like (42), Vocabulary Insertion first targets X, then Y, then Z; if insertion at √ROOT positions is admitted, then the Root would be the first to undergo insertion:

(42) Complex Head

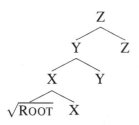

Putting to the side the question of Root insertion, assume that the morphemes $X, Y,$ and Z are suffixes, such that, prior to Vocabulary Insertion, the linearization mechanisms yield the statements √ROOT⌢X, X⌢Y, and Y⌢Z. When Vocabulary Insertion begins, (C3) says that X receives its phonological exponent before Y. There are two consequences of ordering insertion in this way. The first is that, if X is sensitive to Y, it can only be sensitive to Y's synsem features, not to its phonological features; this is because Y receives its phonological form after Vocabulary Insertion applies to X.[2] The second consequence is for Y, which could in principle be sensitive to either X's grammatical features, or to the features of the phonological exponent inserted at X.

Taken together, the consequences of (C3) for allomorphy looking outwards and inwards are summarized in (43); since the attested cases in (43) have all been illustrated above, either in earlier chapters or in section 7.2 of this chapter, the predictions are not illustrated further here:

(43) Predictions of (C3)

    a. Looking **outwards** to synsem features is possible. [examples in section 2.1 above]

    b. Looking **outwards** to phonological features is impossible.

    c. Looking **inwards** to synsem features is possible. (Looking inwards at the identity of a Root is also possible.) [many examples throughout the book]

    d. Looking **inwards** to phonological features is possible. [examples in section 7.2.2 above]

One point of difference among theories that assume (C3) concerns what happens to the features of a morpheme that has undergone Vocabulary Insertion. Recall from the discussion of chapter 4 that Vocabulary Insertion can be formalized in various ways: with rewriting of features, substitution, etc. Among these different options, a key question is whether the synsem features that are referred to in a Vocabulary Item are deleted when the Vocabulary Item applies to a morpheme.

In the theory developed in chapter 4, Vocabulary Insertion substitutes an exponent for a Q variable, with the default assumption being that synsem features are unaffected by this process. Thus, when a morpheme $[\alpha,Q]$ pre-insertion is targeted by a Vocabulary Item $[\alpha] \leftrightarrow$ /-x/, the result is $[\alpha,\text{-x}]$ post-insertion. However, as Bobaljik (2000) and others (e.g. Noyer 1997) have discussed, deleting synsem features on insertion restricts the amount of information that is in principle capable of being referred to when outer morphemes undergo Vocabulary Insertion. With reference to (43c) in particular, the situation is as follows. If Vocabulary Insertion does not delete any features, then (43c) is as it stands above. But if Vocabulary Insertion (or some attendant operation) deletes either (i) all of the features on a morpheme, or (ii) some of the features—e.g., those that are referred to by the Vocabulary Item that applies—then (43c) does not hold. Rather, it is predicted that inwards-looking allomorphy should see either (i) no synsem features (when all are deleted), or (ii) only features that were not deleted during earlier Vocabulary Insertion (if "partial" deletion is assumed).

For reasons discussed in chapter 4, I have adopted the "no deletion" assumption in this work. But, as can be seen from even this cursory discussion, a number of interesting directions in the theory of insertion can be explored in terms of different assumptions about how insertion affects synsem features. Many of these assumptions produce clear and interesting empirical predictions, both for contextual allomorphy, along the lines outlined here, and also for morphophonological processes, especially when phonological rules that appear to refer to synsem features are taken into account. These topics are active areas of current research.

The idea that Vocabulary Insertion proceeds from the inside out is independent of the other conditions (C1) and (C2) that were introduced above. It is also independent of other parts of the theory, in the sense that it is not clear that it follows from other assumptions. However, early work in the theory like Halle and Marantz (1993) connects with earlier models of morphology and phonology in assuming inside-out application, and the assumption that Vocabulary Insertion works this way has been examined fruitfully in much subsequent work (see Bobaljik 2000 for discussion). Whether it can ultimately be understood in terms of other parts of the grammar or not, it remains an important theoretical proposal, one which is open to further investigation.

7.3.4 Summary

The theory of contextual allomorphy that is outlined in this section is based on the idea that, by (C1), syntactic objects are sent to the PF interface in phases, where they are linearized and subjected to the Vocabulary Insertion operation. When the resulting representation is operated on in the PF component, the conditions (C2) and (C3) constrain contextual allomorphy by restricting it to concatenated nodes, and by ordering the process from the inside out, respectively.

Condition (C2) imposes a PF-specific locality relation on contextual allomorphy. It would be falsified by an example in which X-Y-Z shows e.g. suppletive contextual allomorphy at Z that makes reference to X, even with

194 *Contextual Allomorphy, and Blocking*

overt intervening *Y*. Condition (C3) restricts the amount of information that is available at the point of insertion. It would be falsified by a morpheme showing suppletive contextual allomorphy conditioned by the *phonological* properties of an *outer* morpheme.

It is important to emphasize in conclusion that (C1), (C2), and (C3) are independent conditions on contextual allomorphy. That is to say, a theory could accept that they work in tandem, as in the approach summarized in this section; or it could reject one or two while maintaining the other(s), and so on.

7.4 Blocking, Morphemes, and Vocabulary Insertion

Chapter 4 introduces the idea that *blocking* exists in the grammar as a relation among Vocabulary Items. For purposes of review and illustration, recall that the analysis of past tense verbs is based on the Vocabulary Items in (44) applying to the T[+past] morpheme in (45):

(44) Modified Vocabulary Items

   a. T[+past] ↔ -t/{√BEND, √LEAVE,...}⌢__
   b. T[+past] ↔ -Ø/{√HIT, √QUIT,...}⌢__
   c. T[+past] ↔ -ed

(45) Past Tense Verb

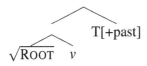

The intuition behind blocking—stated with particular reference to Vocabulary Items and their application to morphemes—is that when a past tense form like e.g. *lef-t* is generated, several conceivable forms are *not* generated. For example, when the Vocabulary Item with the *-t* exponent applies in the context of √LEAVE, the default Vocabulary Item with *-ed* does not (**leav-ed*). Moreover, there is no "double application" of the Vocabulary Items in (44), which would produce forms like **lef-t-ed*. The same thing is true of "regular" past tense forms, since for e.g. √PLAY, Vocabulary Insertion only applies once to T[+past], to produce *play-ed* (and not **play-ed-ed* etc.). A theory of blocking effects must be able to explain why *lef-t* and *play-ed* are grammatical, while **leav-ed*, **lef-t-ed*, **play-ed-ed* etc. are not.

As discussed in chapter 4, Vocabulary Insertion targets Q positions that are possessed by morphemes and morphemes only (*Terminal Insertion*). Moreover, Vocabulary Insertion obeys *Uniqueness*, such that once the Q of a morpheme has been provided with an exponent, there is no further Vocabulary Insertion for that morpheme. Finally, Vocabulary Items are *Ordered* in a way that determines the winner for application at each morpheme. Taken together, these assumptions allow for the derivation of *lef-t*, and rule out the derivation of the ungrammatical forms considered in the last paragraph. Ungrammatical **leav-ed* is not derived because Vocabulary Items compete for insertion, and, due to Ordering, the Vocabulary Item that inserts *-t* wins this competition when T[+past] is local to $\sqrt{\text{LEAVE}}$. The "double application" seen in **lef-t-ed* is ruled out by *Uniqueness*: after the Vocabulary Item inserting *-t* applies to T[+past] in (45), Vocabulary Insertion is done for that morpheme. Since there is not a second T[+past] morpheme in the structure (45), there is no morpheme that the Vocabulary Item with *-ed* could target a second time, so that **lef-t-ed* is not derived. The same reasoning extends, mutatis mutandis, to rule out **play-ed-ed* etc.

In a theory that implements blocking in terms of Vocabulary Insertion, all of the action takes place in terms of morphemes. Thus, it is not the case that the "word" *left* blocks the "word" **leaved*. Rather, the Vocabulary Item that inserts *-t* blocks the Vocabulary Item that inserts *-ed* in the context of $\sqrt{\text{LEAVE}}$, in the way described above. The (hypothetical) word *leav-ed* is thus not itself blocked. Instead, it is not derived by the rules of the grammar in the first place.

The reason to be precise about the locus of blocking effects is that blocking is often taken to be a relation that obtains between words (or perhaps larger objects as well). This intuition, with respect to word/word blocking in particular, stems from the influential work of Aronoff (1976), which looks at complex patterns in derivational morphology. Moving beyond that particular empirical domain, the theoretical issues that surround blocking are part of a larger set of questions about the extent to which competition for grammaticality is part of the grammar of human language.[3]

In order to explicate further the essential properties of the morpheme-based theory of blocking that is developed in this book, I will outline what is at issue in putative cases word/word blocking in the rest of this section.

7.4.1 Blocking and Words: The Intuition

Chapter 1 introduces the *Morpheme Locus Effect*: the idea that a number of crucial grammatical generalizations converge on the morpheme as the key object of analysis. One of the important manifestations of this effect is in the idea that Vocabulary Insertion, which applies only to morphemes, derives blocking. By contrast, many of the most influential discussions of blocking in the field build on Aronoff (1976) in assuming that blocking relations obtain between words, such that "otherwise expected" forms are ruled out via word/word competition. In light of this, it is essential that a morpheme-based theory of blocking be able to account for such generalizations in a way that restricts competition to morphemes. The issues surrounding word/word blocking are complex, because they implicate many topics in the theory of derivational morphology. This section outlines some of the key intutions that have been implemented in this domain, as a way of introducing readers to more detailed discussions like Aronoff (1976) and Embick and Marantz (2008).

Aronoff's (1976) theory of blocking is based on the idea that forms of words fill *cells*, in such a way that when a "special" form occupies a cell, it will prevent an otherwise expected word from being grammatical. The example at the center of his argument involves the relationship between adjectives with -*ous* and nouns with -*ity*, as shown in the following table:

(46) A Pattern in Derivational Morphology from Aronoff (1976:44)

-ous	*nominal*	*-ity*	*-ness*
various	*	variety	variousness
curious	*	curiosity	curiousness
glorious	glory	*gloriosity	gloriousness
furious	fury	*furiosity	furiousness
specious	*	speciosity	speciousness
precious	*	preciosity	preciousness
gracious	grace	*graciosity	graciousness
spacious	space	*spaciosity	spaciousness

Aronoff's idea is that the two columns in the middle—the "nominals" and the -*ity* forms—are competing to express the same meaning; something that we could call "abstract noun". While it looks like -*ity* nouns can be derived from -*ous* adjectives, it appears that only some of the -*ity* derivatives are grammatical. Aronoff's theory says that when the cell for "abstract noun" is filled with an existing nominal, as it is with e.g. *glory*, then the *-ity* form based on that Root is ungrammatical: hence, **gloriosity*. It is important to note that on this approach, **gloriosity* is derived by the rules of the grammar, but rendered ungrammatical by virtue of losing a (word/word) competition with *glory*. (On the other hand, nouns in *-ness* are not listed in cells, because, on Aronoff's theory, they are fully regular; thus, they are always grammatical.)

7.4.2 *Glory*, **gloriosity*, and the Morpheme

The idea that competitions are waged between words like *glory* and **gloriosity* has had a very strong influence on subsequent discussions of blocking. For the purposes of this chapter, I will outline the analysis of *glory/*gloriosity* from Embick and Marantz (2008), which employs blocking defined in terms of Vocabulary Insertion. The essence of this analysis connects with the discussion of blocking earlier in this section: that is, in the same way that forms like **leav-ed* and **lef-t-ed* are not derived (and thus do not need to be blocked), the idea is that **gloriosity* is not derived in the first place.

To start with, a simple noun ("nominal") like *glory* is internally complex in a Root-based theory; it consists of a Root and an *n* morpheme:

(47)   *glory-Ø*

```
        n
       / \
   √GLORY  [n,-Ø]
```

With this analysis of nouns in mind, there are two different structures to consider for the (ungrammatical) abstract noun **gloriosity*. The first structure, (48), is a simple noun of the type that is considered in (47). The second structure is a noun that is derived from an adjective, and is shown in (49):

(48)   Simple Noun   (49)   Deadjectival Noun

To see why *gloriosity* is not derived in these structures, it is necessary to examine some facts about allomorphy in English, and, in particular, about the realization of *n* heads.

In the first structure, (48), the *n* head would have to be realized as *-osity* to derive *gloriosity*. This analysis can be rejected. As shown above in (47), the normal (non-emphatic) *n* head in the context of √GLORY has no overt phonology; i.e., (48) exists, but it is pronounced *glory*.[4]

This leaves the deadjectival noun structure in (49) to consider with respect to *gloriosity*. The Root √GLORY forms an *-ous* adjective, with the structure in (50):

(50)   *glorious*

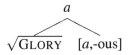

The salient question is what happens when this structure is nominalized with *n*, along the lines of (49).

In order to answer this question, it is necessary to look closely at the distribution of the *-ity* exponent of *n*, since it forms part of *gloriosity*. As shown in the first Vocabulary Item in (51), *-ity* realizes *n* when *n* is local to a number of different morphemes, both Roots and functional heads. For purposes of comparison, *-ness*, which is the exponent of a Vocabulary Item that does not have these contextual conditions, is shown as well:

(51)   Two Vocabulary Items for *n*

$n \leftrightarrow$ -ity   /{√SOLEMN, √CURIOUS,...[*a*,-able]...}⌢___
$n \leftrightarrow$ -ness

The contextual condition for the *-ity* Vocabulary Item contains a number of Roots. These are Roots that form an *-ity* nominal when *n* is Root attached; that is:[5]

(52) Adjective *solemn* (53) Noun *solemnity*

Thus far it has been established that the Vocabulary Item inserting *-ity* applies to *n* only in the context of a highly restricted set of elements, as reflected in (51). Returning to **gloriosity*, it is important to observe that the list for the insertion of *-ity* does not contain the *a* head with the exponent *-ous*. This point is especially clear in forms like *feroc-ious*, *feroc-ity*, which show that *-ity* is Root-attached when it forms abstract nouns:

(54) *ferocious* (55) *ferocity*

When the adjective in (54) is nominalized by the addition of *n*, the result is not **feroc-ios-ity*. Rather, this structure is pronounced *feroc-ious-ness*, as shown in (56):

(56) *ferociousness*

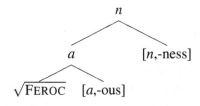

An important observation to be made about (56) is that it is exactly the same structure that was introduced as a possible source of **gloriosity* in (49) above. We now have an answer as to why **gloriosity* is not derived in a structure in which *n* is attached outside of *a*: this structure produces *gloriousness*, as shown in (57) with the category-defining heads shown after Vocabulary Insertion:

(57) *gloriousness*

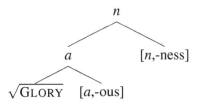

Bringing the different components of this discussion together, then, the main points are as follows. The task that was outlined at the beginning of this section was to derive an analysis of the facts that motivated word/word blocking in Aronoff (1976), but with blocking restricted to interactions among Vocabulary Items. With this in mind, the analysis developed in this section concentrates on two possible structures for *gloriosity*, a basic noun [√GLORY *n*] and a derived (deadjectival) noun [[√GLORY *a*] *n*].

In the first structure, the *n* head is realized as -Ø; assuming that there is no -*osity* exponent of *n*, *gloriosity* is not derived. For the second structure, [[√GLORY *a*] *n*], the focus is on the Vocabulary Item that inserts -*ity*. This Vocabulary Item does not apply to *n* when it is outside of the *a* that is pronounced -*ous*. Rather, the Vocabulary Item with -*ness* applies to *n* morphemes that are attached to that *a* head, because the -*ity*-inserting Vocabulary Item applies only in the context of a specific list of morphemes. It therefore follows that *gloriosity* is not the output of the structure [[√GLORY *a*] *n*]. Instead, *gloriousness* is derived.

Taken together, then, this analysis provides structures and Vocabulary Items for the grammatical forms (*glory, glorious, gloriousness*, etc.). Moreover, it does not derive the ungrammatical forms. And, crucially, it does this in terms of the interaction of Vocabulary Items applying to morphemes, which is to say that it does not involve words blocking other words.

There are many more things to be said about the full analysis of the facts considered in Aronoff's discussion, and about how morpheme-based blocking versus word-based blocking can be compared with each other. In addition, there are a number of implications of the analysis outlined here that warrant careful consideration.[6] For detailed discussion of these matters, and for arguments why morpheme-based blocking is superior to word-based blocking when other phenomena are considered, see Embick and Marantz (2008) and Embick (2010a).

7.5 Non-Affixal Morphology and Blocking

In concluding this chapter, I will introduce a topic that looks at a first glance to provide a challenge for a morpheme-based morphology. The earlier parts of this book are focused on morphemes and their phonological realization via the Vocabulary Insertion operation. It is clear from even the most cursory descriptions of what "morphology" is about, however, that there are other phenomena at play in this part of language as well. In particular, most languages show what is called (descriptively speaking) *non-affixal* or *non-concatenative* morphology. Often, though not always, non-affixal morphology takes the form of a change to a phonological representation, in a way that is correlated with a particular morphological context. To take a specific example, at many points above I have used the English past tense as a test case for the illustration of the mechanics of Vocabulary Insertion. The last time this system was looked at, in section 7.4 of this chapter, the working analysis employed the Vocabulary Items that are shown in (58):

(58) Vocabulary Items

 a. T[+past] ↔ -t/{√BEND, √LEAVE,...}⌢__
 b. T[+past] ↔ -Ø/{√HIT, √QUIT,...}⌢__
 c. T[+past] ↔ -ed

Although it correctly determines the different realizations of the T[+past] morpheme in English, the analysis summarized in (58) does not take into account forms like *gave*, *sang*, and so on, where, according to a standard type of description, the verbs *give* and *sing* show *stem allomorphy* (or a *stem alternation*) in the past tense. This is one of the phenomena that falls under the heading of "non-affixal morphological change".

The kind of stem allomorphy seen in *sang* etc. is only one type of non-affixal morphology. Cross-linguistically, other phenomena, such as the *templatic* effects seen in Semitic (recall the brief discussion of Arabic in chapter 2), would be part of a broader overview of this part of morphophonology. However, the aims of this section are quite narrow: they are to show why it is that theories like Distributed Morphology hold that many types of stem allomorphy are not derived by Vocabulary Insertion, but are instead the result of phonological operations. Importantly, this particular facet of the theory is based on the behavior of non-affixal morphology with respect to blocking, and thus follows directly on the discussion of the last section.

In the next subsections, I will first outline an analysis of the *sing/sang* type of alternation (section 7.5.1), and then look at why it is problematic to treat non-affixal morphology of this type on a par with morpheme-based Vocabulary Insertion (section 7.5.2). Section 7.5.3 concludes with some general remarks on the relationship between (morpho)phonological rules and Vocabulary Insertion.

7.5.1 An Analysis of Non-Affixal Changes

In extending the analysis in (58) to cover *sang* etc., there are two main facts to be accounted for. The first is that the default VI with *-ed* does not apply with $\sqrt{\text{SING}}$; this is clear from the fact that **sing-ed* is ungrammatical (as is **sang-ed*). The second effect to be accounted for is the stem form (where *stem* is used descriptively for "phonological form of a Root"): i.e., the analysis must account for the fact that the Root $\sqrt{\text{SING}}$ surfaces as *sing* in the present tense, and *sang* in the past tense.

For reasons that are discussed in detail in 7.5.2 below, the standard analysis of these two types of effects in Distributed Morphology, which is developed in detail in Halle and Marantz (1993), takes the blocking of *-ed* and the change that produces *sang* from $\sqrt{\text{SING}}$ to be the result of two distinct mechanisms. The first one, blocking the Vocabulary Item that inserts *-ed*, is attributed to Vocabulary Insertion. Specifically, $\sqrt{\text{SING}}$ is entered on the list of the Vocabulary Items that take the *-Ø* exponent of past tense:

(59) Vocabulary Items

    a. T[+past] ↔ -t/{$\sqrt{\text{BEND}}$, $\sqrt{\text{LEAVE}}$,...}⌢___

    b. T[+past] ↔ -Ø/{$\sqrt{\text{HIT}}$, $\sqrt{\text{QUIT}}$, $\sqrt{\text{SING}}$, ...}⌢___

    c. T[+past] ↔ -ed

Making this addition to the Vocabulary Items in (58) produces **sing-Ø* as the past tense of $\sqrt{\text{SING}}$. This is where the second component of the analysis comes in; along with taking the Vocabulary Item that inserts -Ø, $\sqrt{\text{SING}}$ is on a list (or a set of lists) of elements that trigger *Readjustment Rules*. These rules are phonological rules that are triggered by certain morphemes, or that are specified to apply to certain morphemes and not others.

With *sing/sang*, the situation is as follows. Assuming for convenience that the phonological underlying representation of $\sqrt{\text{SING}}$ is the one that surfaces in *sing*, a Readjustment Rule (or a set of such rules) that is triggered by the T[+past] morpheme changes the stem vowel to /æ/. In addition to being triggered by T[+past], this rule must also be stated so that it applies only to certain Roots and not others. I am being neutral about the precise phonological details involved in the *sing/sang* alternation because there are many ways in which the alternation could be analyzed (see Halle and Mohanan (1985) for one). Moreover, one need not assume that the underlying representation is the one seen in *sing*. What is important is that the analysis separates Vocabulary Insertion at T[+past] from the change effected to the phonological form of the Root √SING, as summarized in (60):[7]

(60) Derivation of *sang*

   a. Structure

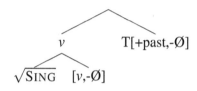

   b. Readjustment Rule(s): change vowel in phonological representation of √SING with rules triggered by T[+past].

Because Readjustment Rules use morphological information in executing phonological operations, they are sometimes referred to as *morphophonological* rules.

7.5.2 Pieces, Processes, Blocking

The analysis outlined in the preceding subsection treats the derivation of *sang* with two distinct mechanisms: Vocabulary Insertion accounts for the absence of the default *-ed*, and a Readjustment Rule accounts for the form of the stem. The general claim behind this analysis is that morpheme-based Vocabulary Insertion and (at least this type of) morphophonological change is executed by different operations in the grammar. This section looks at the motivations for making this distinction.

As a starting point, it is important to emphasize that the motivations are empirical, and not conceptual. All other things being equal, it would be prima facie more parsimonious to treat all "morphological realization" broadly construed with one mechanism, rather than two. Indeed, this type of argument plays an important role in morpheme-less theories like the one that is developed in Anderson (1992). In response to Anderson's approach, Halle and Marantz (1993) argue that a sharp distinction between piece-based Vocabulary Insertion and non-affixal changes is essential to understanding how blocking effects work in the grammar. Thus, the argument is that in spite of its apparent conceptual appeal on the grounds of simplicity, treating all types of morphology with a single mechanism is problematic.

The argument for distinguishing Vocabulary Insertion from Readjustment Rules will proceed in a few steps. The central point is that the realization of morphemes and the realization of non-affixal morphology do not block each other, and thus should be treated with different mechanisms.

A first point to be established can be made with *sing/sang*. Looking only at this verb, it might seem as if the stem change is what is preventing the realization of *-ed*. This is not something that can be stated in a theory that treats Vocabulary Insertion and Readjustment Rules as independent effects. It *could*, however, be encoded in a theory that makes no such distinction. In particular, such a theory could say that it is the change seen in *sang* that blocks the realization of the expected past tense *-ed*. Informally, this would require a Vocabulary Item like (61):

(61)   T[+past] ↔ <stem change>/{ $\sqrt{\text{SING}}$, $\sqrt{\text{RING}}$, ... } __

There are two arguments against this type of analysis. One is relatively limited in its implications, and the other is quite general.

The limited one is as follows. Suppose that we found that in every language, the non-occurrence of an expected, default affix (like *-ed* in the past tense) were accompanied by some kind of stem changing rule. On the face of it, this would look like evidence in favor of treating affixal morphology and non-affixal morphology in the same way; that is, there would be evidence that defaults like *-ed* were not surfacing because they were being blocked by the stem changes. Even within the English past tense, though, there is little reason to think that things work like this. For example, verbs like $\sqrt{\text{HIT}}$ take the *-Ø* Vocabulary Item for T[+past] (*hit-Ø*). With this kind of verb, there is no stem change to block *-ed* for T[+past], but *-ed* fails to appear all the same. The same point can be made in the plural system. In some irregular plurals, the expected /-z/ is not found, and there is a stem change: *mouse/mice* is one of these. But in others, neither /-z/ nor a stem change are found: *moose/moose*.

Taken together, these facts show that there is not always a stem change that blocks an otherwise expected morpheme.

Although suggestive, the argument outlined in the last paragraph is still relatively weak. It shows only that blocking of Vocabulary Items does not require a stem change—and, to the extent that we allow -Ø exponents, as we have at several points in this book, this is relatively unsurprising. But there are more interesting things to say about how morphemes and non-affixal changes interact for blocking. This brings us to the more important and general argument in favor of distinguishing piece-based realization from non-affixal changes. Rather than looking at whether non-affixal changes always block expected Vocabulary Items, as we did immediately above, we can now look at how non-affixal changes relate to *overt* realizations of morphemes. The pertinent questions can be stated in two ways, since in principle non-affixal changes could block affixation, or vice versa; that is:

(62) Questions:

a. Do non-affixal changes triggered by a feature X necessarily block overt realization of X with an affix?

b. Does realization of morpheme X by an affix necessarily block non-affixal changes triggered by X?

If the questions in (62) were answered positively, it would mean that morphemes and non-affixal changes always block each other. This would be strong evidence in favor of treating them with a single mechanism. For this reason, the questions in (62) play a prominent role in Halle and Marantz's (1993) critique of Anderson's (1992) single mechanism theory. In particular, Halle and Marantz argue that there are strong reasons to think that non-affixal changes and Vocabulary Insertion **do not** block each other. Continuing with verbs (and participles) in English, this point can be seen in the fact that there are many Roots which show **both** stem changes and overt affixation in their past tense and participial forms:

(63) tell, tol-d
freeze, froz-en
break, brok-en

Accounting for this kind of "double marking" is straightforward in the theory developed above, where Vocabulary Insertion handles the realization of morphemes like T[+past], and Readjustment Rules account for non-affixal changes. First, √TELL is not on any list for the realization of T[+past], which is thus spelled out as -*ed*. In addition, √TELL is on a list that triggers the Readjustment Rule that produces *tol* in the context of T[+past]. Since the two changes (insertion of -*ed* and the change from *tell* to *tol*) are the result of two distinct grammatical operations, there is no expectation that they should block each other. On the other hand, the double-marking that is seen in (63) is unexpected in a theory that does not distinguish morpheme-based Vocabulary Insertion from stem-changing processes—one of these changes should block the other, if they are treated with the same mechanism.[8]

As emphasized by Halle and Marantz, there are in fact two generalizations about blocking that are accounted for when the theory separates Vocabulary Insertion from Readjustment Rules. While affixes and non-affixal changes sometimes co-occur (*froz-en*, *tol-d*, ...) and sometimes do not (*sang*, *broke*, ...), the pattern with affixes interacting with affixes is much clearer: insertion at morphemes blocks further insertion at that morpheme. This latter point is illustrated at length in the discussion of blocking in section 7.4. There, it was shown how e.g. the insertion of -*t* for T[+past] in the context of √LEAVE blocks the insertion of -*ed*. This kind of blocking between pieces is not piecemeal; rather, it is completely general. Bringing the different lines of this discussion together, then, the key generalizations to account for are those in (64):

(64) **Generalizations about blocking:**

    a. piece-based insertion blocks piece-based insertion; but

    b. piece-based insertion and non-affixal changes do not block each other.

For the reasons that were developed throughout this section and the last, these generalizations can be accounted for in a principled way in a theory that treats affixal and non-affixal morphology with distinct operations (Vocabulary Insertion and Readjustment Rules in Distributed Morphology), but not in a theory that eschews this distinction.

7.5.3 Non-affixal Morphology: Concluding Remarks

The idea that Vocabulary Insertion and Readjustment Rules account for affixal and non-affixal morphology respectively has been explored in a number of different directions. While distinguishing between these two types of morphology is often straightforward, there are some types of apparently "non-affixal" alternations that could very well be handled with Vocabulary Insertion. One direction for further work in this area concerns what criteria can be used to determine whether a particular alternation should be treated with Vocabulary Insertion or with Readjustment Rules.

An illustration of what is at issue is provided by the facts in (65), which are from the Arawakan language Terena (Ekdahl and Grimes 1964, Akinlabi 1996, 2011, Wolf 2006). The realization of first person singular agreement takes the form of nasalization, which spreads from left to right, and is stopped by obstruents (the first column shows 3s forms, which are not nasalized in this way):

(65) Terena 1s Nasalization

3s	1s	gloss
arıne	ãrĩnẽ	'sickness'
emoʔu	ẽmõʔũ	'boss'
owoku	õw̃õ^{n}gu	'house'
ıwuʔıʃo	ĩw̃ũʔĩ^{n}ʒo	'to ride'
takı	^{n}daki	'arm'
paho	^{n}baho	'mouth'

In other person/number combinations (e.g., 1pl, at least with certain hosts), agreement is realized as a prefix. This observation fits nicely with the fact that nasalization spreads from left to right, and the assumption that the structure of the forms in (65) is as shown in (66), with Agr as a prefix:

(66) Agr-[Noun/Verb]

With these points at hand, it is now possible to illustrate why there might be alternative analyses of first person singular Agr: one that attributes the nasalization effect to a Readjustment Rule, and another that treats it with Vocabulary Insertion.

Beginning with the first approach, the analysis says first that the grammar contains a Vocabulary Item that realizes first person singular Agr as Ø-, as shown in (67). Then, a Readjustment Rule triggered by Agr[+1,-2,-pl] would apply to nasalize material to the right of the Agr morpheme. This analysis is parallel to the analysis of *sang* above.

(67) [+1,-2,-pl] ↔ Ø-

The second type of analysis dispenses with the Readjustment Rule, and employs only Vocabulary Insertion. This analysis posits that the exponent of first person singular Agr is an autosegment:

(68) [+1,-2,-pl] ↔ [+nasal]

The floating [+nasal] feature, which is in the (prefixal) position of the Agr morpheme, is then manipulated phonologically to produce the distributions seen in (65). (This manipulation might involve a rule that is identical to the Readjustment Rule required in the first solution).

Choosing between these analyses is not simple. The first type of analysis employs tools that are clearly required elsewhere, since, as we saw above in the discussion of English, both Readjustment Rules and Vocabulary Insertion have independent motivation. Recall, in particular, the double marking seen in e.g. *tol-d*. It might be possible to treat e.g. *sang* by inserting for T[+past] some autosegment(s) to (i) derive *sang*, and (ii) block the insertion of *-ed*. But it is not possible to derive the stem change in doubly marked forms like *tol-d* in this way, since the stem change is effected in the presence of the default *-ed* exponent of T[+past].

The second type of analysis, the one in (68), employs only Vocabulary Insertion, and is thus, according to at least one metric, simpler than the first. At the same time, though, allowing the exponents of Vocabulary Items to be autosegments, rather than restricting exponents to larger objects, constitutes a modification to the theory that warrants careful investigation. Further study is required to determine the predictions made by different theories of possible exponents, and to determine which of these predictions are correct.

The general point that is at issue in this discussion, where to draw the line between Vocabulary Insertion and (morpho)phonology, is an important topic in current research (recall section 7.2.3 above). While it is not possible to report on a consensus view at this point in time, the discussion above is, I hope, sufficient to clarify what is at stake in this part of the theory.[9]

7.6 Conclusions

Contextual allomorphy and blocking are two of the most important topics in morphological theory. They fit together, in the sense that one aspect of contextual allomorphy is that a more specific Vocabulary Item must win out over—i.e., "block", in an intuitive sense—less specified competitors in particular environments. Building on this initial connection, this chapter develops theories of contextual allomorphy and blocking that are centered on the morpheme.

For contextual allomorphy, the morpheme plays a central role because it is the target of the Vocabulary Insertion operation. In the specific theory of contextual allomorphy that is presented in section 7.3 above, patterns of allomorphy in natural language are restricted by the interaction of three independent conditions. Condition (C1) holds that morphemes may interact with each other for contextual allomorphy only when they are in the same cyclic domain, as determined by phase-based spell out of syntactic structures. Condition (C2) enforces a PF-specific, linear requirement on contextual allomorphy, restricting interactions further to morphemes that are concatenated. Finally, the idea that Vocabulary Insertion proceeds from the inside out, given in this chapter as (C3), imposes constraints on the types of information that are visible to Vocabulary Insertion, in a way that predicts directional asymmetries in phonologically conditioned versus grammatically conditioned allomorphy. While these separate conditions may be modified in different ways, or combined or separated to produce different predictions, the most important idea is that the correct theory of contextual allomorphy treats the morpheme (and no other object) as the basic object of phonological realization.

The analysis of blocking effects picks up on this last point. In the theory that is presented in section 7.4, blocking effects in the grammar are hypothesized to derive only from interactions among Vocabulary Items. Since Vocabulary Items apply only to morphemes, this means that the morpheme is the only object that shows blocking effects; there is thus no word/word, or word/phrase blocking.

Beyond giving rise to the hypothesis that the morpheme is the locus of blocking effects, blocking also provides crucial information about the nature of non-affixal alternations in grammar. As discussed in section 7.5, non-affixal morphological changes do not block affixes, and vice versa. This observation is at the heart of an important distinction in Distributed Morphology: that between affixal realization, which is treated with Vocabulary Insertion, and non-affixal morphological changes, which are treated with Readjustment Rules.

In short, the two major phenomena discussed in this chapter converge on the morpheme as the most important unit of analysis, in ways that resonate with the central themes of this book.

Chapter 8
Concluding Remarks

A common way of thinking about how grammars are organized holds that sentences are built out of words, and that words are built out of morphemes. The theory that is developed in this book takes another perspective: sentences are built out of morphemes, and words (to the extent that they are needed at all) are built out of syntactic structures; i.e., they reflect particular way(s) in which morphemes are packaged.

In the particular morpheme-centered view that is developed in this book, there are two types of morphemes in the grammar: the Roots and the functional morphemes. The main emphasis of the book is on how sound and meaning connections are established in terms of these morphemes, with a particular emphasis on functional morphemes and Vocabulary Insertion.

The interplay of sound, meaning, and structure constitutes **the** fundamental issue in the theory of the morpheme. The particular interactions at the center of this book are two phenomena showing that sound/meaning connections are not always one-to-one: allomorphy and syncretism. Allomorphy is a departure from the one-to-one ideal because it shows that a single synsem object can be realized in ways that are not phonologically related to one another; i.e., with suppletive allomorphs. Syncretism is a departure from the one-to-one ideal because it shows that a single phonological exponent can realize distinct sets of synsem features.

Following the general intuition outlined in chapter 1, my goal has been to present the basic properties of a theory in which sound and meaning are connected transparently in the default case, but in which there is enough flexibility to allow for limited departures from the one-to-one ideal, so that constrained theories of allomorphy and syncretism can be developed. The Vocabulary Insertion operation, which is at the center of chapter 4, and developed in subsequent chapters, serves this function by providing a mechanism that adds phonological representations to morphemes. Because they can be underspecified with respect to the morphemes that they apply to, Vocabulary Items are able to account for syncretism; and because Vocabulary Insertion targets morphemes at PF, after they have been assembled into complex objects, contextual allomorphy can be investigated in terms of different types of locality conditions (phase-cyclic, linear) that are part of syntax and PF.

Along the way, several additional elements of the theory are introduced in addition to Vocabulary Insertion (e.g. Impoverishment rules, which are examined in chapter 6). Moreover, some questions about the scope of Vocabulary Insertion are left unresolved; in particular, whether it applies to all morphemes (including Roots); only to functional morphemes; or to some subset of morphemes. With respect to these topics (and a number of related ones that surface in the pages above), my goal has not been to try and provide definitive arguments in favor of one view or another. Rather, I have tried to provide enough theoretical and empirical context for understanding the important questions, so that interested theoreticians can appreciate what is at issue, and direct their attention to the active primary literature in these areas. One reason that I have not attempted to provide strong conclusions on these topics is that the core topic of the book—Vocabulary Insertion, and its relation to syncretism and allomorphy—is compatible with a number of auxiliary theories of related phenomena, and it is not my intention here to determine a comprehensive theory that includes all of these.

My hope is that by outlining the core properties of a theory of the morpheme, and that by taking an open approach towards a number of attendant questions, the book will serve as a stimulus for further work in this part of the theory of grammar. I also hope that in addition to helping readers understand how to do things with the theory in one form, it will help them to undo it (and redo it, and preferably outdo it) in constructive ways. Every aspect of an active theory is subject to continuous question and re-examination; and to the extent that presenting things as I have done here leads to innovations and changes to the theory—even if this means fundamentally changing or rejecting parts that I consider now to be the most central and the most correct—the book will have justified its existence.

Appendix: Fission and Fusion

A.1 Introduction

Early work in Distributed Morphology introduced two types of rules that affect the number of morphemes that are targeted by Vocabulary Insertion (see in particular Noyer (1992) and Halle and Marantz (1993)). The rules are *Fusion*, which creates one morpheme out of two; and *Fission*, which creates two morphemes out of one. To a first approximation, these rules are motivated by two different scenarios:

(1) Two Types of Mismatches

  a. **Case 1:** The morphosyntactic analysis motivates two distinct morphemes, X and Y. In some particular combination(s) of feature values for X and Y, though, there are not two distinct exponents realizing X and Y on the surface. Rather, there appears to be a "portmanteau" realization instead of the expected individual realizations of X and Y. ⇒ This case motivates *Fusion*.

  b. **Case 2:** The morphosyntactic analysis motivates a single morpheme X, with features $[\pm\alpha]$ and $[\pm\beta]$. In particular combinations of feature values, though, there are two (or more) distinct exponents on the surface, corresponding to the different features $[\pm\alpha]$ and $[\pm\beta]$. ⇒ This case motivates *Fission*.

Some simple illustrations of Fusion and Fission rules are given in sections A.2 and A.3. These rules are controversial; there is some question as to whether their effects can be reduced to independently motivated mechanisms (see e.g. Trommer 1997). Since my intent here is primarily to illustrate what these rules do, as an introduction to the primary literature, I will not dwell on possible reductions to other mechanisms here.

A.2 Fusion

Rules for Fusing morphemes prior to Vocabulary Insertion were initially discussed in Halle and Marantz (1993). As described in Case 1 above, Fusion is motivated when what appear to be two distinct morphemes are compressed into one under particular circumstances (i.e., combinations of features on local morphemes). The need for this type of operation is, of course, clear only when there is substantial motivation for the two distinct morphemes in the first place. An example will make these points more precise.

The realization of agreement (Agr) in Latin verbs interacts in complex ways with voice morphology. The present indicative active and passive forms of *laudāre* 'praise' are shown in (2); for the moment, the Agr component and the passive component (i.e., the feature [+pass]) are not segmented in the passive forms:

(2) Present Indicative Active and Passive of *laudāre* 'to praise'

p/n	active	passive
1s	laud-ō	laud-or
2s	laud-ā-s	laud-ā-ris
3s	laud-a-t	laud-ā-tur
1p	laud-ā-mus	laud-ā-mur
2p	laud-ā-tis	laud-ā-minī
3p	laud-a-nt	laud-a-ntur

There are common components to many of the endings here, so that, descriptively, the passive forms add something to what is seen in the active. In particular, it appears that [+pass] is typically realized as *-r*, along with the usual realization of Agr (shown boldfaced in (3)).

(3) Passive and Active

1s passive:	-**o**-r;	cp. Active *-ō*
2s passive:	-r**i-s**;	cp. Active *-s*
3s passive:	-**t**-ur;	cp. Active *-t*
1p passive:	-**mu**-r;	cp. Active *-mus*
2p passive:	-**minī**;	no Active counterpart
3p passive:	-**nt**-ur;	cp. Active *-nt*

(There are some additional complications with the *-r* forms. For instance, linearly, the second person singular form *laud-ā-r-is* shows the *-r-* exponent of passive voice to the left of Agr. I put these to the side, since they do not affect the main point about the motivation for Fusion.)

The common components (*-ō*, *-s*, etc.) suggest that Vocabulary Insertion in the passive typically targets distinct Agr and [+pass] morphemes. For instance, the structure of the 1s Passive is shown in (4), which treats the theme vowel as a realization of *v*, and omits the present tense morpheme (in this particular form, *laudor*, the theme is deleted phonologically):

(4) Verb Structure

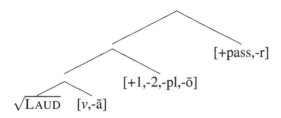

Other person/number combinations can be treated similarly, with one exception: in the 2pl, there is no relationship between passive *-minī* and active *-tis*; moreover, the passive *-r* that appears elsewhere in the system is absent here. Thus, whereas each of the other Agr forms consists of the agreement found in the active in conjunction with an *-r* component, it seems that the 2pl passive is realized with only a single exponent, *-minī*.

The interaction of Agr and [+pass] in Latin falls under Case 1 of (1). The two separate morphemes that are at issue in the majority of the system, Agr and [+pass], are well motivated, and they are realized in most person/number combinations as separate objects. However, in one specific feature combination, they are apparently realized together, such that a Vocabulary Item with the exponent *-minī* blocks both the *-r*-inserting passive Vocabulary Item and the Vocabulary Item with *-tis* that realizes second person plural Agr.

Mechanically, Fusion creates one morpheme (with one *Q* position) from two by combining the features of the two morphemes **prior to the application of Vocabulary Insertion.** A rule for fusing second person plural Agr with [+pass] in this way is shown in (5); in terms of locality, it can be assumed that morphemes have to be concatenated in order to be fused:

(5) Fusion Rule for Latin

$$[-1,+2,+pl,Q]\frown[+pass,Q] \longrightarrow [-1,+2,+pl,+pass,Q]$$

The output of the rule (5) is a morpheme whose features are those of the two morphemes on the left side of the rule. The morpheme that results from Fusion has a single *Q* position, in line with the general assumption from chapter 4 that a morpheme can possess only one *Q*.

An important facet of Fusion rules is that they apply prior to Vocabulary Insertion. By combining features from two morphemes, they allow for the application of a highly specified Vocabulary Item that is specified for features from each. With respect to the analysis of (3), the Vocabulary must contain the items in (6):

(6) Vocabulary Items

$$[+2,+pl,+pass] \leftrightarrow \text{-minī}$$
$$[+2,+pl] \leftrightarrow \text{-tis}$$
$$[+pass] \leftrightarrow \text{-r}$$

The most specific item that can apply to the fused node in (6) is the first one, which inserts the *-minī*. This Vocabulary Item blocks both the one with *-tis* and the one with *-r*, so that its special ("portmanteau") exponent appears at the expense of the two expected ones.

A.3 Fission

Noyer (1992) argues for morpheme "splitting" rules whose effects are in some ways the inverse of Fusion. In Halle and Marantz (1993), such rules are referred to as *Fission* rules.

Schematically, the effects of Fission can be illustrated as follows. Suppose that we have a language that shows agreement for person, number, and gender ($\pm P, \pm N, \pm G$) on verbs. Suppose moreover that there are reasons for assuming that these features originate in a single morpheme (i.e. an agreement morpheme), as shown in (7):

(7) Verb-Agr[$\pm P, \pm N, \pm G$]

A Fission rule takes a single morpheme like this Agr and splits it into two morphemes. For instance:

(8) Fission Rule

$$\text{Agr}[\pm P, \pm N, \pm G] \longrightarrow \text{Agr}[\pm P, \pm G], \text{Agr}[\pm N]$$

An important question concerns how Fission rules are ordered with respect to Vocabulary Insertion. Early motivations for Fission (provided by Noyer

(1992) and Halle (1997), as well as Halle and Marantz (1993)) were closely connected with the idea that morphemes first undergo Vocabulary Insertion, with Fission then applying to the "left over" features; i.e., those that are not affected by that first application of Vocabulary Insertion. (For this reason, Fission rules often work together with a theory of feature deletion or discharge on insertion; recall the discussion of chapter 4). However, the phenomena motivating this type of "interleaved" Fission are too complex to illustrate here; interested readers should consult the primary works.

For purposes of illustration, I will draw on an example in which Fission is applied before Vocabulary Insertion, as this suffices to illustrate the basic properties of this type of rule.

A simple case study is provided by the case inflection of the Australian language Djabugay (see Hale (1976a,b) and Patz (1991); for the analysis presented here, see Embick (2010a)). Like many languages of Australia, this language shows a great deal of phonologically conditioned allomorphy in the case affixes that attach to nouns. Of particular interest in this connection are the genitive and dative cases, which are shown in (9). The genitive alternates between -:n (the colon because it lengthens a preceding vowel) and -ŋun before V-final and C-final hosts, respectively. The dative case alternates in a similar way; in fact, it appears to be simply the genitive exponent, followed by an invariant -da:

(9) Djabugay Genitives and Datives

	case	form	env.	example	gloss
a.	Genitive	-:n	V__	guludu-:n	'dove'
		-ŋun	C__	gaɲal-ŋun	'goanna'
b.	Dative	-:nda	V__	yaba-:nda	'elder brother'
		-ŋunda	C__	ganaŋgirray-ŋunda	'younger brother'

As indicated at the end of the last paragraph, the dative forms look as if they are internally complex: -:n-da and -ŋun-da. If the dative is not decomposed in this way, the generalization that the first component of the dative is identical to the genitive would be missed.

The role of Fission in the analysis of these forms can be seen in the context of some other assumptions. Based on other properties of the language (in particular, based on the forms of other cases, which are not shown here), the language appears to have a single case morpheme on nouns: Noun-CASE. As mentioned in chapter 6 above, morphosyntactic theories of case hypothesize that labels for cases like *genitive* and *dative* are shorthand abbreviations for combinations of features of the type shown in (10), which is taken from Halle and Vaux (1998):

(10) Genitive and Dative Decomposed

	genitive	**dative**
obl(ique)	+	+
str(uctural)	+	+
sup(erior)	−	+
free	+	+

It can be seen in (10) that genitive and dative case morphemes have a large amount of shared feature content: they differ only in the value of [±sup].

To derive the facts in (9), there are two scenarios to consider. The first of these involves what we can think of as "genitive syntax", where the case morpheme has the features shown in the Genitive column of (10). The second scenario to consider is "dative syntax": when this is found, the case morpheme possesses the features shown in the dative column of (10).

The second scenario is the primary one of interest from the perspective of Fission. As noted above with reference to (9), the fact to be accounted for in datives is the presence of an (-:n or -ŋun) morpheme—i.e., the exponent realized in the genitive—followed by *-da*. With this in mind, consider the rule of *Dative Fission* in (11), which applies to dative morphemes to create two morphemes that are each subject to Vocabulary Insertion:

(11)   *Dative Fission:* [+obl,+str,+sup,+free] → [+obl,+str] [+sup,+free]

The morphemes in (11) are realized by the Vocabulary Items in (12).

(12)   Vocabulary Items

    [+obl,+str] ↔ -:n   /V__
    [+obl,+str] ↔ -ŋun /C__
    [+sup,+free] ↔ -da

The most specific Vocabulary Items in (12) that can apply to the first morpheme in (11) are the ones that refer to [+obl, +str]. In this first position, then, the exponents *-:n* or *-ŋun* are realized, depending on the phonological context. For the second morpheme that is the output of Fission, with the features [+sup, +free], the last Vocabulary Item inserts -da.

With genitive syntax, the case morpheme starts with the features [+obl, +str, +sup, +free]. The Fission rule does not apply to this morpheme. The most specific Vocabulary Items that can apply to it are also the first two in (12); thus, genitive syntax yields a single morpheme with the exponent -:n or -ŋun, depending on the phonological context.

The analysis of the two cases considered above is summarized in (13-14):

(13) Case 1: Dative

    a. Case morpheme: [+obl,+str,+sup,+free]

    b. Dative Fission (11): [+obl,+str] [+sup,+free]

    c. Vocabulary Insertion at first morpheme: Insertion of -:n or -ŋun depending on phonological context.

    d. Vocabulary Insertion at second morpheme: Insertion -da

(14) Case 2: Genitive

    a. Case morpheme: [+obl,+str,-sup,+free]

    b. Dative Fission (11): N/A

    c. Vocabulary Insertion: Insertion -:n or -ŋun depending on phonological context.

The use of Fission in this analysis is made necessary by the assumption that there is a single case morpheme on nouns prior to Vocabulary Insertion. Fission then provides a principled mechanical account of why it is that syntactic datives are realized in a way that consists of two morphemes. Of course, if there were substantial morphosyntactic evidence from other domains (or other languages) for holding that "cases" of the relevant type are actually derived from two morphemes in the normal case, then Fission would not be required.

Notes

Notes to Chapter 1

1. Strictly speaking, PF is not specifically tailored to the sound system, as is clear from the existence of signed languages. It thus appears that a certain amount of PF computation is sufficiently abstract to be able to convert syntactic representations into representations that can be executed in either the signed or spoken modalities. How similar the properties of "morphology" are in signed and spoken systems—and how PF-related matters might differ in modality-specific ways—is thus a matter of great theoretical interest. In this work, I will speak of "sound" and "sound/meaning connections", but with the understanding that the framework developed here can be extended to signed languages as a general theory of form/meaning connections.
2. The *lexical vocabulary* and *open class* vocabulary of a language might overlap considerably, but there are some cases in which these two notions do not coincide. For example, *light verbs* like *be* and *go* could be considered to be part of the lexical vocabulary, since a "verb" is a traditional lexical category. At the same time, these elements are presumably not part of the open class vocabulary; and they are certainly not Roots in the theory advanced here; instead, they are bundles of synsem features (i.e., they are functional morphemes). See chapter 2 for discussion of the latter point.
3. Some early versions of the theory explored the idea that phonological material is introduced in PF for all morphemes (references below). A related point is that although it is assumed here that Roots may be specified underlyingly for phonological features, whether or not these features are visible in the syntax is an open question. Empirically, what is at issue is whether or not there are any (narrow) syntactic processes that refer to phonological features; a working hypothesis that has been employed in the current approach is that there are not. At the same time there is some evidence that morphological diacritic features of Roots might be visible to processes like head-movement (cf. Embick 2000). For different aspects of this discussion see Marantz (1995) and Embick (1997, 1998), which explore the idea that Roots are always inserted late (*Universal Late Insertion*).

4. This sense of *spell out* is distinct from the use of this term in syntactic theory, where it refers to the process that sends syntactic representations to the interfaces.
5. The claim that word formation precedes syntax produces some predictions about the ordering of lexical and syntactic processes, of a type that are explored in works like Wasow (1977) and Bresnan (1982). These predictions continue to be discussed in several domains; for example, in the analysis of the differences between so-called adjectival and verbal passives, which plays an important role in Wasow's paper. See Embick (2004) for a non-lexicalist point of view.
6. A useful overview of many of these themes can be found in Carstairs-McCarthy (1992), chapter 2. Carstairs-McCarthy traces the development of lexicalist theories from responses that arose to early work in morphology by Halle (1973), which posits three distinct lists in the grammar. This move is reacted to in various ways by lexicalist theories like Jackendoff (1975), Aronoff (1976), Lieber (1980), and di Sciullo and Williams (1987).
7. See, for example, Pinker and Prince (1988), and many subsequent theories in this vein, particularly those on the "words and rules" side (cf. Pinker and Ullman (2002)) of the so-called past-tense debate (cf. Marslen-Wilson and Tyler (1998)).
8. In a theory that allows Vocabulary Insertion for Roots, it might be possible (depending on further assumptions about contextual allomorphy) to hold that *sang* is part of a Vocabulary Item that applies to a Root $\sqrt{\text{SING}}$ in the context of the past tense morpheme. On this approach, *sing* and *sang* are treated as instances of suppletive allomorphy, along the lines of what is seen in *go/went*. Although an analysis of this type might be necessary for some alternations shown by Roots (i.e., if there is true Root suppletion), it should be approached carefully. Generalizing suppletion ignores the shared phonological properties of *sing* and *sang*. More generally, suppletion should probably be treated as a sort of "last resort" analytically; see Embick and Halle (2005) and Embick (2010b) for some pertinent discussion.
9. In fact, although underspecified Vocabulary Items like those in (17) are required for the analysis of Latin American Spanish, the connection between second and third plural in Spanish is even deeper than the analysis in the text indicates; see in particular section 6.3.3 in chapter 6.
10. Strictly speaking, theories that add phonological representations to morphemes in this way this are only one type of realizational theory. There are

other realizational theories that have rules for realizing synsem features, but that do not employ morphemes (e.g. Anderson 1992).

Notes to Chapter 2

1. Different types of geometries, motivated by analogy with phonological feature representation, have been explored in works like Bonet (1991) and Harley and Ritter (2002), among others. Such representations are intended to account for particular types of "natural class" behavior, as well as patterns of markedness relations among features. While synsem feature geometries have been employed in a fair amount of morphological work, their exact status in the grammar is a matter of debate; see e.g. Harbour (2010) for a critical overview.
2. The idea that categories are defined featurally is of great importance in syntactic theory. See Chomsky (1970) and much subsequent work.
3. For some different applications of this idea, see, for example, Bobaljik and Thráinsson (1998) and Pylkkänen (2002) and references cited there.

    Above (4) I qualified the statement that Mandarin and English differ in terms of packaging [±1] and [±pl] together. This is because a more detailed semantic analysis might reveal that their number features are in fact different, so that e.g. Mandarin uses a [+collective] feature for "number", whereas English does not.
4. For the features involved in dual number, see Noyer (1997, 1998) and Harbour (2008). There appear to be different ways in which dual is encoded featurally cross-linguistically. Consider (i), from the language Lahu (Tibeto-Burman; Matisoff (2003)):

   (i) Lahu Pronouns

person	singular	dual	plural
1	ŋà	ŋà-hɨ́-mà	ŋà-hɨ
2	ŋɔ̀	ŋɔ̀-hɨ́-mà	ŋɔ̀-hɨ
3	yô	yô-hɨ́-mà	yô-hɨ

   This language appears to "add" something to the plural to derive the dual. In addition to its relevance for questions about bundling, this kind of pattern raises the question of how many ways there are of deriving "dual" meanings cross-linguistically.
5. In a traditional way of referring to these ways of expressing distinctions,

the one-word Spanish type is called *synthetic*, while the two-word English type is called *analytic*.
6. With respect to the UFI, it is safe to say that the features of category-defining heads are understudied relative to the features of other domains (e.g., tense, person/number, etc.) mentioned in section 2.2. Although most theories seem to assume that a number of different features are active in this domain, no comprehensive proposals have emerged in the literature.
7. For additional discussion of this matter see the notion of *Pruning* that is discussed in chapter 7.
8. In addition to how polysemy arises from Root-categorizer interactions, there is a further question of what to do when a Root is unacceptable in a particular grammatical category; see section 2.3.4.
9. For discussion of Roots and templates see Arad (2005) subsequent work. There is also an extensive experimental literature (psycho- and neurolinguistic) examining Root-based representation; see e.g. Prunet et al. (2000) for representative discussion.
10. While the text and the examples employed above speak of diacritic features as properties of Roots, such specification is not limited to Roots. For example, the adjectival or participial head Asp[pres] in Latin that is realized as -*nt* inflects as an adjective of the third declension; this information has to be associated with this functional morpheme (or perhaps its exponent) diacritically.

Notes to Chapter 3

1. For some discussion of this idea see Chomsky (1995:334 ff.), where it is framed with reference to the idea that linear order appears to have no effects in narrow syntax or LF.
2. As a notational convention, the label of non-terminal nodes in complex heads will often be left out of tree structures in other parts of this book.
3. For the idea that Agreement morphemes are not syntactic objects, see Iatridou (1990) and Chomsky (1995).
4. Regarding the option without head movement, Koopman (2005) and others have argued that phrasal movement (augmented perhaps with a kind of phonological "leaning" of morphemes) is responsible for the creation of objects of morphological interest. Theories of this type need to be able to give explicit accounts of the relationships between syntactic structures and domains of phonological interaction (see section 3.5 below). But as long

as the locus of Vocabulary Insertion is the morpheme, the assumption that there is no head movement is compatible with the central claims of the present work.
5. That is to say, the standard theories referred to in the text deny the so-called *excorporation* of subconstituents of complex heads.
6. Strictly speaking, these orders are impossible as the *initial* linearization of (21). They could conceivably be found on the surface as the result of later operations that re-order morphemes in restricted ways (the *Local Dislocation* operation in particular); see the references in section 3.2.3 for illustration. Note also that X and Y could be linearized in different directions—X-Root-Y or Y-Root-X—in a way that does not involve tangled branches.
7. The fact that only No Tangling is assumed here is highlighted because a number of research programs in syntactic theory have developed additional conditions on linearization that could be relevant to morphological concerns. For instance, one important aspect of Kayne's (1994) Linear Correspondence Axiom (LCA) is that the linearization procedure is not subject to cross-linguistic variation, so that hierarchical structures determine a fixed order universally. This view thus contrasts with the idea that there is a *Head Parameter* (see Chomsky and Lasnik (1993) and references cited there), by which individual languages differ in terms of how they linearize head/complement and other syntactic relations.
8. By way of contrast, in an approach in which complex words are derived in a component that is not the syntax (e.g., in the lexicon, in lexicalist approaches to morphology), systematic relations between phrasal syntax and affix order can only be stipulated by independent mechanisms that must enforce systematic relations between word-internal structure and the clauses in which those words appear (see e.g. Halle and Marantz 1993 in response to the "checking" theory of Chomsky 1993).
9. A complicating factor in the analysis of comparatives is the complex phrasal syntax that they appear in. This raises a further question that (31) abstracts away from, concerning how the DEG morpheme comes to be affixed onto adjectives in the first place. See the discussion in Embick (2007a).
10. There are other syntactic factors that can affect phonological behavior. A case in point concerns the cyclic domains (phases) of phase theory, which also appear to constrain morphological and phonological interactions. Importantly, cyclic domains in phase theory do not correspond to the informal notion of word either, as a single cycle domain sometimes contains several words in the informal sense, while in other cases a single word contains

several cyclic domains; see Marantz (2007) and Embick (2010a) for pertinent discussion. —)
11. Possible exceptions to the M-Word/phonological word correspondence are not easy to find; Poser (1990) considers a potentially relevant example.

Notes to Chapter 4

1. In some works, Vocabulary Items are described as rules. The emphasis in the present formulation goes against this view in holding that they are objects in memory. As objects in memory, Vocabulary Items can be associated with e.g. frequency information (or other psycholinguistically significant properties), as is characteristic of stored objects more generally. See e.g. Embick and Marantz (2005) and Stockall and Marantz (2006) for some preliminary discussion.
2. The assumption that *all* functional morphemes possess a Q as their initial phonological representation could be modified. For example, in Halle's approach, only certain morphemes have Q as their phonological representation. Others (those that show no allomorphy, i.e., with only one phonological realization in a language) are not subject to the equivalent of Vocabulary Insertion. Empirically speaking, Halle's more restricted view of the scope of Vocabulary Insertion makes different predictions from a theory with Q positions for every functional morpheme (for example, with respect to certain types of phonologically conditioned allomorphy). However, a detailed study of these different predictions has not yet been undertaken.
    On the question of which morphemes possess a Q, one possible extension would be to the Root vocabulary. In particular, if it is determined that some Late Insertion for Roots is required, this can be implemented by treating (certain) Roots as possessing a Q variable, rather than a phonological underlying representation.
3. The non-deletion view says only that Vocabulary Insertion does not delete features. This does not mean that synsem features are present throughout the entire PF derivation. According to standard assumptions, these features must be eliminated at some point between the output of the syntax and the end stages of PF. The precise point of deletion is a matter of some discussion, since it relates to questions about "morpheme-specific" phonological processes that have occupied many phonological theories (see e.g. Kiparsky (1996)).
4. It can be assumed that in the case of e.g. *sing/sang*, the -$\emptyset$ exponent of

T[+past] appears, and a morphophonological rule triggered by T[+past] changes the stem form of this verb. For this second (morphophonological) part of this analysis, see the discussion of chapter 7.
5. Note that this use of the term must be kept distinct from the sense of *cyclic* that refers to the syntactic theory of phases.
6. The forms in (30) also show alternations in vowel length; these are phonological as well.
7. This kind of deletion is sometimes called *radical impoverishment*, or *obliteration* (see e.g. Arregi and Nevins (2007)); see also the *Pruning* rules of chapter 7.
8. One consequence of this analysis of -*m* when the rest of the Latin verbal system is considered is that subjunctive forms behave as if they were [+past], in that they show -*m*. Connections between past tense and irrealis along these lines have been motivated semantically; see e.g. Iatridou (2000) for some discussion.
9. One final note concerning the morphemes that Vocabulary Insertion applies to: the main focus of this and the following chapters is on how functional morphemes receive their phonological form. The morphemes that are examined here and below are all *basic*, in the sense that they are not e.g. composed out of other morphemes. Some work in Distributed Morphology has posited rules of *Fusion*, which create one morpheme out of two; and *Fission*, which split off new morphemes to create two morphemes from a single basic one. A basic introduction to these rules is presented in the Appendix.

Notes to Chapter 5

1. Of course, not all realizational theories share all of the assumptions that are made in this work. In particular, many realizational approaches follow Anderson (1992) in denying the existence of morphemes. See chapter 7 for some discussion of this point.
2. The Spanish agreement example used for illustration in chapter 1 and section 1 of this chapter is examined in further detail in chapter 6.
3. The glosses show underlying phonological representations, which are in some cases altered in the surface forms by phonological rules. I focus in this example only on the first and second person forms, as third person morphemes have a slightly different status in the system (they involve deictic and other semantic distinctions). Here and below, ADV = "adverb";

OBJ = "object"; SUBJ = "subject"; STAT = "stative"; ASP = "aspect"; and CAUS = "causative".

4. Feature overlap of the type appealed to above is not the only scenario in which underspecified Vocabulary Items are motivated. There is also a role for such items in systems where a particular exponent has a default or elsewhere realization; see chapter 6.

5. For more detailed comparison of Late Insertion versus traditional morphemes, see Halle and Marantz (1993) and Noyer (1998).

6. Many of these consequences implicate how Vocabulary Items are ordered with respect to one another. For instance, in some systems of complex person, number, and gender realization, it has been proposed that there are individual Vocabulary Items realizing individual features of these types. Sometimes, it appears to be the case that a Vocabulary Item referring only to e.g. number must be ordered with respect to one referring only to e.g. gender. In cases of this type, it is not possible to appeal to the principle that the number of features referred to in a Vocabulary Item determines the winner of a competition. Noyer (1992) introduces the idea that feature type resolves this kind of competition, with person above number above gender features.

7. The subject and object morphemes appear in different zones in the verbal complex, with these zones showing distinct phonological behaviors (Golla 1970). The presence of /i/ in the object agreement exponent could perhaps be linked to these factors.

8. See also Noyer (1998) for some pertinent discussion of "vague" morphemes.

9. Or, at the very least, the syncretizing morphemes are of the same type and have the same syntactic distribution; see the discussion of *default* Vocabulary Items in the next chapter.

10. See Birtalan (2003) for the morphophonological properties of these exponents. According to Birtalan, the third person possessor shows dialect variation between *-i* and *-n*; only the former is shown in the text.

11. The third person singular subject pronoun has a *-Ø* allomorph whose distribution is not clear; it is ignored in this analysis.

12. The idea that natural classes are important for stating generalizations is one that is familiar from phonological theory. There, for instance, it is expected that while e.g. [+velar] consonants form a natural class, the same is not true of non-velars, so that a rule making reference to [-velar] would be suspect.

13. For additional discussion, see e.g. Halle 1997, which uses binary features that allow for a direct way of encoding the notion of "participant".

14. Other facts from the language may provide some guidelines. For example, Beeler (1976:255) notes that -*wun* also appears as a nominal plural with certain elements (e.g. *he-ẃun* 'these', *ho-ẃun* 'those', *čiči-ẃun* 'children'), suggesting that it is a general purpose plural; this fits with (31), which treats -*wun* as the default non-singular.
15. On the theme of natural classes and the [+part] feature, it should be noted that both of the analyses in the text make use of the feature [-sg]. There might be better ways of defining a natural class of "non-singulars", but these require a more detailed look at number systems. See Noyer (1992) and Harbour (2008) for some relevant discussion.
16. While the class that the Root belongs to determines which set of possessive endings appear, it does not determine how the theme morpheme surfaces. Rather, the realization of the morpheme depends on the identity of the Root; thus, the same theme exponent can be found in different classes:

(i) More Nouns (cited in 1s possessor form; theme boldfaced)

   a. Class 1: tita-**n**-ai 'father'; ei-**l**-i 'eye'; bol-**s**-i 'knee'; nan-**u**-i 'garden'...

   b. Class 2: aŋ-**l**-e 'firewood'; gi-**ŋ**-e; kaua-**k**-e 'dog'; didu-**ak**-e 'skirt'...

   c. Class 3: pok-**k**-a 'chest'; boŋ-**g**-a 'mouth'...

   d. Class 4: aba-**i**-at 'pork'; beta-**m**-at 'sore'; to-**moi**-at 'smell'...

So, for example, *ei* 'eye' and *aŋ* 'firewood' both have the -*l* themes, but the former takes class 1 possessor inflection, and the latter class 2; *kaua* 'dog' and *pom* 'chest' both show -*k* themes, but the former is in class 2 while the latter is in class 3. Thurston speculates (1982:37) that there are twenty categories defined by theme realization combined with class behavior, but makes no claims that his description is exhaustive (1982:87). Nouns also have a grammatical gender, which does not relate in any predictable way to theme class or possessive inflection class (1982:46). A further complication is that verbs show object agreement using the sets of possessive suffixes illustrated in the text. Verbs, like nouns, show both unpredictable theme elements and condition sets of agreement affixes in an unpredictable way. As Thurston notes (1982:43) "[f]or the outsider, the morphology of these suffixes gives a nightmarish quality equally to nouns and verbs in Anêm."

17. The relationship between Roots, themes, and possessor allomorphy is complicated. In part this is motivated by the way in which the theme component relates to the meaning of the Root. It appears to be the case that—at least for some Roots—the theme functions as a sort of classifier, such that the same Root may appear with different themes, each associated with a different interpretation; e.g. *aba-k-e* is 'my pig', whereas *aba-i-at* is 'my pork'. Possessor class changes with the change in theme and interpretation as well, in a way that could shed light on the nature of features like [I], [II], etc.

Notes to Chapter 6

1. See Halle and Marantz for why two *-e* Vocabulary Items are posited for the locative and the vocative.
2. Following Halle and Marantz, (16) simply enumerates the noun class features contextually in these rules. Alternatives might involve decomposing class features like 1, 2, etc. into primitive features, which are then referred to in Impoverishment rules (Alexiadou and Müller (2008) treats inflectional class features in this way).
3. The five nouns in (20) instantiate the five declensions, but represent a subset of the full set of noun types that are found in the language. For the purposes of this illustration I am putting to the side further complications that are introduced when nominal gender and some other morphophonological factors are taken into account.
4. The encoding of Tense and Aspect features could be changed in various ways (e.g. by using binary [±perf]); the main points of this example are not affected by these different options.
5. In (32), the context for the *-v* Vocabulary Item is given as either [+1] or [+2]. With more developed assumptions about the representation of person features (e.g., using a feature like [+participant] for [+1] and [+2] categories; recall section 5.5.3 in chapter 5), the disjunctive contextual condition on the *-v* allomorph could be removed and replaced by reference to a single shared feature.
6. I have not included zero realizations. The past III is described as showing a portmanteaux ("fused") realization of tense and agreement. Even though the overt forms are sometimes quite similar to overt agreement morphemes elsewhere I have not attempted a more detailed segmentation.

Notes to Chapter 7

1. This analysis puts to the side some complications with the *-ō* and *-m* realizations of first person singular (in particular, why the latter appears with both past tenses and subjunctives). See Footnote 7 of chapter 4.
2. Of course, later in the derivation, in the phonology, the phonological exponent of X could be affected phonologically (or morphophonologically) by the phonological exponent of Y, when phonological rules apply. This would be an alternation in the position of X induced by Y, but it would not involve Vocabulary Insertion per se (i.e., it would not be suppletive contextual allomorphy). Some of the apparent cases of allomorphy looking "outwards" to the phonology discussed in Carstairs (1987), for example, appear to be caused by morphophonological rules operating in the manner just described.
3. Beyond the issue of whether competition is found with word/word interactions, another important line of discussion in the field asks whether there are competitions for grammaticality among larger objects (e.g., words versus phrases, phrases versus phrases, etc.) as well. See, for example, Poser (1992), Andrews (1990), Hankamer and Mikkelsen (2005), Kiparsky (2005), Embick (2007a, 2008), and, for a general discussion, Embick and Marantz (2008). Another important question concerns how competition in phonological theory relates to the themes that are examined in this section; see the introductory discussion of Embick (2010a) for some comments.
4. Although there is an emphatic sense of *-osity* that appears to have entered English—so that instances of *gloriosity* can be found on the web—this is a marginal type of derivation.
5. The noun *solemnness* also exists in addition to *solemnity*. In this word, the *n* head realized as *-ness* is attached outside of an *a* head: [[√SOLEMN *a*] *n*]. This outer *n* head cannot see the Root due to these morphemes being in different phase cycles, as discussed earlier in this chapter. Thus, it is realized as *-ness*, not *-ity*.
6. For example, it follows from the theory presented above that the adjective *curious* is (on the simplest analysis) the realization of [√CURIOUS *a*], where the *a* has the exponent *-Ø*, not *-ous*.
7. Although the structure in (60a) shows the *v* head (and a *-Ø* exponent for it), recall from above that this head is Pruned, so that T[+past] and the Root √SING are concatenated when Vocabulary Insertion applies to T[+past].
8. Unless, for example, blocking relations between morphological changes

were stipulated on a case by case basis; this is an unacceptable solution, however, as will be seen shortly in considering (64).

9. For some important prior discussions of these themes see Lieber (1987), which looks at different ways of treating morphological realization autosegmentally; and Carstairs (1987), which argues that stem changing processes and affixes behave differently with respect to certain types of paradigmatic patterns.

    From the point of view of Lexical Phonology, Kiparsky (1996) discusses criteria by which allomorphy and morphophonology might be distinguished from one another. Noyer (1997) addresses this issue as well, in a framework like the one adopted here. For another view of how the morphophonology versus allomorphy issue can be resolved in terms of a different set of assumptions about possible exponents, see Bendjaballah (2003), and the proposals in Lowenstamm (2008), Lampitelli (2010), and related work. Finally, Embick (2010b) examines some morphophonological themes from the perspective of the theory of allomorphy outlined earlier in this chapter.

Bibliography

Adger, D., S. Béjar, and D. Harbour (2003) "Directionality of Allomorphy: A Reply to Carstairs-McCarthy," *Transactions of the Philological Society* 101:1, 109–115.

Akinlabi, A. (1996) "Featural Affixation," *Journal of Linguistics* 32:2, 239–289.

Akinlabi, A. (2011) "Featural Affixes," in M. van Oostendorp, C. J. Ewen, and E. V. Hume, eds., *The Blackwell Companion to Phonology*, John Wiley and Sons, 1945–1971.

Alexiadou, A., L. Haegeman, and M. Stavrou (2007) *Noun phrase in the generative perspective*, Mouton de Gruyter.

Alexiadou, A., and G. Müller (2008) "Class features as probes," in A. Bachrach and A. Nevins, eds., *Inflectional Identity*, Oxford University Press, Oxford and New York, 101–147.

Anderson, S. (1992) *Amorphous Morphology*, Cambridge University Press, Cambridge.

Andrews, A. (1990) "Unification and Morphological Blocking," *Natural Language and Linguistic Theory* 8, 507–57.

Arad, M. (2005) *Roots and Patterns: Hebrew Morphosyntax*, Springer, Dordrecht.

Aronoff, M. (1976) *Word Formation in Generative Grammar*, MIT Press, Cambridge, MA.

Arregi, K. (1999) "How the Spanish Verb Works," ms., MIT.

Arregi, K., and A. Nevins (2007) "Obliteration vs. Impoverishment in the Basque g-/z- constraint," in T. Scheffler, J. Tauberer, A. Eilam, and L. Mayol, eds., *Proceedings of the Penn Linguistics Colloquium 30*, 1–14.

Baker, M. (1985) "The Mirror Principle and Morphosyntactic Explanation," *Linguistic Inquiry* 16, 373–416.

Baker, M. (1988) *Incorporation: A Theory of Grammatical Function Changing*, University of Chicago Press, Chicago.

Beard, R. (1966) *The Affixation of Adjectives in Contemporary Literary Serbo-Croatian*, Doctoral dissertation, University of Michigan.

Beard, R. (1995) *Lexeme-morpheme Based Morphology: A General Theory of Inflection and Word Formation*, State University of New York Press, Albany.

Beeler, M. S. (1976) "Barbareño Chumash Grammar: A Farrago," in M. Langdon and S. Silver, eds., *Hokan Studies*, Mouton, The Hague/Paris, 251–269.

Bendjaballah, S. (2003) "The internal structure of the determiner in Beja," in J. Lecarme, ed., *Research in Afroasiatic Grammar II. Selected Papers from the Fifth Conference on Afroasiatic Languages, Paris, 2000*, John Benjamins, Amsterdam/Philadelphia, 35–52.

Beretta, A., R. Fiorentino, and D. Poeppel (2005) "The effects of homonymy and polysemy on lexical access: An MEG study," *Cognitive Brain Research* 24:1, 57–65.

Birtalan, Á. (2003) "Oirat," in J. Janhunen, ed., *The Mongolic Languages*, Routledge, London and New York, 210–228.

Bloomfield, L. (1933) *Language*, George Allen and Unwin Ltd, London.

Bobaljik, J. (2000) "The Ins and Outs of Contextual Allomorphy," in *University of Maryland Working Papers in Linguistics* 10, 35–71.

Bobaljik, J. (2002) "Syncretism without Paradigms: Remarks on Williams 1981, 1987," *Yearbook of Morphology 2001* 53–85.

Bobaljik, J., and H. Thráinsson (1998) "Two heads aren't always better than one," *Syntax* 1, 37–71.

Bonet, E. (1991) *Morphology After Syntax: Pronominal Clitics in Romance*, Doctoral dissertation, MIT.

Bonet, E. (1995) "Feature Structure of Romance Clitics," *Natural Language and Linguistic Theory* 13, 607–47.

Bonet, E., M.-R. Lloret, and J. Mascaró (2007) "Allomorph selection and lexical preference: Two case studies," *Lingua* 117, 903–927.

Booij, G., and J. Rubach (1987) "Postcyclic versus Postlexical Rules in Lexical Phonology," *Linguistic Inquiry* 18:1, 1–44.

Borer, H. (2003) "Exo-skeletal vs. endo-skeletal explanations: Syntactic projections and the lexicon," in *The Nature of Explanation in Linguistic Theory*, CSLI Publications, Stanford, CA, 31–67.

Borer, H. (2005) *Structuring Sense*, Oxford University Press, Oxford.

Bresnan, J. (1982) "The Passive in Lexical Theory," in J. Bresnan, ed., *The Mental Representation of Grammatical Relations*, MIT Press, Cambridge, MA.

Calabrese, A. (2008) "On absolute and contextual syncretism: Remarks on the structure of case paradigms and how to derive them," in A. Bachrach and A. Nevins, eds., *Inflectional Identity*, Oxford University Press, Oxford, 156–205.

Cameron-Faulker, T., and A. Carstairs-McCarthy (2000) "Stem alternants as morphological signata: Evidence from blur avoidance in Polish nouns," *Natural Language and Linguistic Theory* 18, 813–35.

Carstairs, A. (1987) *Allomorphy in Inflexion*, Croom Helm, London.

Carstairs, A. (1988) "Some implications of phonologically conditioned suppletion," in G. Booij and J. van Marle, eds., *Yearbook of Morphology 1988*, Foris, Dordrecht, 67–94.

Carstairs, A. (1990) "Phonologically Conditioned Suppletion," in W. Dressler, H. Luschutzky, O. Pfeiffer, and J. Rennison, eds., *Selected Papers from the Third International Morphology Meeting*, Mouton de Gruyter, Berlin, 17–24.

Carstairs-McCarthy, A. (1992) *Current Morphology*, Routledge, London.

Carstairs-McCarthy, A. (2001) "Grammatically conditioned allomorphy, paradigmatic structure, and the ancestry constraint," *Transactions of the Philological Society* 99:2, 223–245.

Carstairs-McCarthy, A. (2003) "Directionality and Locality in Allomorphy: A Response to Adger, Béjar, and Harbour," *Transactions of the Philological Society* 101:1, 117–124.

Chomsky, N. (1957) *Syntactic Structures*, Mouton, The Hague.

Chomsky, N. (1965) *Aspects of the Theory of Syntax*, MIT Press.

Chomsky, N. (1970) "Remarks on Nominalization," in R. Jacobs and P. Rosenbaum, eds., *Readings in English Transformational Grammar*, Georgetown University Press, Washington D.C., 184–221.

Chomsky, N. (1986) *Barriers*, MIT Press, Cambridge, MA.

Chomsky, N. (1993) "A Minimalist Program for Linguistic Theory," in K. Hale and S. Keyser, eds., *The View from Building 20: Essays in Linguistics in Honor of Sylvain Bromberger*, MIT Press, Cambridge, MA.

Chomsky, N. (1995) *The Minimalist Program*, MIT Press, Cambridge, MA.

Chomsky, N. (2000) "Minimalist Inquiries: The Framework," in R. Martin, D. Michaels, and J. Uriagereka, eds., *Step by Step: Essays on Minimalist Syntax in Honor of Howard Lasnik*, MIT Press, 89–156.

Chomsky, N. (2001) "Derivation by Phase," in M. Kenstowicz, ed., *Ken Hale: A Life in Language*, MIT Press, Cambridge, MA, 1–52.

Chomsky, N. (2007) "Approaching UG from Below," in U. Sauerland and H.-M. Gaertner, eds., *Interfaces + Recursion = Language?*, Mouton de Gruyter, Berlin and New York, 1–30.

Chomsky, N., and M. Halle (1968) *The Sound Pattern of English*, Harper and Row, New York.

Chomsky, N., and H. Lasnik (1993) "Principles and parameters theory," in J. Jacobs, A. von Stechow, W. Sternefeld, and T. Vennemann, eds., *Handbook of Syntax*, Walter de Gruyter, Berlin.

Clements, G. (1985) "The Geometry of Phonological Features," *Phonology* 2, 223–250.

Corbett, G. G. (2000) *Number*, Cambridge University Press, Cambridge.

Corne, C. (1977) *Seychelles Creole Grammar*, TBL Verlag Gunter Narr, Tübingen.

di Sciullo, A., and E. Williams (1987) *On the Definition of Word*, MIT Press, Cambridge, MA.

Ekdahl, M., and J. E. Grimes (1964) "Terena Verb Inflection," *International Journal of American Linguistics* 30:3, 261–268.

Embick, D. (1995) "'Mobile Inflections' in Polish," In J.N. Beckman et al. eds. *Proceedings of NELS 25:2*, 127-142.

Embick, D. (1997) *Voice and the Interfaces of Syntax*, Doctoral dissertation, University of Pennsylvania.

Embick, D. (1998) "Voice Systems and the Syntax/Morphology Interface," in H. Harley, ed., *MITWPL 32: Papers from the UPenn/MIT Roundtable on Argument Structure and Aspect*, MITWPL, 41–72.

Embick, D. (2000) "Features, Syntax and Categories in the Latin Perfect," *Linguistic Inquiry* 31:2, 185–230.

Embick, D. (2003) "Locality, Listedness, and Morphological Identity," *Studia Linguistica* 57:3, 143–169.

Embick, D. (2004) "On the Structure of Resultative Participles in English," *Linguistic Inquiry* 35:3, 355–92.

Embick, D. (2007a) "*Blocking Effects* and Analytic/Synthetic Alternations," *Natural Language and Linguistic Theory* 25:1, 1–37.

Embick, D. (2007b) "Linearization and Local Dislocation: Derivational mechanics and interactions," *Linguistic Analysis* 33:3-4, 303–336.

Embick, D. (2008) "Variation and morphosyntactic theory: Competition fractionated," *Language and Linguistics Compass* 2:1, 59–78.

Embick, D. (2010a) *Localism versus Globalism in Morphology and Phonology*, MIT Press, Cambridge, MA.

Embick, D. (2010b) "Stem alternations and stem distributions," ms., University of Pennsylvania; http://www.ling.upenn.edu/~embick/stem-ms-10.pdf.

Embick, D., and M. Halle (2005) "On the status of *stems* in morphological theory," in T. Geerts and H. Jacobs, eds., *Proceedings of Going Romance 2003*, John Benjamins, Amsterdam/Philadelphia, 59–88.

Embick, D., and A. Marantz (2005) "Cognitive Neuroscience and the English Past Tense: Comments on the Paper by Ullman et al." *Brain and Language* 93.

Embick, D., and A. Marantz (2008) "Architecture and Blocking," *Linguistic Inquiry* 39:1, 1–53.

Embick, D., and R. Noyer (2001) "Movement Operations after Syntax," *Linguistic Inquiry* 32:4, 555–595.

Embick, D., and R. Noyer (2007) "Distributed Morphology and the syntax/morphology interface," in G. Ramchand and C. Reiss, eds., *Oxford Handbook of Linguistic Interfaces*, Oxford University Press, 289–324.

Golla, V. (1970) *Hupa Grammar*, Doctoral dissertation, University of California at Berkeley.

Halle, M. (1973) "Prolegomena to a Theory of Word Formation," *Linguistic Inquiry* 3–16.

Halle, M. (1990) "An Approach to Morphology," in *Proceedings of NELS 20*, GLSA, 150–184.

Halle, M. (1997) "Distributed Morphology: Impoverishment and Fission," *MIT Working Papers in Linguistics* 30, 425–449.

Halle, M. (2002) *From Memory to Speech and Back: Papers on Phonetics and Phonology 1954-2002*, Mouton de Gruyter.

Halle, M., and A. Marantz (1993) "Distributed Morphology and the Pieces of Inflection," in K. Hale and S. Keyser, eds., *The View from Building 20: Essays in Linguistics in Honor of Sylvain Bromberger*, MIT Press, Cambridge, MA, 111–176.

Halle, M., and A. Marantz (1994) "Some Key Features of Distributed Morphology," in A. Carnie, H. Harley, and T. Bures, eds., *Papers on Phonology and Morphology*, MITWPL 21, Cambridge, MA, 275–288.

Halle, M., and A. Marantz (2008) "Clarifying ''Blur'': Paradigms, defaults, and inflectional classes," in A. Bachrach and A. Nevins, eds., *Inflectional Identity*, Oxford University Press, Oxford and New York, 55–72.

Halle, M., and K. P. Mohanan (1985) "Segmental Phonology of Modern English," *Linguistic Inquiry* 16, 57–116.

Halle, M., and B. Vaux (1998) "Theoretical Aspects of Indo-European Nominal Morphology: The Nominal Declensions of Latin and Armenian," in *Mír Curad: Studies in Honor of Calvert Watkins*, Innsbruck.

Halle, M., and J.-R. Vergnaud (1987) *An Essay on Stress*, MIT Press, Cambridge, MA.

Halpern, A. (1992) *Topics in the Placement and Morphology of Clitics*, Doctoral dissertation, Stanford University.

Hankamer, J., and L. Mikkelsen (2005) "When Movement Must be Blocked: A Response to Embick and Noyer," *Linguistic Inquiry* 36:1, 85–125.

Harbour, D. (2008) *Morphosemantic number: From Kiowa noun classes to UG number features*, Springer, Dordrecht.

Harbour, D. (2010) "Descriptive and explanatory markedness," *Morphology*.

Harley, H., and E. Ritter (2002) "Person and number in pronouns: A feature-geometric analysis," *Language* 78:3, 482–526.

Harris, J. W. (1991) "The exponence of Gender in Spanish," *Linguistic Inquiry* 22:1, 27–62.

Harris, J. W. (1998) "Spanish imperatives: syntax meets morphology," *Journal of Linguistics* 34, 27–52.

Hayes, B. (1990) "Precompiled Phrasal Phonology," in S. Inkelas and D. Zec, eds., *The Syntax-Phonology Connection*, University of Chicago Press, Chicago, 85–108.

Hyman, L. (2003) "Suffix ordering in Bantu: A morphocentric approach," *Yearbook of Morphology 2002* 245–281.

Hyman, L., and S. Mchombo (1992) "Morphotactic constraints in the Chichewa verb stem," in L. Buszard-Welcher, L. Wee, and W. Weigel, eds., *Proceedings of the Eighteenth Annual Meeting of the Berkeley Linguistics Society*, volume 2, Berkeley, University of California, Berkeley Linguistics Society, 350–364.

Iatridou, S. (1990) "About Agr(P)," *Linguistic Inquiry* 21:4, 551–577.

Iatridou, S. (2000) "The Grammatical Ingredients of Counterfactuality," *Linguistic Inquiry* 31:2, 231–270.

Jackendoff, R. (1975) "Redundancy Rules and the Lexicon," *Language* 51:3, 639–671.

Jakobson, R. (1936) "Beitrag zur Allgemeinen Kasuslehre," in E. Hamp, F. Householder, and R. Austerlitz, eds., *Readings in Linguistics II*, University of Chicago Press, 51–95.

Jakobson, R., and M. Halle (1956) *Fundamentals of Language*, Mouton, The Hague.

Kaye, A. S. (2007) "Arabic Morphology," in *Morphologies of Africa and Asia*, volume 1, Eisenbrauns, Winona Lake, Indiana, 211–248.

Kayne, R. (1994) *The Antisymmetry of Syntax*, MIT Press, Cambridge, MA.

Kiparsky, P. (1982) "Lexical Morphology and Phonology," in Linguistic Society of Korea, ed., *Linguistics in the Morning Calm: Selected Essays from SICOL-1981*, Hanshin, Seoul.

Kiparsky, P. (1996) "Allomorphy or Morphophonology?" in R. Singh and R. Desrochers, eds., *Trubetzkoy's Orphan*, John Benjamins, Amsterdam/Philadelphia, 13–31.

Kiparsky, P. (2005) "Blocking and periphrasis in inflectional paradigms," *Yearbook of Morphology 2004* 113–135.

Klein, T. B. (2003) "Syllable structure and lexical markedness in creole morphophonology: Determiner allomorphy in Haitian and elsewhere," in I. Plag, ed., *The Phonology and Morphology of Creole Languages*, Niemeyer, Tübingen, 209–228.

Koopman, H. (1984) *The syntax of verbs*, Foris, Dordrecht.

Koopman, H. (2005) "Korean (and Japanese) morphology from a syntactic perspective," *Linguistic Inquiry* 36:4, 601–633.

Kornfilt, J. (1997) *Turkish*, Routledge, London and New York.

Kramer, R. (2009) *Definite Markers, Phi-Features, and Agreement: A Morphosyntactic Investigation of the Amharic DP*, Doctoral dissertation, University of California, Santa Cruz.

Lampitelli, N. (2010) "Nounness, gender, class and syntactic structures in Italian nouns," in R. Bok-Bennema, B. Kampers-Manhe, and B. Hollebrandse, eds., *Romance Languages and Linguistic Theory 2008. Selected papers from Going Romance, Groningen, 2008*, John Benjamins, Amsterdam/Philadelphia, 195–214.

Lapointe, S. (1999) "Stem selection and OT," *Yearbook of Morphology 1999* 263–297.

Leumann, M., J. B. Hofmann, and A. Szantyr (1963) *Lateinische Grammatik, auf der Grundlage des Werkes von Friedrich Stolz und Joseph Hermann Schmalz; 1. Band lateinische Laut- und Formenlehre*, Beck'sche Verlagsbuchhandlung, München.

Lewis, G. (1967) *Turkish Grammar*, Oxford University Press.

Lieber, R. (1980) *The Organization of the Lexicon*, Doctoral dissertation, MIT.

Lieber, R. (1987) *An integrated theory of autosegmental processes*, State University of New York Press, Albany.

Lieber, R. (1992) *Deconstructing Morphology*, University of Chicago Press, Chicago.

Lowenstamm, J. (2008) "On little n, $\sqrt{}$ and tyes of nouns," in J. Hartmann, V. Hegedus, and H. van Riemsdijk, eds., *The Sounds of Silence: Empty Elements in Syntax and Phonology*, Elsevier, Amsterdam, 105–143.

Marantz, A. (1984) *On the Nature of Grammatical Relations*, MIT Press, Cambridge, MA.

Marantz, A. (1988) "Clitics, Morphological Merger, and the Mapping to Phonological Structure," in M. Hammond and M. Noonan, eds., *Theoretical Morphology*, Academic Press, San Diego, 253–270.

Marantz, A. (1995) "A Late Note on Late Insertion," in *Explorations in Generative Grammar*, Hankuk Publishing Co., 357–368.

Marantz, A. (1997) "No Escape from Syntax: Don't Try Morphological Analysis in the Privacy of Your Own Lexicon," in A. Dimitriadis, L. Siegel, C. Surek-Clark, and A. Williams, eds., *Proceedings of the 21st Penn Linguistics Colloquium*, UPenn Working Papers in Linguistics, Philadelphia, 201–225.

Marantz, A. (2001) "Words and Things," handout, MIT.

Marantz, A. (2010) "Locality Domains for Contextual Allosemy in Words," talk handout, New York University.

Marlett, S., and J. Stemberger (1983) "Empty consonants in Seri," *Linguistic Inquiry* 14:4, 617–39.

Marslen-Wilson, W., and L. K. Tyler (1998) "Rules, representations, and the English past tense," *Trends in Cognitive Sciences* 2:11, 428–435.

Marvin, T. (2002) *Topics in the stress and syntax of words*, Doctoral dissertation, MIT.

Matisoff, J. (2003) "Lahu," in G. Thurgood and R. J. LaPolla, eds., *The Sino-Tibetan Languages*, Routledge, London and New York, 208–221.

Murphy, G. L. (2002) *The Big Book of Concepts*, MIT Press, Cambridge, MA.

Muysken, P. (1981) "Quechua causatives and Logical Form: A case study in markedness," in A. Belletti, L. Brandi, and L. Rizzi, eds., *Theory of markedness in generative grammar*, Scuola Normale Superiore, Pisa.

Newell, H. (2008) *Aspects of the morphology and phonology of phases*, Doctoral dissertation, McGill University.

Noyer, R. (1992) *Features, Affixes, and Positions in Autonomous Morphological Structure*, Doctoral dissertation, MIT.

Noyer, R. (1997) *Features, Positions and Affixes in Autonomous Morphological Structure*, Garland, New York.

Noyer, R. (1998) "Impoverishment Theory and Morphosyntactic Markedness," in S. Lapointe, D. Brentari, and P. Farrell, eds., *Morphology and Its Relation to Syntax and Phonology*, CSLI, Stanford.

Noyer, R. (2005) "A constraint on interclass syncretism," *Yearbook of morphology 2004* 273–315.

Odden, D. (1993) "Interaction Between Modules in Lexical Phonology," in *Phonetics and Phonology 4: Studies in Lexical Phonology*, Academic Press, 111–144.

Oltra-Massuet, M. I. (1999) *On the Notion of Theme Vowel: A New Approach to Catalan Verbal Morphology*, Master's Thesis, MIT.

Oltra-Massuet, M. I., and K. Arregi (2005) "Stress by Structure in Spanish," *Linguistic Inquiry* 36:1, 43–84.

Pak, M. (2008) "The postsyntactic derivation and its phonological reflexes," Doctoral thesis, University of Pennsylvania.

Pardee, D. (1997) "Ugaritic," in R. Hetzron, ed., *The Semitic Languages*, Routledge, London and New York, 131–144.

Partee, B. H., A. ter Meulen, and R. E. Wall (1993) *Mathematical Methods in Linguistics*, Kluwer, Dordrecht.

Paster, M. (2006) *Phonological Conditions on Affixation*, Doctoral dissertation, University of California at Berkeley.

Patz, E. (1991) "Djabugay," in B. J. Blake and R. Dixon, eds., *The Handbook of Australian Languages*, volume 4, Oxford, 245–347.

Pesetsky, D. (1979) "Russian Morphology and Lexical Theory," ms., MIT.

Pesetsky, D. (1985) "Morphology and Logical Form," *Linguistic Inquiry* 16, 193–246.

Pinker, S., and A. Prince (1988) "On language and connectionism: analysis of a parallel distributed processing model of language acquisition," *Cognition* 28, 73–193.

Pinker, S., and M. Ullman (2002) "The past and future of the past tense," *Trends in Cognitive Sciences* 6:11, 456–463.

Poeppel, D., and D. Embick (2005) "Defining the relation between linguistics and neuroscience," in A. Cutler, ed., *Twenty-first century psycholinguistics: Four cornerstones*, Lawrence Erlbaum.

Poser, W. J. (1985) "Cliticization to NP and lexical phonology," in *Proceedings of WCCFL*, volume 4, 262–72.

Poser, W. J. (1990) "Word-Internal Phrase Boundary in Japanese," in S. Inkelas and D. Zec, eds., *The Phonology-Syntax Connection*, The University of Chicago Press, Chicago, 279–288.

Poser, W. J. (1992) "Blocking of Phrasal Constructions by Lexical Items," in I. Sag and A. Szabolsci, eds., *Lexical Matters*, CSLI, Stanford, CA, 111–130.

Prunet, J.-F., R. Béland, and A. Idrissi (2000) "The Mental Representation of Semitic Words," *Linguistic Inquiry* 31:4.

Pylkkänen, L., R. Llinás, and G. L. Murphy (2006) "The Representation of Polysemy: MEG Evidence," *Journal of Cognitive Neuroscience* 18:1, 97–109.

Pylkkänen, M. (2002) *Introducing Arguments*, Doctoral dissertation, Massachusetts Institute of Technology.

Roberts, J. R. (1987) *Amele*, Croom Helm, New York.

Saussure, F. de (1986) *Course in General Linguistics*, Open Court, Chicago and La Salle, Illinois.

Schlenker, P. (1999) *Propositional Attitudes and Indexicality: A Cross-Categorial approach*, Doctoral dissertation, MIT.

Schlenker, P. (2006) "Ontological symmetry in language: A brief manifesto," *Mind & Language* 21:4, 504–539.

Selkirk, E. (1982) *The syntax of words*, MIT Press, Cambridge, MA.

Sproat, R. (1985) *On Deriving the Lexicon*, Doctoral dissertation, MIT.

Stockall, L., and A. Marantz (2006) "A single-route, full decomposition model of morphological complexity: MEG evidence," *Mental Lexicon* 1:1, 85–123.

Svantesson, J. (2003) "Khalkha," in J. Janhunen, ed., *The Mongolic Languages*, Routledge, London and New York, 154–176.

Taft, M. (2004) "Morphological decomposition and the reverse base frequency effect," *The Quarterly Journal of Experimental Psychology* 57(A):4, 745–765.

Thurston, W. R. (1982) *A Comparative Study in Anêm and Lusi*, Pacific Linguistics, Canberra.

Travis, L. (1984) *Parameters and Effects of Word Order Variation*, Doctoral dissertation, MIT.

Wagner, M. (2005) *Prosody and Recursion*, Doctoral dissertation, MIT.

Wasow, T. (1977) "Transformations and the Lexicon," in P. Culicover, T. Wasow, and A. Akmajian, eds., *Formal Syntax*, Academic Press, New York.

Wehr, H. (1976) *A Dictionary of Modern Written Arabic, edited by J. Milton Cowan*, Spoken Language Services, Inc., Ithaca, New York, 3rd edition.

Wiese, R. (1996) *The Phonology of German*, Oxford University Press.

Wolf, M. (2006) "For an autosegmental theory of mutation," in L. Bateman, M. O'Keefe, E. Reilly, and A. Werle, eds., *University of Massachusetts Occasional Papers in Linguistics 32: Papers in Optimality Theory III*, GLSA, Amherst.

Index

ℛ-Meanings, *see* Roots, Lexical Semantic Meaning of
↔, 9
⌢-operator, *see* Concatenation

Accidental Homophony, 8, 26–28, 114, 118–119
    versus Syncretism, 26–28, 125–127, 166–167
Activity Corollary, 182
Affixation, 60–67, *see also* Complex Heads
    postsyntactic, 12, 67, 73, 225
Allomorphy
    Contextual, 11, 29, 92–93, 96, 102–107, 162, 170–194
    Inwards/Outwards Sensitivity, 172–173, 192–193
Amele, 157–161
Anêm, 134–136, 229, 230
Arabic, 45, 48–49
Architecture of the Grammar, 3–5, 13–17, 20–21

Barbareño Chumash, 131–134
Blocking, 19, 96–98, 194–202
Bracketing paradox, 24, 79–82
Bundling, *see* Features, bundling of
Category, 31, 43–47, 56, 180, 221, 223
    Categorization Assumption, 44–47
    Category-Defining Head, 43–47, 179–183, 197–200

Checking Theory, 225
Classical Greek, 36–39, 124
Competition, *see* Vocabulary Insertion
Complex Heads, 12, 18, 23–24, 43–44, 60–70
    Linearization of, 71–79
    Order of Insertion in, 99–100, 179, 191–193
Concatenation, 71–73
    and Allomorphy, 178, 183–191
Concepts, 8, 41, 47, 49–51
Cyclic Domains, *see* Phases
Cyclicity
    "Inside Out", *see* Inside-Out Insertion
    Derivational, *see* Phases

Decomposition, *see* Full Decomposition
Derived Nominal, 179–183
Diacritics, 51–54, 224
Directionality, *see* Allomorphy, Inwards/Outwards Sensitivity
Discharge of Features, *see* Features, Deletion/Non-Deletion of
Dissociated Morpheme, 65, 68, 101
Djabugay, 217
Double Marking, 87, 96–98, 205–206, 208, *see also* Blocking

Encyclopedia, 16–17, 19–21, 47, 112

Exponent, 9, 85, *see also* Vocabulary Item

Features, 6–7
    Active, 33, 36–40, 122–125
    Binary, 6–7, 32, 37, 40, 116, 230
    Bundling of, 34–40, 124–125, 130–131, 160, 223
    Deletion/Non-Deletion of, 107–109, 226
    Interpretable, 32–40, 54
    Morphological, *see* Diacritics
    Phonological, 6–7, 41–43
    Synsem, 6–10, 32–40, 49–51, 91–92, 122
    Unary, 101, 156
Fission, 213, 216–219, 227
Full Decomposition, 17–19, 21, 29
Full Specification, 116–117, 121–125
Functional Morpheme, 7, 9–11, 15, 32–40
Fusion, 213–216, 227

German, 164–165
Gerund, 179–183
Gloriosity, 196–200

Haitian Creole, 175
Head Movement, *see* Affixation
Heads
    Cyclic, 47, 179–183
    Non-Cyclic, 180–183
Hungarian, 173, 184
Hupa, 114–125, 161–162

Identifier (Non-Phonological), *see* Index

Idiomatic Meaning, 16
Impoverishment, 125, 139–165
Index, *see* Roots, Indices of
Inherent Specification, 53
Inside-Out Insertion, 99–100, 173, 179, 191–193
Interface Transparency, 22–24, 30, 79, 82

Khalkha, 130–131
Korean, 174–175

Lahu, 223
Late Insertion, 8, 10, 24–28
Latin, 25, 42, 52–53, 100–109, 151–153, 186–189, 214–216, 224
Level 1 and Level 2 Affixes, 83
Lexical Category, 7, *see also* Roots
Lexical Information, 12–17
Lexicon, 13–15, 22–23
    Bloomfieldian, 14–15
Light Verbs, 43, 55–56, 221
Linear Order, 71–79, *see also* Concatenation
Listedness, 12
Lists, 11–17, 19
Local Dislocation, 73, 225
Locality
    Affixation, *see* Complex Heads
    Allomorphic, *see* Concatenation, Phases
Lowering, 67

M-Word, 67–70
    Relation to Phonological Word, 82–83, 226
Macedonian, 155–157, 163–164
Mandarin Chinese, 34–35, 223

Memory, 1, 4, 6, 10, 17–22, 41, 54, 111–112, 171, 226
Mirror Principle, 24, 73–82
Mismatches, 24, 79–82, 213–219
Mongolic, 129–131
Morpheme, 1–219, *see also* Functional Morpheme, Root
    Order, 73–79
    Traditional, 19, 111–112
Morpheme-Locus Effect, 28–30
Morphophonological Rule
    versus Vocabulary Insertion, 206
Morphophonological Rule, 18, 83, 165, 170, 190, 193, 203–208, 232
    versus Vocabulary Insertion, 208

No Tangling, 72, 76–78
Non-Affixal Morphology, 11, 201–208
Non-Lexicalist Theory, 13–15, 21
Norwegian, 143–146

Obliteration, 227
Oirat, 129–131
Open Class Vocabulary, 7, 221
Ornamental Morpheme, *see* Dissociated Morpheme

Phases, 47, 83, 178–183, 225–227
Phonological Exponent, *see* Exponent
Polish, 148–149
Polysemy, *see* Roots, polysemy of
Pruning, 185, 188–190, 224, 227, 231

Q Variable, 89–90, 98
Quechua, 74–79

Readjustment Rule, 202–208, *see also* Morphophonological Rule
Realizational Theory, 10, 19, 24–28, 111–113, 119, 222, 227
Roots, 7–9, 41–56
    and the *Encyclopedia*, 16
    Category of, *see* Category
    Indices of, 8, 42, 51
    Lexical Semantic Meaning of, 47–51
    No Decomposition of, 49
    No Synsem Features, 49
    Polysemy of, 16, 48, 167, 224

Separation Hypothesis, 111
Seri, 175
Seychelles Creole, 127–129
Sign (Saussure), 8
Spanish, 25–28, 39–40, 45, 53–54, 62–66, 112–114, 141–143, 153–155, 222
Stem, 55
    Allomorphy, 18, 201–208, 232
    Suppletion, 42–43
Subset Principle, 95
Subword, 67–70, 83, 87
Suppletion, *see* Stem, Suppletion
Syncretism, 19, 25–28, 111–167
    "Deep", 149–161
    Minimizing the Vocabulary, 166
    versus Homophony, 125–127
Syntactic Terminals, 5–11, 15–17, 19–21, 56, 68, 112

Templatic morphology, 48, 201
Terena, 207–208
Terminal Insertion, 98, 195

Exponent, 9, 85, *see also* Vocabulary Item

Features, 6–7
- Active, 33, 36–40, 122–125
- Binary, 6–7, 32, 37, 40, 116, 230
- Bundling of, 34–40, 124–125, 130–131, 160, 223
- Deletion/Non-Deletion of, 107–109, 226
- Interpretable, 32–40, 54
- Morphological, *see* Diacritics
- Phonological, 6–7, 41–43
- Synsem, 6–10, 32–40, 49–51, 91–92, 122
- Unary, 101, 156

Fission, 213, 216–219, 227
Full Decomposition, 17–19, 21, 29
Full Specification, 116–117, 121–125
Functional Morpheme, 7, 9–11, 15, 32–40
Fusion, 213–216, 227

German, 164–165
Gerund, 179–183
Gloriosity, 196–200

Haitian Creole, 175
Head Movement, *see* Affixation
Heads
- Cyclic, 47, 179–183
- Non-Cyclic, 180–183

Hungarian, 173, 184
Hupa, 114–125, 161–162

Identifier (Non-Phonological), *see* Index

Idiomatic Meaning, 16
Impoverishment, 125, 139–165
Index, *see* Roots, Indices of
Inherent Specification, 53
Inside-Out Insertion, 99–100, 173, 179, 191–193
Interface Transparency, 22–24, 30, 79, 82

Khalkha, 130–131
Korean, 174–175

Lahu, 223
Late Insertion, 8, 10, 24–28
Latin, 25, 42, 52–53, 100–109, 151–153, 186–189, 214–216, 224
Level 1 and Level 2 Affixes, 83
Lexical Category, 7, *see also* Roots
Lexical Information, 12–17
Lexicon, 13–15, 22–23
- Bloomfieldian, 14–15

Light Verbs, 43, 55–56, 221
Linear Order, 71–79, *see also* Concatenation
Listedness, 12
Lists, 11–17, 19
Local Dislocation, 73, 225
Locality
- Affixation, *see* Complex Heads
- Allomorphic, *see* Concatenation, Phases

Lowering, 67

M-Word, 67–70
- Relation to Phonological Word, 82–83, 226

Macedonian, 155–157, 163–164
Mandarin Chinese, 34–35, 223

Memory, 1, 4, 6, 10, 17–22, 41, 54, 111–112, 171, 226
Mirror Principle, 24, 73–82
Mismatches, 24, 79–82, 213–219
Mongolic, 129–131
Morpheme, 1–219, *see also* Functional Morpheme, Root
    Order, 73–79
    Traditional, 19, 111–112
Morpheme-Locus Effect, 28–30
Morphophonological Rule
    versus Vocabulary Insertion, 206
Morphophonological Rule, 18, 83, 165, 170, 190, 193, 203–208, 232
    versus Vocabulary Insertion, 208

No Tangling, 72, 76–78
Non-Affixal Morphology, 11, 201–208
Non-Lexicalist Theory, 13–15, 21
Norwegian, 143–146

Obliteration, 227
Oirat, 129–131
Open Class Vocabulary, 7, 221
Ornamental Morpheme, *see* Dissociated Morpheme

Phases, 47, 83, 178–183, 225–227
Phonological Exponent, *see* Exponent
Polish, 148–149
Polysemy, *see* Roots, polysemy of
Pruning, 185, 188–190, 224, 227, 231

Q Variable, 89–90, 98
Quechua, 74–79

Readjustment Rule, 202–208, *see also* Morphophonological Rule
Realizational Theory, 10, 19, 24–28, 111–113, 119, 222, 227
Roots, 7–9, 41–56
    and the *Encyclopedia*, 16
    Category of, *see* Category
    Indices of, 8, 42, 51
    Lexical Semantic Meaning of, 47–51
    No Decomposition of, 49
    No Synsem Features, 49
    Polysemy of, 16, 48, 167, 224

Separation Hypothesis, 111
Seri, 175
Seychelles Creole, 127–129
Sign (Saussure), 8
Spanish, 25–28, 39–40, 45, 53–54, 62–66, 112–114, 141–143, 153–155, 222
Stem, 55
    Allomorphy, 18, 201–208, 232
    Suppletion, 42–43
Subset Principle, 95
Subword, 67–70, 83, 87
Suppletion, *see* Stem, Suppletion
Syncretism, 19, 25–28, 111–167
    "Deep", 149–161
    Minimizing the Vocabulary, 166
    versus Homophony, 125–127
Syntactic Terminals, 5–11, 15–17, 19–21, 56, 68, 112

Templatic morphology, 48, 201
Terena, 207–208
Terminal Insertion, 98, 195

Terminal Node, *see* Morpheme
Transparency, *see* Interface Transparency
Turkish, 176–178

Ugaritic, 146–147
Umlaut, 164–165
Underspecification, 26–28, 113–121, 127–137, 139–140, 142, 145, 149–157
   and "Defaults", 146–149
   and Impoverishment, 161–165
   and *Full Specification*, 121–125
Uniqueness, 98, 195
Universal Feature Inventory (UFI), 32–40, 91

Vocabulary, 9, 15–17, 19, 85, 88, 96, 112–113, 121, 127, 139, 161–162
   Minimization of, 112, 113, 119, 166–167, 177
Vocabulary Insertion, 4, 9–11, 24–28, 85–167
Vocabulary Item, 9–11, 26–28, 42, 85–87, 125
   Ordering of, 92–96
   Specification of, 121–122

Word, 3
   "Structural", *see* M-Word
   Informal notion of, 3
   Phonological, 82–84

CPSIA information can be obtained
at www.ICGtesting.com
Printed in the USA
BVHW040354080221
599130BV00019B/52